Beyond the Bosphorus

British Drivers on the Middle East Routes

Beyond the Bosphorus

British Drivers on the Middle East Routes

Dave Bowers

First published 2015

Copyright © Dave Bowers 2015

All rights reserved. No part of this publication may be reproduced, stored in a retrieval system, or transmitted, in any form or by any means, electronic, mechanical, photocopying, recording or otherwise, without prior permission of the copyright holder.

Published by
5M Publishing Ltd
Benchmark House
8 Smithy Wood Drive
Sheffield S35 1QN, UK
Tel: +44 (0) 1234 81 81 80
www.5mpublishing.com

A catalogue record for this book is available from the British Library

ISBN 978-1-910456-02-6

Book layout by Forewords, Oxford

Printed and bound in India by Replika Press Pvt. Ltd.

Disclaimer

Every effort was made to contact the copyright holders of these images. In some cases, despite repeat attempts to make contact, it was not possible to locate the copyright holder. If you are the copyright holder of an image that we have not attributed to you, please contact the publisher immediately for inclusion.

Contents

Acknowledgements vii
1. Introduction 1
2. The Right Stuff 5
3. Taking the Plunge 13
4. Pat Seal 37
5. How Different Trucks Performed 43
6. Mechanical Mishaps 61
7. Different Loads 73
8. Perils of Winter 85
9. Hazards of the High Ground 95
10. Desert Travel 105
11. Working Internal Routes – Saudi Arabia 117
12. As Far As You Could Go: Afghanistan and Pakistan 127
13. Venturing Behind the Iron Curtain 133
14. Tricks of the Trade 139
15. Life on the Road 147
16. Camaraderie 161
17. When It All Went Wrong! 169
18. Crossing Borders 173
19. Guardians of Law and Order 185
20. Con Tricks and Scams 191
21. Local Traffic and Road Hazards 199
22. Accidents 209
23. Family Matters 221
24. Changing Political Situations 225
25. The End of the Road 233

Dedication

This book is dedicated to the memory of those truck drivers who tragically never made it back from a journey out to the Middle East, and also for those who have subsequently passed away. They will always be remembered by those who drove alongside them all those many years ago.

Acknowledgements

Writing a book would appear to be a fairly solitary occupation in many ways, but not always. Seeing the job through called for valuable assistance which was generously provided by those I arranged to interview. Then, of course, there was the need to obtain approval that the project was heading in the right direction, and many of those I contacted were also helpful in providing just the right sort of encouragement needed to complete the job, particularly when things were not going as smoothly as they should have done!

First of all, I would like to extend my thanks to Ashley Coghill for his support throughout the project. He supplied a marvellous launch platform to the book by loaning hundreds of photographs which he had collected over the years that illustrate what it was like to take part in the Middle East trucking enterprise. It was Ashley's own publication, *The Long Haul Pioneers* which set the precedent for my own book on a similar subject. Without his encouragement it's unlikely *Beyond the Bosphorus* would have made it into print.

In addition, I was off to a good start when Ash suggested some names of former Middle East drivers who would be good to contact, and my thanks also go to David Miller and Ken Ward in particular. They were the first to be interviewed, ands as well as providing many fascinating stories of their times as Middle-East drivers, they were also immensely encouraging at a time when completing the book seemed to stretch out towards infinity.

Which it didn't. In fact, the pace soon quickened after I had started to contact other ex-Middle-East drivers, who kindly gave up their time to be interviewed, a process which largely took place over the telephone with all the inconvenience this may imply! Their time was so generously given in supplying so much information as well as additional photographs and documents.

Completing all the text involved many hours of work, often into the small hours, and even though this would seem to be solely an author's due burden, this wasn't strictly true. My wife, Sarah, spent many hours proofreading the script. Her only objection being that she now knew more about lorries and long-distance road haulage than any woman should reasonably be asked to assimilate or endure!

In many ways, writing this book was an attempt to preserve a historical record of what it was like to drive all the way to the Middle East, or alternatively, to take on the internal routes of the Arabian Peninsula for months at a time.

It is a truism that history is essentially incomplete, so I would like to comment on the basic truth that it's been impossible to include the stories of everyone who took part in the Middle East trucking experience. Hopefully, reading the accounts of others will allow them to reflect and relive their own experiences of the days when they were young and free to explore a way of life which was so exciting compared with what they'd previously experienced until that so formative time of their lives.

Thanks also go to the staff of 5M Publishing for making such a good job of the publication process which was achieved with minimal delay and commendable professionalism by all concerned.

It is hoped everyone who reads this book will enjoy following the adventures and experiences of those who have contributed to this book.

Photo Credits

COPYRIGHT UNKNOWN denotes that the owner of the photograph could not be found.

If you are the copyright holder of an image that is not credited to you please contact us at you2us@5mpublishing.com so we can update the credit list. Every effort was made to contact copyright holders for all of the images used in this book, so we would be delighted to include you in the list below if you have been inadvertently omitted.

AC	Ashley Coghill	IT	Ian Taylor
AG	Anglo Continental	ITY	Ian Tyler
BC	Bob Carter	IW	Ivor Whittall
BR	Bill Robins	JB	John Buffham
BRO	Brian Robertson	JC	Jerry Cooke
BRS	British Road Services	KP	Kelvin Parfitt
CB	Chapman & Ball	KW	Ken Ward
DB	Dave Bowers	MC	Mark Chevalier
DAY	FA Dayson	MD	Mike Dunstan
DM	David Miller	MH	Malcolm Howe
DS	Des Seal	MM	Martyn Moulsdale
DT	Dave Tickle	OR	Oryx Freight Lines
EW	Wilson Birdale Transport	PB	Peter Bamford
FH	Fred Hodgkins	PR	Paul Rowlands
FT	Fred Topham	RDB	Robert Dods-Brown
GB	George Brooke	RG	Richard Garn
GH	Gerry Holmes	RH	Robert Hackford
GHA	Glen Harley	RP	Roger Pierce
GF	Geoff Frost	RR	Redcliffe Roadways
GK	Gerry Keating	RS	Ray Scutts
GP	Gordon Pearce	RW	Roger Williams
GR	Graham Ryan	SH	Spiers and Hartwell
GS	Gordon Summers	SN	Simon Normanton
HG	HG Brown	TT	Terry Tott
HL	Howard Leighton	UC	Union Cartage

CHAPTER 1

Introduction

In recent years there has been much interest in the long-distance road haulage routes that became collectively known as the Middle East runs. The objective of this enterprise, which really got into its stride during the mid-seventies, involved using trucks and trailers to deliver goods and materials all the way from Europe to the countries of the Middle East; notably Iraq, Iran, Saudi Arabia, the Gulf States of the Arabian Peninsula, with some deliveries going as far as Afghanistan, and Pakistan being the most distant country of all!

As suggested by the title of this book, travelling across the waters of the Bosphorus straits in Old Istanbul was a defining feature of travelling any of the different Middle East routes. This was achieved by boarding one of the drive-on/drive-off ferryboats that transported trucks and also any other vehicles together with passengers across the busy sea lane of the Bosphorus.

The Bosphorus could be crossed at a considerable height above the waters by driving across the suspension bridge built in 1973 which linked Europe and Asia. But this wasn't the preferred option: the approach roads to the bridge had not been properly developed, so the ferry service remained the route of choice for drivers long after the construction of the bridge was completed. Using the ferry came with the advantage of this form of transport being an enjoyable experience in itself, as the views to be seen when crossing the Bosphorus offered an unsurpassed panorama of Istanbul together with all of its splendid Islamic architecture, with many towering mosques, minarets and Ottoman palaces to be seen along the shoreline and the far horizon!

It could be said that crossing the Bosphorus became a rite of passage for any new driver passing this way. And whether they were outward-bound to the Middle East or inbound back to Britain, taking a stopover in Istanbul was an ideal opportunity to indulge in a well-deserved rest and some eastern-style recreation.

There were times when crossing the Bosphorus and also passing through Turkey altogether were bypassed by choice owing to political and internal issues, so travelling by roll-on/roll-off ferries from Greece to Syria became an attractive option, providing shorter overall journey times and far less time spent behind a steering wheel, while enjoying the comforts of shipboard life.

The boom years of transporting goods out to the Middle East lasted from 1975 until 1982, and it is from this era that most of the drivers who have contributed to this publication have provided their reminiscences of what soon became the greatest adventure of their lives. The stories they have recounted include the good times and the bad times; moments of elation as well as those of despair; and in particular, the high value placed on the comradeship or 'camaraderie' that existed between drivers, which could make light of even the most tricky situations or difficult working conditions which could always be anticipated somewhere along the way!

It was decided to limit the time-span covered by this book to the Middle East run's glory years between 1975 and 1982 when the business was in its prime, with a seemingly unending convoy of trucks passing from East to West and then back again, with new internal transport systems developed to serve throughout the Arabian Peninsula.

Many of those who were interviewed expressed the view that any stories they provided should not be exaggerated in any way, which may have something to

The approach to the vehicle ferry on the Bosphorus. BR

Europe. AC

do with a certain television series that concerns the work activities of North American truckers. In this television series there has always been a tendency for commonplace events to be blown out of all proportion by the commentator suggesting these are chillingly life-threatening when this is patently untrue! A tank of diesel fuel requires an awful amount of encouragement before it will explode in an engulfing fireball destroying everything in its path!

On the other side of the same coin, the bravery of those drivers who were prepared to drive thousands of miles to those far distant destinations should not be in any way understated. They endured hours and hours of solitude that often lasted from dawn until dusk each day, with the possibility of some form of hazard suddenly occurring around each bend in the road or when a rapidly approaching vehicle coming the other way threatened a nose to nose, high-speed collision.

The story of how Michael Woodman and Bob Paul trail blazed the Middle East route in 1964 with a Guy Warrior and started Astran International is well known and as this topic has been extensively covered to good effect in Ashley Coghill's book, *The Long Haul Pioneers*, which engagingly tells the story of how Astran, a firm that's still involved in the freight haulage business today, first set the ball rolling by hauling freight to the Middle East, half a century ago.

Following on from what Ashley managed to achieve so successfully concerning the history of Astran together with the firm's drivers and sub-contractors, the intention of this publication was to throw the net even wider and draw attention to many other British operators and drivers who took on the challenge of travelling the Middle East routes, as reflected in the book's choice of title.

Whichever of the many firms that the Middle East drivers worked for, they had to adapt as quickly as they could to a wandering lifestyle which must have seemed very strange at first, as they were no longer working a regular day and perhaps tramping a few hundred

Introduction

miles a week; they were taking on journeys covering upwards of 8000 miles, and maybe as many as 10,000 miles on each round trip; deliveries that took a month to six weeks to complete, and maybe a lot longer if things went well! And all the while they would be continually aware of the sobering reality that any kind of mechanical breakdown, road accident, or intractable problems with local officialdom could seriously disrupt the timing of their trip, dashing any hopes of returning home to their loved ones by a prearranged date or to meet a promise they had made to attend a particular occasion or function.

Some took to the unusual style of life that the Middle East run offered like ducks to water, as they became so carried away with the adventure of what they had become involved with, the passage of time did not seem to matter at all – prompting a blissful unawareness of any other way of making a living which lasted until the day arrived when they finally decided to call it quits and declare an end to their great adventure. This could be due to family commitments, ill-health, incapacity, or simply admitting to themselves that they had finally had enough of roughing it out there!

Not everyone took to the life of course, and for many, their first trip was also their one and only trip, as this wasn't the life for them: a big mistake that ultimately resulted in handing over a truck's ignition keys after arriving home in Blighty, to seek alternative employment at a rather less demanding pace! But this was by no means something that could be described or classified as failure, as they always had the reassurance to fall back on that they had given a most difficult and demanding job their very best try.

So what was the incentive that explained why many ordinary working blokes from all over the United Kingdom subsequently found themselves driving lorries over thousands of miles across Europe and then all the way across the lands of the Middle East? The motivation to introduce this form of transport can be traced to a significant improvement in the trading position of the oil-producing Middle East countries

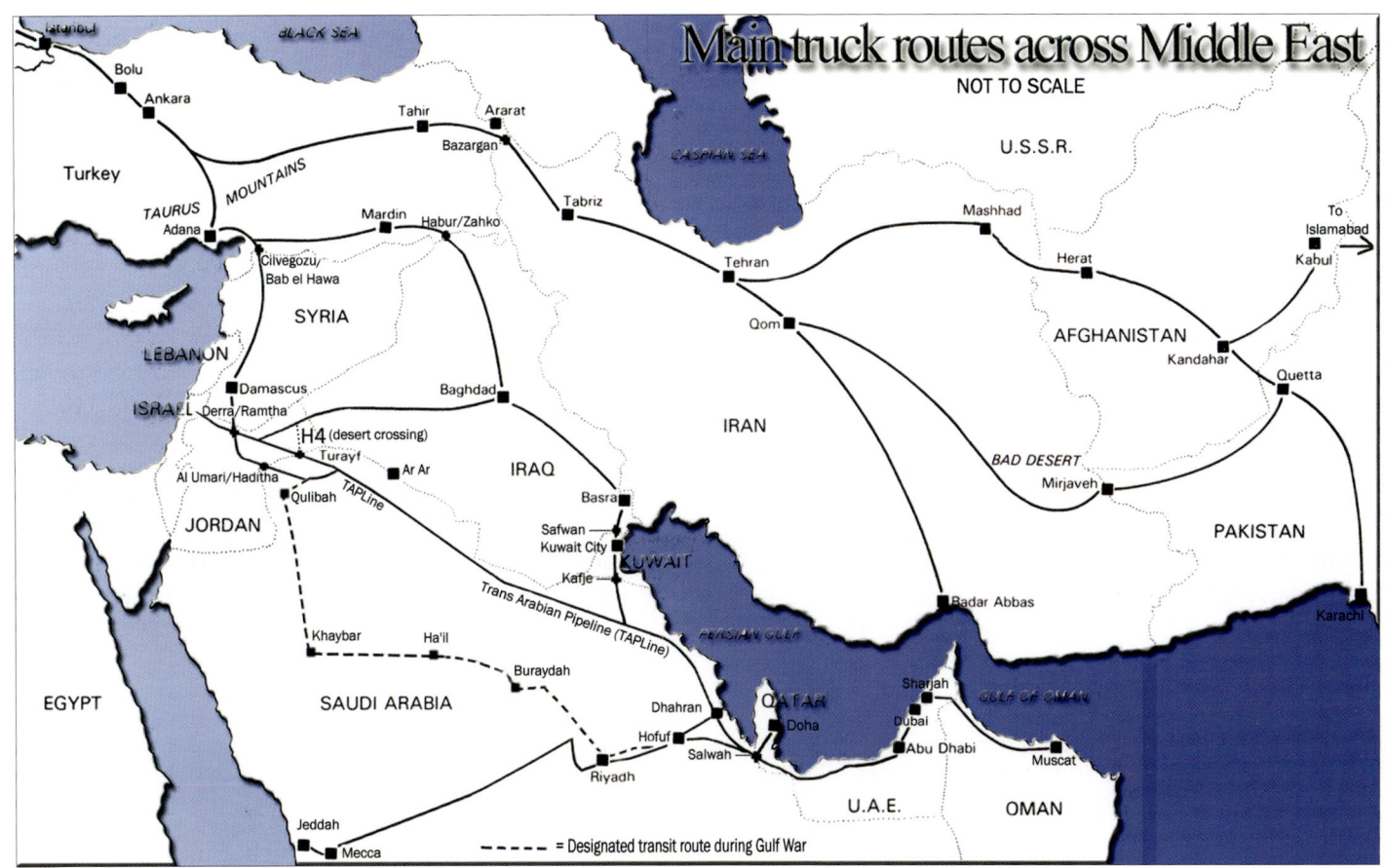

The Middle East. AC

with the rest of the world due to the increases in oil revenues that made these countries so rich.

With so much money coming into the coffers of those Middle East countries, the time was ripe to go on a spending spree. But although the money was there in abundance, getting any Western goods out to the Middle East was difficult at the time owing to a particular restriction that had been applied to transporting goods by ship from Europe. This situation occurred because the Suez Canal had been blockaded by the Egyptian government as a reprisal for the American support given to Israel during the Six Day War between Israel and Egypt in 1967.

The Suez Canal was sealed off to any through traffic by shipping from 1967 to 1975, so rather than ships being allowed to pass from the Mediterranean to the Red Sea along this man-made waterway, any ships carrying cargoes bound for the Arabian Peninsula ports along the shores of the Persian Gulf or the Red Sea had to make a long detour around the coast of Africa, adding many thousands of miles to the sea journey, delaying the delivery of cargoes, and increasing the cost of shipping due to the extra time and the increase in fuel that the longer sea journey demanded.

In October 1973, the Organization of Arab Petroleum Exporting Countries (OPEC), comprising Saudi Arabia, Kuwait, Bahrain, Qatar, United Arab Emirates, Iraq, Syria, Egypt, Algeria and Tunisia, announced an embargo on the supply of oil from these countries, which was in response to the support given to Israel by the United States during the Yom Kippur War of 1973, when the Israelis defeated Egyptian and Syrian forces.

This will be remembered in the United Kingdom as a time when all registered motorists were issued petrol ration coupons with the intention of preserving remaining petrol and diesel fuel stocks, although these coupons were never actually used, as following a new agreement with OPEC in March 1974, the embargo was abandoned, and the supply of oil was increased – to the intense relief of the rest of the world!

The increase in the price of oil per barrel made the oil-producing member nations of OPEC very rich in the process, and as a direct consequence of the sudden increase in national affluence, the floodgates were opened to all sorts of goods and commodities being ordered by any of the OPEC countries, particularly those in the Middle East.

The oil-rich countries went on a spending spree, and so began a period of rapid social and economic development, with six-lane highways, modern housing developments, hotels and educational establishments springing up, as if these had been built overnight.

During this period of rapid expansion the only answer that could be found to the Suez Canal closure was to use road transport to ship in any goods and supplies by road from Europe, and so the first phase of the Middle East run commenced, although the dependency on trucks was partially relieved in 1975 when the blockade of the Suez Canal was lifted, resulting in far more goods arriving by sea in ports such as Jeddah in Saudi Arabia. However, unloaded cargoes began stacking up in the docks due to the large amounts that were being delivered, which the underdeveloped port facilities could not cope with, so many ships would have to ride at anchor for many months before they could be unloaded.

So began phase two of the Middle East run, with trucks transporting cranes and other equipment from Europe to improve the efficiency of the dockyards when unloading ships to clear the logjam of undelivered cargoes. And then to complete the deliveries, British, other European, and many Pakistani drivers were employed to make deliveries throughout Saudi Arabia as well as the smaller Gulf States.

The development of internal transport services on the Arabian Peninsula attracted a new influx of British drivers who were drawn to tax-free wages which amounted to several times what they could expect to earn in the UK. So there was no shortage of volunteers for these fixed-term contract jobs, with British transport firms and drivers being at the forefront owing to this country's long-established involvement with the Middle East oil-producing countries.

This publication is largely based on a series of interviews with those who drove the Middle East routes in the earlier years, although of course, it has not been possible to interview everyone who took part in this remarkable story of long-distance truck driving, but it is hoped that the reminiscences of those who have contributed to this publication will keep the story of the Middle East runs alive so these tales can be passed down from one generation to the next.

Many of today's drivers would have welcomed the chance to follow in the footsteps of the pioneers who travelled along the desert tracks and the poorly surfaced mountain roads of the Middle East some forty-odd years ago and it is hoped the following pages make the best job of bringing this great adventure to vivid life!

CHAPTER 2

The Right Stuff

What personal qualities did it take to become a Middle East driver? Imagine what it would have felt like to set off from somewhere in the United Kingdom for the very first time on a journey that was going to take you several thousand miles in one direction, and then after reaching the destination where the truck would be unloaded, and maybe after taking a breather for a day or so, you would set off to accomplish the same journey but in a reverse direction, before finally arriving back at home at least a couple of weeks later. This was a task that could only appeal to a particular breed of committed, single-minded individuals!

After arriving home and then enjoying a few days' rest with your wife, family and friends, it would be time to head off again to one of the English Channel ports at the start of a new overland trip, perhaps to the same destination you had driven to on a previous occasion, although possibly somewhere completely different, which required an extra degree of caution owing to the need to learn a new route and cope with any complicated navigational issues this posed, as well as any different rules and regulations that may now apply at the border posts of any countries that you had not visited before!

The strain of living on your wits for weeks on end could exert a psychological toll, as could the effects of loneliness together with the culture shock of being somewhere which seemed to be so uniquely foreign.

In most walks of life it is fairly easy to predict how long a particular task is going to take, but not so when it came to the Middle East runs, as a trip could be subject to so many unpredictable disruptions along the way, such as breakdowns, delays at border crossings, etc.

To provide their drivers with some kind of guidelines on how long a trip could take, PIE International Carriers suggested 14 days for a round trip to Istanbul, 30 days for Tehran, 24 days Baghdad, 28 days Riyadh, 38 days Kabul and 44 days Karachi, although whether a driver could achieve these times was quite literally in the lap of the gods! If fate was to play a few tricks along the way then this could extend the journey for a good long while before the reassuring sound was heard once more of your truck's wheels rolling on to the steel decking of a ferry boat that was shortly to depart on its way back to dear old England!

Perhaps representing those who had more resilience than the average person in the street, some drivers regarded going out to the Middle East as the heaven-sent opportunity of a lifetime, a chance to finally pursue their own previously frustrated spirit of adventure, as they drove along the ancient highway through Turkey, Iran and onwards that is still known in a historical sense as 'The Silk Road'!

David Miller, one of the most experienced veteran drivers of the Middle East run, was asked what personal qualities he thought were essential for this extremely demanding job, skills that ensured each run stood every chance of reaching a successful conclusion, with a safe outward and homeward journey, and the goods delivered on time and all still in as good condition as when the journey started:

'More than 75 per cent of the Middle East truck drivers were either ex-Merchant Navy, like I was, or they were ex-Services. What we all had in common could be described as a difficulty in settling down into any normal sort of civilian job. But when we were out on any Middle East run, it was as if we were in Heaven. Only quite a small proportion of those who went out to the Middle East were in fact career truck drivers. There were guys with full-on university degrees working happily alongside guys who had had no formal education at all; out-and-out villains working happily alongside guys who were born with silver spoons in their mouths. But they had the same degree of self-reliance and independence which united them all and made any differences between each other seem to be so unimportant. Get a group of these people on the piss in the bar at the back of the Mocamp Hotel and just let the stories roll! Only later, as the numbers of those out on the road increased, did we suffer from the bullshit merchants, who hadn't a clue what they were doing.

'It was an extraordinary job which attracted extraordinary people, and that for me was the single best part of it. In 1973, when I first made my hesitant way out eastwards,

there were probably a hundred blokes, almost all Brits, who were involved in the job and I think it's fair to say there were very few pillocks to be counted amongst them at all.

'But by the early eighties, that number had increased to perhaps five thousand drivers of all nations, and the pillock factor had grown exponentially. Many of us, and I was one of them, preferred to run on our own, or only alongside particular friends we knew well. As the quantity of companies that became involved increased over a period of time, new drivers would be sent out, often with completely unsuitable vehicles to drive, or vehicles which had not been properly prepared for such a difficult trip. They were then told by their employer to 'Look out for an Oryx, a Grangewood, an Astran or an Altrex driver, and they will show you the way'. Now that was OK as far as it goes, because we all had to start off somewhere, but the fact was, you were working for the man who paid all your wages, and therefore your first responsibility was to him. I always used to say: "You can follow me with the greatest pleasure, but only if you can keep up, and if you break down, I'll get you to somewhere safe, but then you will be on your own." Some did come along with me following this simple rule, and some did not, and if they thought that I was a miserable bastard, then so be it. If someone applied for a job with a Middle East firm, their name would always be run past whichever drivers were at hand at the time. So it was tough on the pillocks, as they wouldn't be asked to come along after the boss had heard a bad report from the others.'

So what could be said to describe the wrong approach? David continued with the following recollection of state-owned British Road Services' (BRS) flawed attempt at tapping into this extremely lucrative form of revenue, wherein the dead hand of outdated management behaviour and stagnant union practices no doubt scotched their chances of success with this venture before the first convoy of trucks had set off on its way!

'I remember one winter trip when I came across some vehicles belonging to British Road Services Overland in the mountains of Romania. The idea that the state-run and operated BRS company could get into the Middle East business must have been dreamed up by some poor, demented executive; someone who I imagine had got hold of a particularly good sample of hallucinatory drugs on the day he came up with this proposal, as he then went ahead and ordered the purchase and equipping of some Leyland Marathons. The trucks were given into the care of some fully unionised, M6 motorway warriors, who were freshly off the well regulated Barnsley night trunk run. These particular boys were soon on their way towards Tehran, the capital city of Iran, but they only managed to get as far as Romania where the diesel in their fuel tanks froze solid, this being in mid-winter. Naturally, this sort of occurrence fell under the heading of a mechanical problem to their instilled way of unionised thinking and past experience. So this was no part of their established employment contract as BRS drivers, and they did the wisest thing and retired to stop in a hotel. Somehow or other, they managed to get a message back to their base at Northampton, and they settled in to await the arrival of a BRS fitter who was coming all that way in a service van to solve the problem of the frozen fuel tanks – his arrival most probably coinciding with the arrival of spring – by which time

As a nationalised company, British Road Services proved to be less well adapted to the work than private haulage firms. BRS

the problem would have been solved by the arrival of warmer weather. It goes without saying the red and white Marathons which were operated by BRS were not a feature of the Middle East job for very long at all.'

However, at least two of the BRS liveried trucks were reportedly seen after the drivers had in fact successfully made deliveries to destinations somewhere in Saudi Arabia.

Many drivers doing trips out to the Middle East would have welcomed the opportunity to drive long hours in countries such as Turkey where the number of driving hours was not subject to any restrictions, although of course this could result in drivers overstretching themselves by driving almost non-stop for periods of up to twenty-four hours.

Even when a truck was standing stationary the driver was often left with the responsibility of looking after the security of the vehicle and its load, as the sole guardian and protector.

It could be said that the secret to maintaining peace of mind and physical wellbeing required the ability to step back from the job at well-regulated intervals, taking a day off once in a while, and maybe deciding not to sleep in the cab in favour of a hotel bed every so often. Also important was generally looking after yourself by remembering to follow daily routine activities, such as taking the time for an invigorating wash and brush-up at certain times of the day.

If a driver had not been able to revitalise his spirits when faced with the latest in a series of unforeseen misfortunes, then he could very well end up in deep trouble, as Ken Ward described with the following story on how important it was to look after your self and wellbeing in the face of trouble and adversity:

'I came across a driver who was crying beside his truck because two of his tyres were flat. So I started off by calming him down and then saying, "Let's have a cup of tea, and then we'll sort out your problem.' He was filthy dirty, and I

View over the Bosphorus at the Harem landing stage where many trucks were parked awaiting the ferry. RW

could see it was his approach to the job which was getting him down so badly. I always made a point of washing myself every morning and every night. And if I had had a rough week, then I would treat myself by staying in a hotel which was paid for out of my expenses.'

Knowing how to look after yourself properly assumed increasing importance as the miles sped by. The further a driver was away from their home, the more the pressure built up that could cause them to succumb to stress and physical and mental exhaustion. Even the most well-travelled routes remembered from previous occasions could then appear to be a chore which was simply impossible ever to achieve!

Many of the haulage firms sending their trucks eastwards became increasingly alarmed when nothing was heard from a driver after a few days of delay since they were due back at home. As time went on, the conclusion these firms then had to grapple with was: had the truck had been abandoned somewhere en route – because driver was inexperienced, or ill-prepared, or perhaps fundamentally ill-suited to the challenge of the job?

This situation became very serious in time, and the overnight parking places of stopovers such as the Mocamp in Istanbul accumulated abandoned trucks

Aydin's garage where many Middle East trucks were repaired with lots of common sense and improvisation. RW

his employer, as he decided to vandalize his truck in order to avoid continuing on with the journey for his own personal, but undisclosed, reason:

'A new driver was recruited, and a Volvo F89 was tooled up so it was ready to go, and off he went, but then the firm received a call from the driver when he was in Belgrade saying he was having some mechanical problems, and after that, a telex arrived from Istanbul saying the engine of this guy's truck had blown up.'

Ian had been trained as a mechanic in the British Army, so he was just the sort of bloke to be sent out on the next plane to Istanbul so that any mechanical problem could be resolved. Ian then met up with the driver at the famous Londra Mocamp where so many drivers stopped, where he was surprised to discover the truck he had come all that way to repair was nowhere to be found.

Adopting a discreet line of questioning, he finally established what had happened since the driver of the broken-down truck arrived in Istanbul. Ian now knew the driver had no intention of pushing on towards his final destination. He also discovered the broken-down Volvo F89 had been taken to a garage run by a Turkish bloke called Aydin – someone who was well respected for the quality of his repair work by many Middle East drivers.

'When we lifted the cylinder head,' said Ian, 'we found something to back up what we later learnt about this driver already being a known troublemaker when he worked for other firms. He had sabotaged the truck after running out of cash, which had all been spent on drink. So what did he do next? He raised the cab on the F89 and then he removed the end of the hose running between the turbo and the inlet manifold. In anticipation of the engine being ruined, he dropped some steel bolts down into the manifold, so when the engine was started, the bolts were blown into the engine's cylinders. This act of sabotage took place shortly before the lorry had been driven across the suspension bridge over the Bosphorus. I immediately knew buying any new parts that

and trailers, which were clearly identifiable by the thick layers of dust that collected over time. Any further hopes of these lorries returning home to resume service were often scotched by the theft of so many parts, such as wheels and batteries, for spares or to be sold elsewhere.

Some drivers sabotaged their own trucks in a ham-fisted attempt to make it seem as if they were not the ones who were responsible for the failure to complete the trip. If they did not have the money to buy a ticket to fly back to Heathrow, then there was always the opportunity to cadge a ride home with another driver after preparing a plausible sob story that evoked sympathy!

More darkly, trucks and trailers would disappear somewhere out there, as pre-planned by crooked owners, with the incentive of conducting criminal and insurance fraud, as the vehicle and the contents would never be seen again. At a lower level of criminal activity, the truck, trailer and the load would eventually turn up somewhere, but not the driver; he would have already done a runner with any money that had been given to him to cover day-to-day running expenses.

Ian Taylor remembers an inexperienced new driver whose very first trip went terribly wrong for

we needed to repair the engine was out of the question, as the import duty applied to any spare parts from abroad being brought into Turkey made these very expensive to buy over there. However, Aydin managed to remove the one and only damaged piston, which still had a bolt embedded in the top. He then smoothed down the top of the piston on his lathe, and he also replaced two damaged valves, so when he had finished, that engine ran again just like a Swiss watch. Another of our drivers then finished off the delivery to Baghdad and the truck eventually returned home.'

Another of Ian's stories on drivers being unprepared for what lay ahead concerned three drivers of brand-new Scammell Crusaders which were operated by Reeds Transport: two of these drivers bowed out after crashing in Yugoslavia, and the third driver didn't do much better, as his truck was badly damaged when a moment's inattention resulted in it being stuffed into an unyielding earth bank along a stretch of road in Turkey and suffering much damage. Having better than average driving skills and constantly maintaining a vigilant approach were essential requirements of the job!

As well as the qualities that the driver possessed to see the job through, these had to be matched by the employer being equally committed to supplying sufficient support and back-up facilities if anything happened to go wrong. This was something that Michael White always did his best to adhere to in order to assist any of his White Trux employees when travelling out to the Middle East run.

'You had to have good back-up all the way there and all the way back. Our vehicles were always quite newish, although lots of people were sent out there driving these old, ramshackle trucks; so they had lots of breakdowns, of course. But we didn't have any problems of this sort over the eight years we were out there. It also helped that when we began sending out loads to the Middle East, this was for established customers that we already knew well. I would minutely plan out the routes in advance, and I even went out myself as the second driver in the truck which was sent with our first load. We did all our own survey work, taking a section of the route at a time so we could get a full grasp of the situation on the ground, while taking account of any problems that had been identified. It was a personal type of business in those days, and if any drivers had problems en route, our agents would always help them out because they knew me personally, and that is how it all worked.

'I normally sent out one vehicle every two days, which meant we could have thirty vehicles on the Middle East

Aydin and his mechanic hard at work on a broken-down truck. DM

route at any one time. If a driver had a problem, then he would know another driver was running somewhere behind him, or another one would be coming along shortly in the opposite direction. I never sent out my trucks as a convoy, as this was only asking for disaster. One boy's a boy, two boys are half a boy, and if there are three boys, then there's no boy in charge at all!'

Self-reliance was something Bob Carter of Trans UK always looked for in any drivers he selected for an interview, this being seen as something which was hugely important at a time when a driver could be out on his own for weeks at a time. This was when telexes were the only viable form of communication across many parts of Europe as well as the remoter

Robert Dods-Brown, a pioneer of the Middle East runs who was known for his friendly disposition and professionalism. AC

be interviewed for this publication. Robert was always well respected by his peers as a Middle East driver. He was someone who definitely exhibited the Right Stuff with all the mental and physical attributes the job could possibly require. Sadly, this was not to be, as after suffering a series of strokes over a period of time, Robert passed away on 17 February 2014.

Robert's funeral provided an insight into his reputation for being so well respected, both as an individual and as a Middle East driver. This was something Ashley Coghill, a very close friend of his, was to describe at length at Robert's funeral where over 400 mourners attended his local village church. And later on, many tales were told of his professionalism and adventures, as an owner driver, in the Scania trucks he always favoured for the job! Ashley summed up Robert's approach to the job as follows:

'His passion and enthusiasm stood out, as he was always as keen as mustard; driving the Middle East routes was all he wanted to do. I once asked him if he would consider driving out there again, and the answer came back "Yes, yes, yes". This was even before I had finished what I was saying! That was providing of course everything would have been the same as it was over forty years ago in the old days!'

Robert Dods-Brown with his Volvo F86 before he took to the long-distance Middle East routes. RDB

hinterlands of the Middle East! The telex service was available in those days, but only at a few locations that were widely spaced out. Bob also made a point of taking on any drivers who had already acquired a degree of proficiency in one or more foreign languages.

When being recruited as drivers for Middle East work, their selection as suitable for employment rested on them satisfying a wide range of variables, although of course these factors could only be verified by how well they performed on their first trip to far-off destinations such as Tehran, Baghdad or Jeddah, which of course sorted out the men from the boys, and clearly identified those who possessed the right stuff to see the job through to a satisfactory conclusion!

It had been planned that Robert Dods-Brown would be one of the Middle East drivers who would

As for a good number of Middle East drivers, the spirit of wanderlust that drove them on to take up this specialist type of work had already been firmly established in foreign climes during their work as military personnel, sailors or in various other roles abroad.

Robert took himself off to Australia when he was aged twenty-one, where he drove tipper trucks up in the distant Northern Territory, followed by a spell driving massive Mack articulated trucks carrying manganese from mines down to the docks.

After spending two years down under, there was a change of pace when Robert decided to further develop or advance his driving career by obtaining a HGV licence here in the UK. This was achieved simply enough, and Robert began making routine agricultural delivery jobs around his home county of Cambridgeshire.

Passport details – Robert Dods-Brown. A document that frequently needed to be renewed by Middle East drivers! RDB

But rather predictably, the urge to venture far and wide soon made its presence felt, and Robert undertook a second period of employment in Australia. He then returned home once more and expanded his horizons with some continental work, which then led to the prospect of tackling some Middle East overland trips. That prospect turned out to be even more exciting than driving through the remote, wild outback of Australia!

Robert contacted Chapman & Ball International of Stoke-on-Trent as he had heard from other drivers that this was a good company to work for, and he was signed up as an owner driver with the proviso that his newly bought Scania 110 was to be painted up in the firm's dayglo-style orange livery with contrasting black lettering.

The first Middle East trip Robert undertook was fairly modest as this involved taking a load of chemicals on what he would later consider to be a rather short run in terms of distance out to Istanbul. Any apprehension that Turkey wasn't a good place to be in was soon dismissed as Robert enjoyed some much-appreciated leisure time relaxing and chatting with other drivers at the Mocamp before successfully making his way home ... the only problem being that it took a whole month to unload the chemicals due to administrative problems! Nevertheless, Robert was entranced by this roaming way of making a living that also paid so well!

Transporting a load of Massey-Ferguson tractors to Baghdad in Iraq came next, and Robert's horizons were further expanded with a trip to Jeddah in Saudi Arabia, and as a reward for helping the crew of a ship to unload its cargo, a berth was provided for the return trip to the UK with his truck safely stored below decks!

Positively encouraged that this was the sort of life that he wanted to lead, Robert eventually replaced the Scania 110 with a more powerful V8-engined 140, also painted up in Chapman & Ball's colours. In addition to Robert's name emblazoned on the headboard, this truck featured the cartoon character of a genie sitting on a flying carpet – something that identified Robert's truck as the 'Arabian Cruiser' – which became a familiar sight to drivers of all nationalities as he travelled across Europe and along the Middle East routes.

Robert's Scania 140 and the tilt trailer in Chapman & Ball livery was chosen by Corgi to duplicate as a 1:50 scale model in the firm's Intercontinental Hauliers range.

Robert would have been the first to admit that he had enjoyed the best years of the Middle East overland story, and no doubt he would have spent many hours mulling over his numerous exciting adventures!

Robert Dods-Brown's Scania – one of an increasing number of Middle East trucks immortalised as scale models. TJ MODEL TRUCKS ©

There was a parting of the ways with Chapman & Ball later on when Robert took on new work with Spiers and Hartwell of Evesham; one of the underlining reasons for this move to another firm was that it provided regular work to his favourite destination, Doha, the capital city of Qatar.

For many drivers on Middle East work, and particularly those like Robert who were self-employed, 1979 proved to be a bit of a disaster, as the collapse of work taking loads out to Iran came as a consequence of the fall and expulsion of the ruling Shah in that year. This resulted in a stampede of trucks heading towards alternative destinations throughout the Arabian Peninsula in order to make up for any loss of any Iranian revenue.

After a lot of heart-searching, it was time to call it quits, particularly as what could be described as the 'cowboy era' was now in its full swing. Robert was not the sort of person to lower his standards of professionalism: either when it came to getting the job done properly, or meeting the expectations of those who had entrusted him to carry their loads safely and on time, over so many thousands of miles.

So ended the career of one of the most pleasant and unassuming characters of the Middle East era, with quite a few regrets over the ensuing years that those days were finally over.

Sadly no long with us, Terry Tott once played a jam session with Showaddywaddy. Many recall his improvised guitar sessions out on the road. TT

CHAPTER 3

Taking the Plunge

The mid-seventies saw a flood of goods and materials transported by road overland to Middle East destinations, with trucks and trailers bearing the different registration plates of so many European countries taking part. Such was the attraction of becoming involved in this form of road haulage business, anyone possessing a truck driving licence must surely have weighed up the prospects of giving it a try. The financial benefits amounted to far more than truck driving in the UK could ever pay. But this had to be balanced out by all the hardships that had to be endured along the way, as driving a truck all the way to Middle East destinations was never going to be easy!

Beside the handsome pay that was on offer, travelling overland by truck to the Middle East routes provided the opportunity to travel to many exotic-sounding locations, such as Istanbul in Turkey, Damascus in Syria, or Herat in Afghanistan; the sort of places that were only vaguely remembered from within the covers of school geography books but would now seem real when viewed through a dust-coated, fly-splattered windscreen! The opportunity to travel so widely was a rare privilege in the days when taking a package holiday to Benidorm each year was as exciting as it could get for most people; particularly anyone who was taking home the sort of average wage that a lorry driver earned at the time!

Some would take to the challenge like ducks to water, but not everyone was up to the task. A good number fell by the wayside as their confidence in what they were doing so far from home suddenly collapsed like a trapdoor. Then there was the slow build-up of home-sickness that became just as off-putting as time went by. Also the culture shock of having to deal with so many different ways of doing things and unfamiliar social situations, such as dealing with officials at border crossings that seemed to require an infinite amount of patience and sophisticated diplomatic skills. And of course there was the ever-present language difficulty of making yourself understood, or understanding what you had been told, which was never going to make life easy! When these factors were working together, this could soon erode away the will to keep on going with the job at hand!

There was also the more immediate shock to the nervous system of getting involved in road accidents, or simply observing any serious road accident or a near miss along the way, incidents that could so easily crush the spirit to travel this far again owing to the repeated dangers to life and limb!

It was usually that very first trip that determined whether a driver had the innate abilities and fortitude to assume such an independent lifestyle. This involved living in a lorry's cab from dawn until dusk through most days of the week except for a short break at noon for a brew-up and a simple meal cooked up on a Calor

Ken Ward and Graham Streak smile for the camera before setting off in their Scania 141 trucks to make another delivery for Grangewood's. KW

Gas stove. The truck cab then took on a new role after sunset as this was somewhere to eat and sleep as well as shelter from the excesses of heat and cold according to the seasons of the year.

The following descriptions detail the experiences of a number of drivers who managed to overcome the drawbacks of taking to such an unusual, yet fulfilling lifestyle.

DAVID MILLER

David set off on his first trip as the boom in road transport to the Middle East was still getting underway. He was aware of his good fortune in taking on this type of work from day one, particularly as everything dropped into place so easily:

David Miller, someone who now looks back on his times on the Middle East runs as the opportunity of a lifetime. DB

'I had come ashore from earning my living at sea so I could get married and I was employed as a lorry driver for a firm called Thompson's Transport down in Devon. I was working with a good friend of mine, a driver called John Craig, and one day when we were on our way back from Scotland, we decided to stop off at the M6 motorway services near Carlisle. I picked up a copy of the Automobile Association's Drive magazine featuring an article describing a Middle East trip which Dick Snow made to Afghanistan with the Astran company. We decided this was what we also wanted to do, so I spoke to Bob Paul at Astran and asked him if he could give us both a job. He responded by asking whether either of us had any Middle East driving experience, to which the answer was sadly "No". So he then said to me: "No, sorry, no can do if you have no experience of this sort of work." '

But David and John were not about to give up so easily, and the plan they cooked up to achieve this most important objective involved buying any maps they could find detailing the routes and place names to be found along the Middle East route, such as Istanbul and Tehran. Their intention was to swot up on the geographical details, and after learning and memorising as many details as they could on all the possible routes to Middle East destinations, they would then be able to pull a flanker by convincing someone in authority with a haulage firm that they were already fully versed in the Middle East haulage business with a fund of experience that suggested beyond doubt they were fully tried-and-tested, seasoned drivers.

'After mugging up on all the maps, I spoke to Bob Paul again, who had clearly forgotten about my earlier enquiry. I said, "Yes we've been [here]" and "Yes we've been [there]." So Bob said, "Super, I know couple of my subbies who are looking for drivers at the moment: J and T International, also another firm called Eileen Ellingham Middle East, so I'll give you call back after I've talked to them in a few minutes." After Bob came back to me, I was offered a job on the spot with Eileen Ellingham – the name of the firm was taken from the founder's wife. So later on, I called round to pick up the truck at their yard, which was in Southall, London. This turned out to be a Scammell Crusader with a trailer on tow which had already been loaded up with oil drilling pipes and was now bound for Basra in Iraq. This was a British-spec, right-hand drive truck, and it was the only right-hander I ever drove out to the Middle East, the rest of them were all left-handers. The boss, John Ellingham, said to me: "Well, you know what you're doing, so off you go." He then handed me a briefcase containing all of these *strange bits of paper which I'd never seen before. Looking at all my paperwork gave me the first clue to what it was that I needed to do next – the paperwork marked all the border crossings along the route that had been chosen, so I knew which way I had to go, and I set off for the first destination, which was Dover. The paperwork also revealed I had a cross-channel ferry booking from the port in Dover, so off I set, and after arriving there I caught the ferry to Zeebrugge. I met some other truck drivers on the ferry who asked me where I was off to, so I told them that I was going to Basra in Iraq, to which they replied I must be completely mad going that far away in a truck!*

'Crossing the border into Turkey was wonderfully chaotic, although I didn't have anything to compare this strange experience with at the time. On reaching the waterfront in Istanbul, I crossed the Bosphorus taking the ferry for Kadıköy and reached the eastern shore. I travelled all the way to Basra in Iraq and then back to the UK, going all the way without seeing another British truck for a long while until I arrived back in Istanbul, where I stopped overnight at the Londra Mocamp.'

So from his earlier sea-faring days with the Merchant Navy, David was ready to further extend his worldwide travels as captain and crew complement of a Scammell Crusader that was soon ranging far and wide through many distant lands of the Middle East, taking on a job that served him very well until this sort of trade began falling away in the mid-eighties.

MARK CHEVALIER

Mark's road haulage career cranked up a gear from making local UK deliveries after he met some drivers who convinced him that doing some continental deliveries would be a good idea. So Mark made a few continental runs, which brought him into contact with drivers who were driving a good deal further on to Middle East destinations. This also convinced Mark that it was time to spread his wings, and he set off to make his first trip to Tehran in 1973.

Suitably impressed that he was now on to a good thing, Mark talked his brother Andy into coming along on the next trip run, and as this also worked out well, they began trading as Middle East transport specialists the Chevalier Brothers, and when repeat orders started to roll in, they began to recruit other drivers to drive their trucks to Middle East destinations.

Mark described some more details on how the firm developed from having a truck each, for Andy and himself over the next few years:

'We started off with two MAN 16.232 I bought, the ones which still had a column gearchange which wasn't a bad move in one way, as this type of gearchange did leave plenty of room for anyone sitting in the cab. My brother Andy and I traded from Chevalier Brothers' base in Box Hill, London. We worked as owner drivers first of all by carrying some loads for Cantrell's in Europe before taking on the bulk of our work with the Davies Turner firm of freight forwarders in Battersea, which was mostly groupage work, by which time we were employing some of our own drivers.'

LES RIVETT

After taking a job with the firm of Spiers and Hartwell, Les's first Middle East trip got off to a poor start after he arrived in Dover, when he mistakenly drove into the entrance for the Eastern Dock rather than the Western Dock, a mistake which was down to not reading the paperwork he had been provided with quite as well as he should have done! Clearly a novice at this sort of work, Les suffered the embarrassment of being escorted by the police to the correct entrance of the Western Dock, where he managed to board a ferry a couple of hours later than his planned departure time!

After crossing the Channel, it looked as if things were going well for Les now that he was driving across the continent at last; he had met up with an experienced driver who offered to take Les under his wing by showing him a suitable route to take across Europe. This driver's destination was to Basel in Switzerland, which seemed to be a step in the right direction towards Les's final destination in Baghdad. So he gratefully followed along in the other driver's wake. But as this was Les's first attempt at driving abroad, it took a while to become accustomed to driving on the right-hand side of the road, so he was driving more slowly than he would normally have done, and it wasn't long before the taillights of the truck in front disappeared over the horizon, never to be seen again, leaving Les to find his own way towards Switzerland, and on his own again!

Thankfully, Les remembered the more experienced driver's instructions, which he rigidly stuck to as he travelled on towards Basel, but on reaching the Swiss frontier, he was told in no uncertain terms he wasn't allowed to transit across Switzerland: the paperwork he was carrying detailed the lorry's load at twenty-one tons, which exceeded the permissible weight limit for trucks using the Swiss road system in those times.

Les had no option but to turn back and then take an alternative route through Germany, which required a new transit permit, resulting in further delay until he managed to contact his boss in the UK so this documentation could be forwarded on.

Despite being so inexperienced, Les eventually made it to Baghdad while accompanying another novice driver who came from Germany, someone Les aptly named 'Herman the German'.

'I just loved the job,' Les remarked. 'I did this type of work for five years from 1975 to 1980. This involved travelling to Doha in Qatar, Dubai, Kuwait, Jeddah in Saudi Arabia, also to Baghdad, as on my first and later trips. My largest job involved taking thirty-six loads of desalination plant equipment down to Doha and also to Kuwait. As a way of undercutting what the competition had on offer to do this particular job, my boss offered to do the first run out to the Middle East for the customer in just thirteen days. This timescale was achieved, as by the time the two German engineers turned up to begin installing the desalination plant, the first of the Spiers and Hartwell trucks had already arrived and was about to be unloaded.'

MIKE DUNSTAN

Rather unusually for a British-born driver, Mike's first employment as a Middle East driver was with a foreign firm, the Dutch company of Butrako, whom he joined in 1975. It was his British nationality that opened the doors to being offered a job with this firm:

'Butrako were looking for British drivers as it was far easier at the time to obtain the necessary visas for British drivers to enter Saudi Arabia than it was for those of any other nationalities. My first trip was in a Spanish-built Pegaso – Butrako had about twenty of these trucks at the time. Pegasos had a good, roomy cab, which was handy, but their engines were gutless and the trucks were rather prone to suffering from breakdowns at regular intervals.'

Mike was accompanied by another Brit driver, John 'Percy' Harris, who came from Stroud: another 'first-tripper', although the pair of them soon wised up as they went along, building up some much-needed confidence in their abilities and also their navigational skills as they travelled across Europe, then through Turkey, and by

Mike Dunstan beside his Butrako Ford Transcontinental stretching his legs after climbing out of the cab. MD

following more experienced Middle East drivers for a while through Syria, they crossed into Jordan by taking a road that skirted along the shoreline of the Red Sea.

One of the high points of this part of the run occurred when Mike met up with Dick Snow, one of the drivers featured in the BBC's DVD documentary on the Middle East run, the recently released *Destination Doha*. Dick was driving an Astran truck when they got chatting at the Jordan/Saudi Arabia border at Haret Ammar, and Mike was most appreciative of Dick's helpful hints on driving and the sort of desert conditions they were about to encounter further along the route they were taking into Saudi Arabia. Mike commented:

'I was loaded in the open TIR style, which meant the load wasn't, or didn't need to be, properly sealed to clear any customs procedures. I was carrying parts of a crane tower that was going to be assembled at the docks in Jeddah so that it could be used for unloading any shipping that came into the port. This was where the money in Middle East haulage was at the time. It was important to relieve the backlog of all the cargoes that had been shipped in, and this could only be achieved by bringing in more cranes and any other heavy lifting gear which was needed. Unbeknown to us at the time, we were away from home for three months before we were flown home. What Butrako hadn't told us when

we'd taken on the job was they also intended setting up an internal transport service in Saudi, for which they needed the services of people like us as drivers for their trucks. So the fact that we weren't going home for such a long time came as a real surprise!'

GORDON SUMMERS

On arriving home after enduring a long, hard Middle East trip, it would be reasonable to assume anyone with sense would have more than just reason to delay going out there again, although this sort of logic seemed to fade away after a few days of leisure at home according to Gordon's comments on this subject:

'Every time I got off the ferry at places such as Ostend, I would think to myself, "You must be off your head going all that way," but whenever I got back home at the end of my trip, I would be looking forward to going out again on the next one.'

GRAHAM 'CARTY' CARTMAIL

Graham's ambition to drive to Middle East destinations came as a one-off opportunity that he grasped with both hands after he was approached by Jenkinson's, a Salford-based haulage firm:

'My first trip was with the late Ronnie Jackson. He was driving his Mercedes-Benz 14-18, and I was driving a Mercedes 19-24 that I'd been given. I suppose you could say it was a case of the blind leading the blind in many ways, as we were both so inexperienced. I was on my way to Tehran, and Ronnie was going to follow the southerly route which would take him down to Kuwait.

'We started off by taking the Ipswich to Rotterdam ferry. But we were in trouble as soon as we had left the ferry behind. What started to cause us problems was that there were not as many motorways in Holland as you would expect to find nowadays. So after coming out of the docks in Rotterdam, we came across these four-metre high bridges on the ordinary roads we were travelling on, which were so low, we couldn't drive under them, our trucks were so tall. So there was a lot of reversing to do in order to correct our mistakes when we'd gone the wrong way and arrived at any of those low bridges. But we eventually managed to find our way onto a motorway. Later on, we caught the train in Germany that carried the TIR lorries: this was the only way to get across this country if you hadn't got a permit that allowed you to travel on by road, and these weren't

Gordon Summers relaxes after a long day at the wheel. GS

available to us at the time, as only so many permits could be issued, and these had all been used up. Continuing by road through Austria and Yugoslavia went smoothly enough until we had reached the Yugoslavia/Bulgaria border. There was a long delay before we could cross the frontier, and this was followed by an even longer wait of over two or three days after we had arrived at the Bulgaria/Turkey border, although we were getting used to the long delays of this kind by now.'

Possessing the sort of patience that a long-term convict might have developed to retain their sanity and peace of mind would be a good description of the sort of fortitude and resilience that Middle East drivers had to adopt in order to withstand the many hours, if not days, when they would be left waiting at border crossings to clear customs and immigration formalities. These frontiers could be choked by long lines of trucks that stretched back for miles awaiting processing, all the while inching forward, but only by a few feet at a time.

Passing through the Turkey/Iran border at Gurbulak/Bazargan was a particularly notorious, lengthy experience, with backlogs of standing trucks parked nose to tail in queues trailing back for miles along the approach road on both sides of the frontier. The lack of any proper eating, washing and toilet facilities added to the displeasure of having to wait standing around or sitting in cabs for long periods of time while enduring the summer heat or the freezing cold winter conditions. Not surprisingly, arguments soon flared up should anyone have the audacity to make an attempt at jumping the long queue of trucks!

Graham remembers that his first border crossings were the worst feature of his newly chosen career. However, once he had mastered all the formalities of dealing with the paperwork and the officials, everything began to fall into place, and after completing a few successful trips, his status as a novice driver was soon dismissed. He began passing on his newly acquired knowledge to any new drivers that the firm took on, and Les Higgins was always grateful for the seasoned advice he received from the likes of Graham and other drivers.

LES HIGGINS

Les joined Jenkinson's after Graham had tipped him off that one of the regular drivers would no longer be going on a trip that was already planned due to a bout of ill-health; so recognising that here was an offer that was unlikely to occur again, Les signed on the dotted line when presented with his future employment contract:

'Graham went with me on my first run,' said Les. 'We knew each other as we'd previously worked together at a firm called Richardson's, so we knew we could get on well enough. This was to be my one and only trip as far as I was told at the time, which seemed like the opportunity of a lifetime.'

Les picked up all the unfamiliar export and customs paperwork including a *carnet de passage* that detailed his vehicle. The purpose of the carnet document was to avoid the need to pay any import duties when a vehicle was transiting through a country rather arriving there as the final destination, in which case the payment of import taxes would then apply. Obtaining a carnet allowed a vehicle to be temporarily imported into a country without requiring a cash deposit to be paid at the entry border which would then be refunded at the exit border, providing of course the vehicle did leave the country! In addition, drivers transiting a country would use a separate document known as a triptych to cover the temporary admission of a motor vehicle through a country. The difference between the carnet and a triptych was that the latter contains a set of forms, and as implied by the name, these are in triplicate. When used to temporarily import a vehicle into a country, one of the forms was stamped on entering a country, the second form was stamped on leaving a country, and the third copy was retained by the driver.

Under the Convention on International Transport of Goods Under Cover, more commonly known as *Transports Internationaux Routiers* or TIR, which was agreed and concluded in 1975, the transportation of goods in sealed vehicles, trailers or containers is permissible from one country to the next without the need for time-consuming border checks at any intermediate border posts. This agreement existed between all Middle East countries with the exception of Iran, which still required a recoverable cash payment as a guarantee.

Returning to Les's story, in January 1977, he set off in a three truck convoy accompanying Graham Cartmail and a third driver, Steve Swaine, with all three of them driving their firm's well-prepared DAF 2800s. The destination was Saudi Arabia, a country so far away and beyond Les's comprehension, this may as well have been somewhere on the dark side of the moon! But Les had the reassurance he was in safe hands all the way:

'They were both nice lads to go with on my first run, as they soon taught me all I needed to know about the job, what to expect, and they also managed to keep me out of any trouble. We were loaded with huge sections of water plant valves which needed to be delivered to a water pumping station in Jeddah in Saudi.'

The Jenkinson's trucks had set off in the depths of mid-winter, and Les's first encounter with poor weather conditions wasn't long in arriving; a fierce snowstorm was encountered as they passed through Bulgaria. So they decided to call a halt until the storm had blown over, and after the trucks had crawled to a halt, Les applied the handbrake on his, which was standing on a steep slope, as this was the only suitable stopping place on offer. However, after climbing out of the cab, the truck and the loaded trailer began rolling backwards, picking up more speed.

'I was then told to get back in and put on the dead man's handle, so back into the cab I climbed as fast as I could! It was all a bit hair-raising, as if I hadn't managed to stop the truck and the trailer from rolling backwards quickly enough it would have gone down a steep ditch and become stuck fast and unmoveable. Luckily, the truck did come to a stop, but I was only just in time!

Travelling through Europe allowed Les to take in the changing scenery as well as the cultural shifts that occurred along the way, and crossing the border from Bulgaria to Turkey was a real eye-opener!

'It took a two-day wait to get through the border into Turkey at Kapıkule. I had never seen anything like this place at all. There was this sea of churned-up mud everywhere, with people running about all over the place! But after we got going again, travelling down the road to Istanbul was a truly evocative moment! Everything seemed so foreign for someone who came from the West Midlands. I remember coming across a mosque with a minaret standing beside it and you could hear the muezzin calling the faithful to prayer as I drove by through the next town which was called Edirne. I learnt more about what was going on in the world on my first Middle East trip than I ever managed to attain during the years when I went to my local grammar school.'

For first-timers, the experience of entering a world that was so different from what they had encountered so far would have reached its zenith when confronted by the awe-inspiring panorama of the Bosphorus waterfront after arriving in Istanbul – once the capital city of the Byzantines, and the seat of power of the Ottomans until the beginning of the last century. This magnificent city has the unique distinction of straddling the continents of Europe and Asia. The highlight of this city's amazing vista then comes to life when the towering mosques and minarets are cast into dark silhouettes by a blood-red sky at sunset.

Les remembers running the gauntlet of the many hordes of street urchins that hung about outside the Harem Hotel in Istanbul on the off chance their pleas for a few coins or one or two cigarettes would be successful, or they would win a small cash payment for shining someone's shoes.

Spending an evening at the famous, or rather infamous, West Berlin nightclub of Istanbul, was a 'must see' for many drivers, where belly dancing was one of the attractions that went down well with the all-male clientele of this well-known drinking den. There was also the chance to get on familiar terms with any of the so-called 'hostesses', who were only too keen to socialise with any drivers round the tables in the bar for the price of a drink, with the distinct possibility of a more personal form of adult entertainment if an agreement was made and the price was right! One of the hostesses was immediately distinguishable as part of her arm was missing, and another had only one eye after losing the sight in the other one. No doubt their career had been ultimately determined by their unfortunate injuries rather than a matter of personal choice.

One driver who shall remain nameless soon discovered that spending some recreational time with one of the hostesses at the West Berlin nightclub meant his journey became a very stop/start affair as he searched out all the chemists along the way home! No doubt he was not the first of many who became similarly embarrassed, particularly if the consequences of their brief liaison had to be eradicated for obvious reasons by the time they arrived home!

After heading west as far as Ankara, Turkey's capital city, Les and company branched southwards towards the Taurus mountain range, then south-eastwards into Syria. Les was impressed by Graham and Steve's grasp of the local languages. So after asking them how they had become so fluent, Les was immediately put in his place when Graham explained that the only 'tongue' they couldn't understand was the one that Les exhibited with his West Midlands accent that seemed to be so incomprehensible to them at times!

With many miles of desert driving already behind Les and his mates, they were finally drawing closer to their destination at the port of Jeddah on the Saudi coast. The approach of civilisation was apparent when Les came across the first set of traffic lights to be encountered since they had left Bulgaria hundreds of miles further back down the road. This was where Les got into an argument over who had the right of way with the Arab driver of an old 6x4 Mercedes truck that came along at the same time and decided to settle the matter by slewing his truck sideways in a vicious sideswipe that was intended to shove Les's truck clean off the road. For which there was only one answer, and that was to respond in kind:

'I gave him a "bit of trailer" each time he did this to my truck. I could see him in my rear mirror, sitting in his cab and shaking his fist at me. Later on, I spoke to Graham about what happened, and he said the same thing had occurred to him when he came across the driver in the Mercedes some time later. Graham managed to push the other truck right off the road, where it became stuck in a bank of soft sand, which then put a stop to the problem from Graham's point of view, as the driver couldn't get his truck restarted. It took us a whole week to unload when we were in Jeddah, and by the time we went back down the same road, there was the Mercedes truck again, still stuck fast up to its axles in all that sand. Through incidents such as this, I

learnt a lot from Graham and Steve on my first trip, which did me a lot of good in the long run!'

KEN WARD

Grangewood Transport was one of the firms that successfully pioneered transporting perishable foods in temperature controlled, refrigerated trailers all the way out to the Middle East. Ken was recruited to work for Grangewood's by the firm's transport manager, Tom Tomlinson, who had taken a liking to the young Yorkshire man. Ken had been offered a considerable wage increase which amounted to a sum, startling for the times, of £82 for a five-day week – double what he was earning with his present employer. More significantly, this put Ken in just the right place to take on the job of a lifetime as far as he was concerned, as Grangewood's had begun making deliveries of refrigerated food supplies to a few Middle East destinations.

Ted Bryce was the first Grangewood's driver to venture out on a Middle East trip and he had set off from Rotterdam in Holland with a consignment of refrigerated cheese to be delivered in Saudi Arabia. This journey was in stark contrast to Ted's normal duties with Grangewood's, as he usually drove the shunter to manoeuvre trailers about the yard, a job which involved driving just a few kilometres each week rather than thousands of miles over a few weeks!

Ken recalled his very first trip driving a Volvo F88 to Saudi Arabia carrying a refrigerated delivery for the Grand Metropolitan Hotels group:

'This firm had a contract supplying food to work camps out in Saudi Arabia, and this journey went well enough for me from then on. Grangewood's were very active in most Middle East markets, and as my first trip was a success, I did well working with this company, and there was never a shortage of work for me to do with this firm.'

JEFF KEDWARD

In 1975, Jeff Kedward realised that the work he had been doing previously had begun to dry up for owner drivers delivering steel made at the Llanwern steelworks in South Wales, so he began scouting around for alternative employment, which eventually encouraged him to consider heading out towards the Middle East. Jeff's first load came his way after he had contacted a firm called PKS Transport of Bury St. Edmunds, and this involved taking a trip out to Iran driving his own Volvo F88, as previously used for hauling steel from South Wales, and this enterprise proved to be more of a success than he could ever have imagined:

'I hadn't even got a passport before I made that very first trip,' said Jeff. *'After making my decision to go all the way with this type of work, I decided to just run with it from then on, as this seemed to be such a good way of making a living.'*

So Jeff was happy to take on a second load on his return, which was for John Evans Transport of Newport. The route he travelled in his F88 on this occasion was a lot longer than previously. This took Jeff to Iran once more, and then he travelled on southwards towards the Persian Gulf coast, and after reaching the port of Bandar Abbas, he delivered some engineering equipment at a Wimpey construction company site where a large oil storage project was being built by the firm.

On the strength of the first couple of trips being successful, Jeff began a long association as an owner driver with the firm B and T Hicks International, of Newport, South Wales, as still managed by Brian and Terry Hicks at the time of writing.

There was one particular aspect of the Middle East job that Jeff always found extremely annoying. This

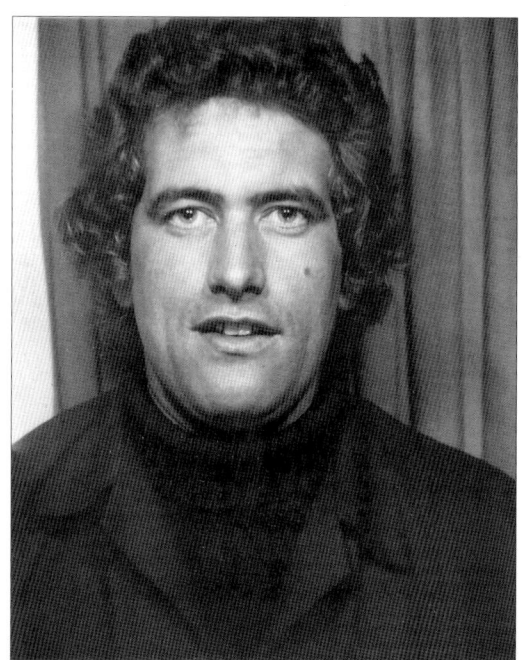

Ken Ward, someone who soon realised the value of making good friends with drivers of other nationalities. KW

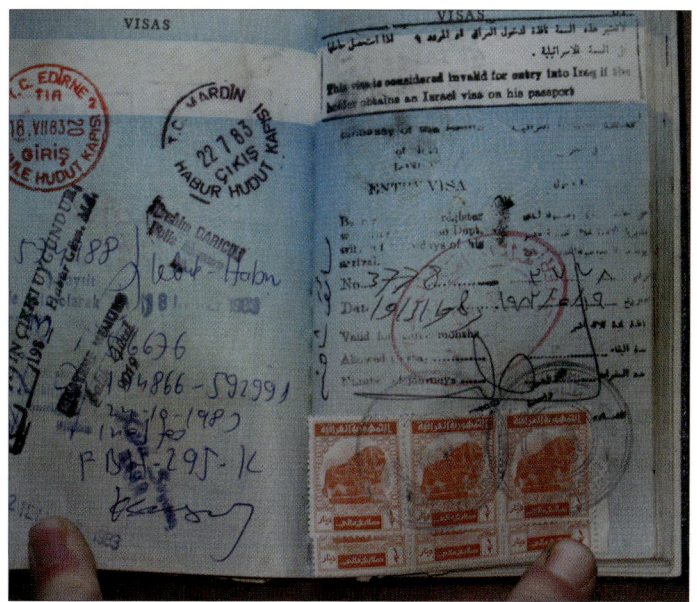

Jeff Kedwards' passport attests to many hard-won miles plying back and forth from the Middle East. DB

often made its presence felt when he was relaxing after the strain and discomfort of driving all those many thousands of miles on some of the roughest roads imaginable. After finally arriving home, he would head off down to his neighbourhood pub where he would be greeted by someone who cheerily announced: 'So when are you going back out there again?' or words to that effect! This sort of comment seemed to suggest that driving all the way out to the Middle East was just an ordinary sort of job, and barely worthy of comment! The truth being exactly the opposite of course, so this was something Jeff did not want to hear at all as he tried to unwind by sinking a few pints down at his local!

PETER BAMFORD

For many younger Middle East drivers, completing their first trip was something they could look back on with a justifiable sense of pride and elation. This was an experience they wanted to share with all their friends no doubt, perhaps assuming the role of a conquering hero which stood them in good stead for a free pint or two after recounting tales of derring-do when travelling across Europe and then through the 'badlands' of the Middle East? But many of the mature drivers, whom Peter represented during the early eighties, adopted a much more relaxed attitude to the job. According to Peter's point of view, the only difference to running any trips around the UK, or for that matter driving on the continent, was that the distances involved tended to be a bit longer! Also the view seen through a truck's windscreen was rather different at times, as you would not expect to see any camels wandering about in the vicinity of any British or European roads!

Peter went on to explain his mellow and so distinctly mature approach to seeing the job through:

'My first job out to the Middle East was not what I would choose to call a step into the unknown. As far as I was concerned, it was just an extension of what I had already been doing for a long while, taking many haulage loads all over the continent, so it felt as if I was going just that little bit further than I normally would have done. I was forty-five years old at the time, so all that "I'm off to the Middle East" bravado didn't appeal to me at all.'

Peter worked for Mick Smith of Preston, a firm that he came to respect for its professionalism in the business; working for any cowboy outfit was not Peter's chosen way of doing things! Over a period of time, Peter had noticed a fall-off in the standards of care that some less well-focused Middle East haulage operators began to offer their customers. The lure of rich pickings seemed to have resulted in a less disciplined or less fully prepared approach to doing the work. According to Peter, this happened at a time when many operators and drivers were getting in on the act without taking much time or applying much thought to what they were letting themselves, or their drivers, in for at the

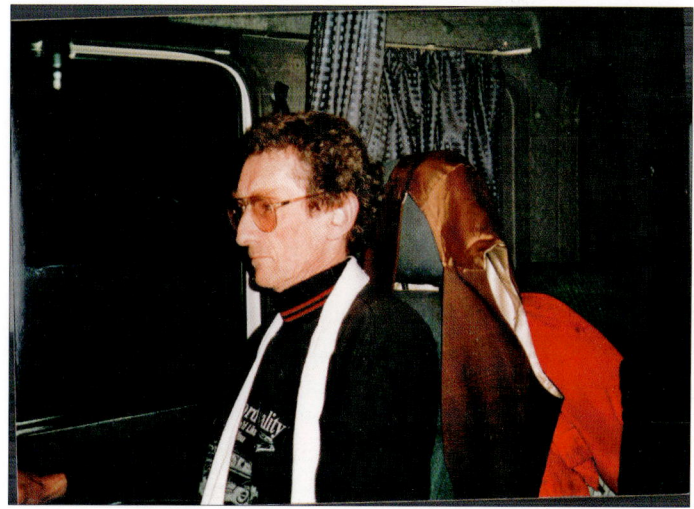

Peter Bamford's approach was rather different than most; with a few more years under his belt, the cash rather than adventure was his main objective. PB

time. So drivers were being sent out with very little awareness of what they were up against, and they were woefully unprepared for any difficult situations that they encountered. Not that some of the drivers were completely blameless, as they could also have the wrong approach to the job, as Peter went on to explain:

'There were some real cowboys about during a period which I would call the "fiddle boom" years. Someone would drop a wad of two thousand pounds into the hand of an inexperienced driver and tell them to go and collect a Fiat truck and a loaded trailer, which had been left standing fully loaded somewhere down the road in a lay-by. And off they would go, but maybe they would only get as far away as Ostend in Belgium, where they would blow away all the running cash they had been given by gambling it away in a casino, so they would then dump their truck and trailer at the side of the road, as they no longer had any money to go on with the trip. It seemed at times as if only the established firms, such as Astran, who originally ploughed the Middle East routes, could manage to do a proper job of delivering the goods so that everything arrived and was still in good order.'

It could be said that most individuals could have a tipping point when the stresses and strains of taking on such a demanding job suddenly reached breaking point, resulting in sheer panic and causing them to race their truck home with all possible haste. Peter remembers one driver who became so disturbed by the experience of living from day to day on his nerves, that the only way he could find to calm down his fears was to put his foot down and drive as fast as he could, covering an immense distance of about 1500 miles between Istanbul and the United Kingdom in slightly over two days by driving virtually non-stop, by day and also by night!

KEITH BURSON

Keith Burson's first Middle East run took place in 1975 when he was working for the firm of Richard Read Transport of Longhope in Gloucestershire. That firm then went into a consortium with two other hauliers to set up a new company that traded as Vijore Middle East Transport – which also comprised a firm by the name of Jones and the Vick Read haulage companies. Keith was already well versed with a background of driving low-loaders, tipper trucks and refrigeration work, and so he felt confident about taking on his first Middle East delivery, which involved travelling to Baghdad and delivering three animal feed mills:

'We all had ERFs on that first trip, with the exception of Tony Jones who drove a Foden with a 180 Gardner engine. As can be imagined, the Foden was an underpowered lorry, so it wasn't a very clever choice for going all that way to Baghdad in Iraq! Richard Read was driving an ERF with a 220 Cummins, and there was a fourth driver in another ERF, Peter Harborn, who's passed away now. My ERF was an A-Series with the 'bubble' extension on the back, a Jenning's-supplied sleeper cab, which I have to say wasn't much good at all: it was uncomfortable to sleep in, although I was lucky in one way, as I only had to do the one trip in that lorry. I was given an ERF European with a 355 Cummins engine and the 15-speed Fuller gearbox for my next trip, which was a much better truck than my old ERF A-Series, which did at least get me there and back!'

On Peter's inaugural trip, the Gardner 220 engine of his ERF began to overheat every so often, a problem that was not corrected until after he had returned. It was recommended by the engine's manufacturer that a set of twin air filters should be installed on the engine, and the plastic pipes on the range-change gearbox changed for copper versions, which unlike the plastic pipes, would not melt when subjected to the intense heat of driving along in scorching desert conditions, a modification that was successful on Peter's later trips to the Middle East in his ERF.

BRIAN ROBERTSON

After deciding to take up the challenge of setting off on his first Middle East run, Brian's next move was to buy a second-hand Scania tractor unit in 1976. The decision to go on this venture had been most positively influenced by a friend's enthusiastic suggestion that maybe the two of them should team up and commence making deliveries to faraway places such as Tehran, as this was a change in direction that promised to be very financially rewarding:

'My first response to this suggestion was, "Where's Tehran?" said Brian. *'The distance to Iran was at least four or five times more than I'd ever had to drive on the continent, which is something I'm still doing today to make a living. I bought a 110 Scania, but not one with a sleeper cab, although this truck did have some sleeping accommodation in what was called a "couchette" in those days. I went out on my own in the end, as my mate who'd suggested I should go out with him all the way to Iran decided he didn't want to go in the end! On my way out of the country, I met up with two blokes at Dover who offered to help me out. One of them*

Brian Robertson relaxes by the Red Sea when working for Chevalier Brothers. BRO

was going to Syria, the other one was going to Istanbul, and they were both taking the route which I'd already decided to take through Czechoslovakia and Hungary, so I went with them, which went fine.

'Later on, after successfully managing to get all the way to Ankara, which is in the middle of Turkey, without too many problems along the way, I came across the famous signpost everyone remembers, as the pointer on the left-hand side of the sign points in the direction of Iran, and the one on the right-hand side points to Iraq. This was where I met up with an Austrian driver who came alongside my truck and shouted across to me: "Are you going to Tehran?" to which my answer was "Yes" so he replied "Follow me" and off we went.

'That first trip went OK, but when I got back home, I said to my wife that I wouldn't be going back out there to the Middle East ever again. But then, after a few weeks of thinking the matter over, I began to realise my life was getting rather boring in comparison to what I'd just experienced, so just doing local work in the UK wasn't going to be enough. So that was that, off I went again on my second trip!

'Unloading at destinations all across the Middle East continued until I finally decided to pack the job in, which took me until 1984. There was the attraction of earning all that money of course as well as enjoying the adventure that went with travelling so far away. Many of us had never seen so much cash in our lives, and the running money you were provided with was so good as well! You could get all the way to Tehran and back for as little as £200–£300 in the early days, and with diesel costing just two pence a gallon in some of the Gulf State countries, this meant you still had lots of spare money to keep for yourself.'

Les Higgins made the point that the success or failure of a trip, from both the perspective of the driver and the haulier back home, could so easily depend on whether enough running money had been provided up front to see a job through to a satisfactory conclusion:

'I know of one mean-spirited boss from another firm who sent one of their drivers out to the Middle East with just £200 in his pocket to cover all his expenses, so you could imagine how long that trip lasted. You needed to take along many more times that amount, even in those days.'

GEOFF MORGAN

Geoff's interest in taking on deliveries to foreign destinations was prompted along the same lines as described for Jeff Kedward. They were both looking to pick up new work following the Llanwern steelworks strike in 1980 when there was no longer a need for steel deliveries from this foundry.

After obtaining a passport for the first time to take on continental work, Geoff was in a position to hitch his X-registered DAF 2300 DKS to a trailer carrying a load of aluminium for MAT Transport, which he successfully delivered to Belgium. So after taking some more loads bound for European destinations, Geoff contacted B and T Hicks Transport of Newport to see if they could offer him any Middle East work:

'I was advised to take a month's food with me,' said Geoff. 'And after coming away from the firm's offices after making the decision to go, I decided maybe it would be best to keep my wife in the dark about where I was actually going and how far away this was from home. So before I set off, I told her that I was going to be doing a few internal runs in the UK over the next couple of weeks. After loading my trailer, I followed another Hicks' driver down to the port in Dover, with my truck carrying the other driver's canvas trailer tilt and its frame on top of my load. He could not fit his tilt on his trailer because of the bulky load that he was carrying. This consisted of three large reels of electrical cable that were too large to be covered by a canvas tilt and its supporting frame.

'The only real problem I had on the outward journey was due to the other driver really having a liking for his drink, and come four o'clock every afternoon, wherever we just so happened to be, off he would go to see if there was any drink *available, and he would disappear into the nearest pub as soon as he could! That would be him, finished for the rest of the day. This meant I would also have to call it a day by pulling over for the night, as we were travelling together, and this sort of behaviour by the other driver lost me lots of valuable running time!*

'*My first run took place in the winter months, and after leaving Austria behind, we reached the border with Yugoslavia. A customs man then came along saying "Problem," as we attempted to cross the frontier. He went on to tell us that the other bloke's trailer needed a special type of permit as this was a quite a bit wider than you would usually find with a normal-sized stepframe trailer. As such, the trailer and its load were classed as an abnormal load. This load was being carried open TIR style, so it didn't need to be sealed beneath a tilt or kept inside a closed container-type body.*

'*If I hadn't been carrying the other bloke's tilt on my trailer, then the delay that occurred in getting hold of the necessary permit wouldn't have held me up at all: I could have just kept on going and left the other driver and truck behind. But I had to stop with him and wait until a special permit had been arranged for his load, and for an escort car to be provided, because his truck and trailer had now been reclassified as carrying an abnormal load. The escort car did not arrive until three days later when this bloke turned up in a little yellow Fiat 500 car, a service which then cost us £600 from our fund of running money. So we set off at last, although not for very long, as the escort driver in the small Fiat said he needed to stop for his breakfast, which he did. So we decided to press on, and that was the last we ever saw of him; he hadn't caught us up by the time we arrived at the National Hotel in Belgrade, so it was obvious he had disappeared for good. We continued on without him all the way to the Bulgarian border, which went just fine without having any official escort.*

'*We then travelled on to Iraq without too much difficulty other than the other driver's four o'clock stops for a few drinks, so after we arrived, I decided he wasn't the sort of bloke I wanted to follow home after losing so much time on the outward journey. After dropping off our loads, I decided to come back on my own.*

'*On arriving home at last, I was in for a lot of trouble from my wife, as she had found out by then how far I had gone, which was all the way to Iraq. I had been away for six weeks rather than the original fortnight that I had deliberately told her about before I left on that trip!*'

The rigours of that first journey were not to be forgotten all that easily, and Geoff was most reluctant to repeat what had been a challenging experience when he was asked to make another Middle East trip at very short notice. But the money tipped the scales with so many bills and other household expenses that always needed paying. So off Geoff went with another load even though he would have much preferred finding some local work:

'*On my next trip, which came only three days later,*' said Geoff, '*I cried my eyes out just before setting off. But once you were on the boat and you had finally left England behind, then you would soon settle down to what needed to be done, which was always a very good way of making a living.*'

ALAN DAYSON

Alan Dayson's haulage firm is based near the M6 motorway at Southwaite near Carlisle, and this family firm is still in business today operating haulage services on both internal UK and European work. Alan recollected:

'*Our first Middle East run took place in 1977 with one of our Scania 111s carrying a load out to Tehran. My driver who took on the job was called Harry Robinson, and he still lives nearby in Carlisle today. Harry was held up in some snow on his way out to Iran and I remember it took him a full three days to cross the Turkey/Iran border due to the massive backlog of trucks that were waiting to go through customs due to the bad weather conditions that had been holding things up. This turned out to be our one and only run to Tehran because the Iranian Revolution occurred shortly afterwards in 1979. So we decided to operate our fleet of six Scania 111 and 112 trucks to some of the other Middle East destinations which were available.*'

Ruling out deliveries to Tehran or other Iranian destinations for the immediate future, and maybe a lot longer, was a sensible decision to make: following the overthrow of the Shah of Iran who ruled the country until he was deposed by a well-supported uprising in 1979, all haulage work to Iran ground to a halt, with the country's borders tightly closed to all intents and purposes. This left many drivers and their trucks trapped inside the country while they waited for the political situation to settle down.

Alan successfully redirected the firm's haulage activities towards the less volatile Gulf States, where many loads were despatched by export agents and hauliers to satisfy the almost insatiable demand for any Western-made goods and supplies.

'All the docks were blocked with ships that were waiting to be unloaded,' said Alan. 'It was a case of either flying anything into the country that was urgently needed, or alternatively, sending it out to them by road transport. The political situation in the Gulf States was far more stable than it was in Iran in those days, and this worked out very well for us. In fact British and many other West European haulage firms were favoured because the Saudis didn't want to see any drivers from the Communist countries entering their country.'

CHRIS STEPHENSON

Chris Stephenson was one of Alan Dayson's pioneer drivers and his first run commenced in 1978. Like many other drivers, this was his first venture beyond the borders of the country of his birth!

'I was carrying a load of security fencing that needed delivering to the city of Doha, which is in Qatar, one of the Gulf States. After arriving in Germany, my truck was loaded on the train that took me through that country, as we couldn't get the permits to travel by road. This is where I met up with an owner driver called John Kemp, and after he had asked me where I was going, he kindly offered to look after me when he realised I was on my first trip. He said to me: "I'll tell you where to go, but don't try and follow directly behind me, as you won't learn the route otherwise, which you will need to know the next time you come this way taking this same route." I thought maybe I would never see him again after we had set off because I could no longer see his truck in front of me, but true to this driver's word, every so often he would stop and wait for me at a place further down the road we had already agreed to. We stayed together in this loose convoy fashion all the way down to Saudi Arabia, which is where we finally parted company, and feeling more confident, I did the last leg of the journey by myself to reach the final destination. Not that it was at all difficult. There are so few roads to take when you are travelling through Saudi, it would be very difficult to get lost with so few alternative routes available.'

GERRY HOLMES

After driving in the UK and taking on some European work, Gerry took a job with the newly established firm of H.J. Atlas of Avonmouth, a firm that had set its sights on the Middle East becoming a growing business venture, a choice that was motivated by the nationality of the firm's owner according to what Gerry reported:

'The guy who owned and set the firm up from scratch was called "Houshang Jafari", although we all used to call him "Hussein". He was an Iranian who came over here to this country as a student, and later on, set up his own transport business. Hussein was a very clever man and also an astute businessman. Being an Iranian meant he was at a considerable advantage when it came to making contacts over there and knowing the tricks of the trade. After we had arrived at an Iranian destination such as Tehran, there would always be a quick turnaround for any of our trucks so

HJ Atlas was founded by an Iranian who had the local contacts as well as the business acumen that guaranteed success. The identity of the driver beside the DAF is unknown. GH

we were soon heading back home again. This was Hussein's native land and he knew the language together with the local business customs. I started out with H.J. Atlas in 1978. Our loads included Singer sewing machines from Scotland, and replacement engines for tanks used by the Iranian army. I also remember taking prefabricated sections of buildings as wide loads. This Iranian guy was a good payer when it came to making up our wages, and you always knew you would never end up with any faulty paperwork that could so easily have complicated matters and caused long delays.'

FRED HODGKINS

Fred Hodgkins was working as a tanker driver for the Total petroleum firm at Langley near Slough in April 1976 when a workmate, Peter Burgess, took on a new job for Frank Willis that was to take him out to the Middle East, which then set Fred off on the very same path:

'When Peter returned from his first trip, I was eager to hear about all his experiences out there. I was immediately hooked by his account of this amazing trip that took him out to Tehran. So I decided this was the life for me as well! Someone had told me about a MAN 232 tractor unit that had been abandoned at the Londra Mocamp in Turkey. This truck was already in the process of being "topped", which meant that it was going to be taken back to the UK on the back of another truck. This recovery work was done by Freddie Noble as he was making his own way back to the UK. I needed this truck to set myself up as an owner driver, and it was fortunate that the amount I'd gathered together to make an offer to buy the MAN was accepted by the owner after the truck arrived back in this country. It was also fortunate that it didn't need to be repaired, as it turned out to be in good condition. The main reason it had been abandoned wasn't a breakdown, the driver had simply "lost his bottle", or maybe he'd spent all of his running money after reaching the Mocamp in Istanbul, so he then dumped the truck and made his way home.

'This second-hand MAN was only eight months old when I bought it, and it was soon ready to take to the road after I'd done all the preparations for my first trip. I soon established myself with a firm called Welham International of Fleetwood, and my truck was painted in their orange livery before I set off for Tehran in June 1976 while carrying a load of Black & Decker power tools. After arriving in Tehran, the first person I began chatting to went by the name "Teherani" Barney, and he gave me some very valuable advice on the do's and don'ts of the job. What a character he turned out to be, and I'm still in touch with him now.'

On leaving the ferry behind at Zeebrugge, Fred decided he had a natural flair for the job as he successfully navigated his way through the streets and highways of Brussels without any problems, which was more difficult than it is today as there wasn't a ring road at the time. Crossing the German border proved to be more challenging: the phrase *Welcomen bis Deutschland* began to seem rather hollow after Fred had locked horns with a cantankerous customs official who seemed intent on causing him as much trouble as possible:

'He was the most arrogant, ignorant and impatient geezer you could imagine. I was saved from matters getting out of hand between us when a Brit driver offered to help me out by sorting through all my documents so these could then be presented in the correct order, as demanded by the customs man. This was a good lesson which I took care to remember from then on, as it was so important to get the hang of sorting out your paperwork, as this meant you were home and dry whenever you had to cross any of the national borders along the way!'

Fred was also helped out by other Brit drivers as he crossed through Germany and he fell in with a couple of White Trux drivers who were following the same route he was taking in the direction of Tehran:

'These two drivers certainly took the pressure off me, and they made my first trip a lot more relaxing,' Fred explained. 'We stopped at various well-known haunts along the way, such as the National Hotel, then the Londra in Istanbul. Crossing the border into Turkey at Kapıkule was an experience I will always remember: it took hours of queuing before we eventually made it into the muddy heap of a parking area just after you had crossed the border and finally arrived in Turkey. This was where I met someone who introduced himself as a representative of the Young Turk import export agency. He helped out when I was asked by the customs men to open my truck up for an inspection. The customs men told me I was supposed to pay for the privilege of this inspection, which I then did, but after a few hours of standing about, none of the customs men came out to inspect my load as they were too busy. So that was that, I had paid up for an inspection which never happened! Together with the two White Trux drivers, we eventually landed up at the Londra Mocamp in Istanbul, where I finished off my long day with a very welcome shower and a hot meal.

'I recall the Mocamp was where you would meet up with what could be loosely referred to as "technical advisers".

The drivers who had been here, there and also everywhere else, the "I've got the T-shirt" types, who would try to give the impression that they knew everything while not actually knowing anything that really mattered at all. What they liked best was to use all the running money which they had been given to test out the quality of the Efes lager that was served in the bar. By the smell of them, they had clearly run out of any money for buying themselves some soap so they could have a good wash! I was told these people were known as "one-trippers" on account of them never being seen again after making the one trip. But I did get to meet some of the really genuine characters who went on to provide me with lots of really sound advice – such as Gerry Whelan for example, who pulled for Astran, someone who has sadly passed away. I also met many of the lads who were working for PIE International Carriers: Dave Telford, Rodney Walsh (The Ace) and Dave McCuller. They were really nice chaps who represented a clique which I really wanted to belong to, and which wouldn't march off down the road without me going with them as well!'

After crossing the Bosphorus by ferry, Fred headed across the hundreds of miles of road that crosses Anatolia, the steep climb over Bolu proving a challenge for his MAN which only had a 232 engine, so the truck was straining badly through the lower set of gears all the way. The MAN's engine wasn't as powerful as it should have been for this sort of terrain, which alarmed Fred, as he was left wondering whether his new-found running mates from PIE were about to leave him behind as they raced on towards Ankara. But they faithfully kept to their promise of easing off on the throttle and going just a bit slower than they normally would have done in their powerful Volvo F89s, so Fred just managed to keep pace on any steep inclines, such as the one over Bolu mountain. Fred was even accused of speeding at one stage, even though this was most unlikely given the lack of engine performance:

'There was an incident in Erzincan when I was stopped by two policemen, supposedly for speeding, but I wasn't going that fast at all. So I got myself involved in an argument with them, which started off with us all getting along and having a laugh, but things started to go badly wrong when they decided to nick me for parking my truck instead of for speeding, despite them being the ones who had stopped me in the first place! Little did I know at the time, these coppers were regularly stopping trucks and demanding baksheesh from any truck driver who happened to come their way. At Bazargan, which is on the Turkey/Iran border, I was greeted by a nasty, officious little policeman, who pulled a gun on me because I had driven my truck just a couple of inches over the white line that was outside his office. I was left wondering why jumped-up nobodies such as this bloke couldn't try to make any visitors to their country welcome instead of setting such a bad example by behaving so badly.'

On reaching his journey's end in Tehran, Fred presented his documents to the import agent, and he was pleased that everything went smoothly when his trailer was unloaded without any hassle. On the way homewards, however, with nothing in the back weighing down the trailer's suspension, there were times when Fred was sure he was about to be shaken to bits, with his back, arms and legs taking the strain whenever the truck and trailer rattled through deep potholes. It was like driving through a minefield as he backtracked across Iran, Turkey, Bulgaria and Yugoslavia, before arriving in Austria where he could enjoy the sheer bliss of driving on decently maintained roads that were smoothly coated over with newly applied asphalt!

Fred remarked in summary: *'One of the lessons I learnt was to be always patient with any officials I came across, and to take it on the chin if there were any problems, all the while remembering that I was British, and therefore had to be polite at all times.'*

JOHN BUFFHAM

John's first trip went fine on the outbound leg but the journey home was a lot more trying after the bloke with whom he was travelling suffered a mechanical failure with his truck which made life very difficult for them both for a good long while:

'I took a Scania 110 on my first trip, which involved travelling with a driver who was a friend of mine, Bob Thompson, and he was driving his own DAF. We travelled together down to Saudi at first, which is where Bob unloaded, and I then went off separately to make my own delivery in Doha. I met up with Bob on my way back through Saudi, and this was where the rear axle of his DAF lorry seized and packed up, so his truck wouldn't move any further at all under its own power. We had to dig a large hole in the desert sand using shovels so we could drop the truck's rear axle in order to release the trailer from the fifth wheel on Bob's truck. We then managed to pull his truck onto the back of my empty trailer so we could take it home. Bob's trailer was then left in a compound so it could be picked up later on and brought home by another truck.

'On the basis of that first successful run, I bought a Volvo F88 to follow the same route I had taken to Saudi. This turned out to be a good truck as it never missed a beat other than requiring a new water pump, which I fitted myself. I was a vehicle fitter by trade, and even though I never had many problems with my own truck, I always enjoyed the challenge of doing some repair jobs for any other people I came across during the years when I worked the Middle East, which in my case lasted from 1977 to 1982.'

PAUL ROWLANDS

Paul's life on the road is well documented in the book that he wrote himself about his experiences – *Not all Sunshine and Sand*. He started out in 1975 and he worked for Bob Carter's Trans UK Haulage firm until 1979:

'My introduction to the Middle East run came about after getting to know Bob Carter and I began working for his firm, Trans UK. Bob was a really nice guy to work for and my first trip was a wonderful introduction on what this job actually involved. It had been so well organised by Tony Wall and Tom Scott, who put everything together before we had set off. There was never any expectation or pressure to go on and do huge mileages each day. All that Bob really

Bob Carter, head of Trans UK. AC

asked of us, or what really mattered to us all, was to make sure we all managed to get there and get back safely!'

BOB CARTER

The summer of 1975 was a defining moment for Bob Carter as his Trans UK Haulage firm had earned the opportunity to take a number of loads out to Iran. In addition to one of the firm's trucks, a Volvo F88 driven by Lenny Baylam, Bob invited a number of sub-contractors to come along; these being Terry Blakesley driving a DAF 2800, Paul Rowlands driving a Fiat 619 for Mitchell Rowlands (who wasn't related to Paul – the surname being a coincidence), and Bob Crofton-Sleigh also driving a Fiat 619. Bob hired four tandem axle tilt trailers from the Rentco firm, and he came along to provide support to the convoy driving his Humber Sceptre car that was used as the support service vehicle, with Colin Staydon coming along as the navigator. Bob's other objective in coming along was also to learn all he could about working the Middle East routes to further develop this as a source of useful income for Trans UK.

The deliveries called for two vehicles to go to Abadan at the head of the Persian Gulf while the other two

Paul Rowlands with Bob Carter's son in Felixstowe in April 1975 at the start of his first trip. PR

On the train to Cologne: Lenny Baylam chaining up his Trans UK F88. BC

Bazargan. Bob Carter's Humber with Colin Staydon being approached by an Iranian who wanted to buy it. BC

terminated their journey in Tehran. That venture proved to be successful, with three of the trucks managing to earn a bit more revenue by picking up backloads on the way home through Germany, and the fourth one by picking up a return load elsewhere, carrying a broken-down truck for another haulage firm. This was such a success, Bob was confident that securing backloads was a viable proposition. Not a popular trend, as many firms preferred travelling back empty, although Trans UK drivers often secured backloads, varying from different types of fruit according to the harvest season, to timber, chipboard and tractors as a source of extra revenue.

Bob's poor old Humber did not fare all that well and took a real pounding from the heavily overloaded roof rack laden down with spare parts and provisions, as the roof panel collapsed under the strain when the car was ploughing along the badly potholed roads of Anatolia!

Nevertheless, Bob's car was much admired when it reached Iran. The reason for this was that the Rootes' 'Arrow' saloon car was licence-built in the country at that time and was sold under the Paykan name. And when the Humber was only a few yards across the border into Iran at Bazargan, Bob was besieged by an Iranian intent on buying this car. The Humber Sceptre was the upmarket version of the range, so it had many luxury features that were lacking on the more basic version built in Iran.

Representing Bob's wish to take a hands-on role with any breakdowns and repairs that affected his vehicles, when a Trans UK Volvo F88 driven by Steve Cooper broke down on another overland trip, Bob jumped into his Range Rover and drove across Europe to recover the stricken Volvo, which involved using the Range Rover as a tow truck for a good few miles!

Not surprisingly, the weight of the F88 proved a bit too much for the struggling Range Rover, particularly as the steering was almost unmanageable due to the weight transfer from the front to the rear axle. This did not impress the German police at all, who put a stop to

Looking like a seventies' pop group: an unknown driver on the left poses with Lenny Baylam, Bob Crofton-Sleigh, Paul Rowlands and Terry Blakesley. BC

Trans UK's depot in Felixstowe. BC

the rescue attempt by insisting this could only continue with the assistance of a proper wrecker truck rather than the Range Rover! So a local tow truck arrived and it was used to haul the Volvo to the Belgium border. But only that far, as once out of Germany, Bob hitched up the Volvo behind the Range Rover once again to continue the uneven struggle of towing it home at a slow but steady pace!

Trans UK's fleet of F88s had a tendency to suffer excessive damage on the poorly maintained roads of the Middle East, and another recurring problem concerned overheating when crossing any of the high mountain passes found in Turkey. The support brackets for the fuel and air tanks often broke which resulted in delays when repairs were needed before a trip could continue. Replacement trucks included two MAN 16.240s which were followed by four Fiat 619s.

The Fiats were thought to be unsuitable when first examined, as these came with day cabs installed. However, the local Fiat dealer offered to have the four trucks converted so that sleeper cabs were installed, which proved a great success. Bob's drivers now looked forward to a good night's sleep after a long day's drive!

Those Fiats earned Bob's respect and his drivers liked these trucks for their powerful, no-nonsense engines and the very effective exhaust brakes which removed some of the strain from the truck's conventional braking system. The additional retardation effort provided by the exhaust brakes was good for the drivers' peace of mind when descending the steep mountain passes, as this left a most useful reserve of braking effort from the standard air braking system.

Trans UK vehicles were easy to spot out on the roads as Bob wanted to give each of these a measure of individuality, which was provided by naming the trucks after Dartmoor stallions, and the accompanying tilt trailers were also easy to identify with the words 'My lady ...' followed by a woman's forename, as borrowed from friends, office employees, or drivers' wives, etc.

IVOR WHITTALL

The opportunity to drive a decent motor was something Ivor had wanted for so long; he had been given one worn-out old warhorse after another, so that he loathed it every time he climbed into a cab. He had noticed

Taking the Plunge

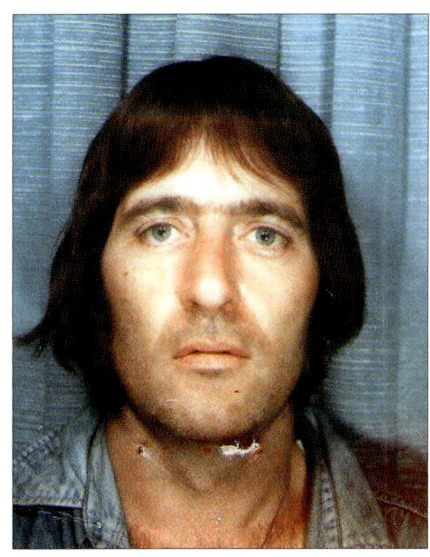

Ivor Whittall, another rock-star lookalike poses for his passport picture! IW

that many of the lorries going out to the Middle East looked to be newer and in far better condition than the ones he was used to driving on UK work, and he also noticed that these were well maintained because of the distances covered and the need to avoid any costly breakdowns along the way. So the opportunity to drive something that was newer and in better condition was what tipped Ivor into making his first Middle East trip:

'I had become sick to death of working for any firm that was still running old wagons, such as an Atkie with a 150 engine I had been given on one occasion, which was a real "shed" in every sense of the word. One day when I was down on Preston docks and had stopped off at the café, another driver told me a firm called Jackson's was taking on some new drivers. This was a firm of builders which wanted to get into road haulage. I drove for them in the UK first of all before Billy Jackson and Edgar Jenkinson approached me to ask if I would like to drive one of the firm's trucks out to Kuwait. I was given a brand-new DAF 2600 to drive, which I thought was just marvellous, particularly as it was fitted with a sleeper cab. My DAF attracted lots of interest at the time; people would want to climb in it and take a look around the cab because it was so modern! Even though this truck did not have air conditioning or a night heater, as you would now expect to find on a modern truck, as far as I was concerned, it was just like driving my own Rolls-Royce!

'My first trip was to take a load of special cement that was used for something or other in the oil industry. I remember the value of the cement was only about £800 in total, although the cost of the haulage on top of this amount was £5500, almost seven times as much!'

Ivor went on to explain why the urgently needed cement had to be delivered by road, irrespective of the huge cost this involved:

'Any shipping containers arriving in any of the Gulf ports by sea could not be unloaded for months at a time, as the docks were full of cargoes waiting to be delivered somewhere else. Everything that arrived by ship was costing so much in demurrage fees! So this was why so much stuff had to go out there by road, in spite of what this had cost. The oil-rich Gulf States had plenty of money to burn, so even though the road transport from Europe was expensive, this didn't seem to matter at all. I remember loads and loads of eggs were being sent out to Saudi by truck in refrigerated containers, so this left me thinking, why is it they haven't got any chickens of their own out there? I couldn't get my head round this situation at all!

'On the way out, I ran for a while with a couple of lads who had been out to the Middle East before. But this wasn't much of a help to me, as I soon noticed they were delaying me by only driving for about six hours across a full day

Ivor Whittall soaking up some rays to balance out his suntanned elbow after resting it on the window ledge while driving over many sunny hours! IW

instead of the twelve hours or more which was available. So I chose to run on my own from then on. Not that I'm antisocial in any way, it was just that they kept on pulling over and stopping for one reason or another.'

IAN TAYLOR

Ian's first Middle East trip was for Brit European, a firm that used the Carmans name on its trucks. Shortly after confirming with his boss that he had a passport, Ian set off in a Volvo F88 that he had prepared for the journey together with two other Carmans drivers who were also going to Baghdad. This trip to Iraq had been set up in just a month, and given his lack of experience, had left Ian pondering on how lightly his employer considered the practicalities of sending novice Middle East drivers all that way with little in the way of training or any other preparation! Preparing the Volvo that was to take Ian to Baghdad did not fill him with all that much confidence, as the truck he had been given for this massive undertaking had already been withdrawn from everyday road use and it had then been used as the yard shunter, a job that didn't require all that much with regard to reliability as it was never more than a few yards from the firm's in-house workshop where it could have been repaired so easily!

'This truck was an F88 with a 240 engine and an 8-speed 'box. The other two Carmans' trucks were also F88s, but these were new and had the more powerful 290 engines. However, keeping up with them was never a problem for me, as the volume of traffic was such that we couldn't run together all day anyway, so we would just meet up again some time later at a prearranged point.'

GORDON SUMMERS

When Gordon took on his first Middle East job, little could he have known that this was the start of an odyssey which was about to take him many thousands of miles before he decided to call it quits after arriving back from his last Middle East trip.

'I first went to the Middle East as a twenty-two-year-old in 1976. This was after I'd spent some time carrying loads of wild game meat from Scotland to Germany. One day when I was on the ferry to Germany, I started talking to a couple of blokes who knew all about driving out to the Middle East. What they had to say immediately attracted my full attention as this seemed to be such an interesting job. So they gave me the contact details for their boss, Frank White of Edinburgh. I did the Middle East from 1976 right up to the First Gulf War after the invasion of Kuwait in 1990.

'I started off on my first trip with Frank's DAF 2800, which was a truck I learnt to like very much. Later on, I drove a MAN 232 out to the Middle East for DJ McIntosh, but this was the one and only truck which I never got on with at all. It had column change gears, and as my legs are somewhat shorter than average, the foot pedals were too far away for me to use properly, so maybe I should have stuck some wooden blocks on the pedals! That truck was a nightmare for me to drive. I finished off my Middle East time with Scanias and Ivecos, and I also drove an Iveco for a while as an owner driver.'

It was just as well Gordon liked driving the DAF 2800, as he was about to be thrown in at the deep end for his very first trip, which took him almost as far as anyone could go on the Middle East run. His destination was somewhere that he'd never even heard of, and reaching it involved driving all the way to Afghanistan!

'That first run for Frank White in a DAF 2800 involved taking a full load of Addis thermos flasks to Afghanistan.

Ian Taylor's F88 on his first trip near the Bulgarian border. John Mudd and Bob Matthews brewing up. IT

I left my home in Scotland and the UK taking a wee bag with me that contained some changes of clothes, also a carrier bag that had some food in it, and a Collins road map of Europe so I could navigate for at least a part of the way. By the time I had got to Istanbul, I was thinking, "It can't be much further," as I had reached the end of my road map of Europe by the time I got there. Little did I realise I was less than half way there at the time! I followed a couple of blokes all the way to Ankara, where one of them split off to go south to Iraq, so I followed the other guy on to Tehran. From there I was on my own, and I was feeling more than a bit lonely. This was a lonely, lonely job, which was something you had to get used to. But if you did one trip and you didn't drop the truck and head off for home, then you had done OK. You might then take a second trip so you could take a look at what you had done the first time. But if you then took on a third trip, that was it, you were hooked so you couldn't give up the job!'

Dave Reynolds about to set off in his Scania 112M for Whittle International. AC

MARTYN MOULSDALE

Martyn Moulsdale began his Middle East career in 1979 with the firm of Harrison's based in Brierley Hill in the West Midlands. The extent to which foreign travel was an unknown quantity to Martyn can be appreciated by the following statement which underlines how much he had to learn of the basics from day one:

'The first time I went abroad, I asked the guy who I was running with, how long I would be driving on the opposite side of the road. It didn't take me long to realise that this wasn't simply a job which I had taken on, it was really a great adventure!'

Martyn Mousdale on the way home from Baghdad and a long way from Wales! MM

George Brooke drove this DAF for Concorde Express. GB

Malcolm 'Corky' Gittus about to set off in the Spiers and Hartwell Fiat. SH

Dick Snow and Ken Searle, two drivers who knew how to enjoy a life out on the road! COPYRIGHT UNKNOWN

Mick Prigg's Fiat. Now deceased, Mick was one of the pioneers of the route to Pakistan. BC

Jerry Cooke today with his hobby ERF that's been restored like the ones he drove in Saudi. DB

CHAPTER 4

Pat Seal

Of all the British drivers who went out to the Middle East there was one name that shone out as the very spirit of self-reliance and individuality. Sadly Pat Seal is no longer with us, although it is fair to say he often is at least in spirit whenever a few veterans of the Middle East get together to mull over old times, as his name is often mentioned with comradely admiration and respect.

Pat was always instantly recognisable thanks to his long, unkempt hair and bushy beard of striking ginger hue. He deliberately cultivated a down-at-heel scruffy appearance, which is said to have prompted his mother to declare that he looked like a tramp of the road. Another comparison that was equally appropriate according to his brother, Des, was that of a Viking warrior who could have stepped out of a longboat with a serpent figurehead rather than the prized Volvo F88 that he drove; the only further refinement to complete the image would have been a Viking helmet decorated with a set of cow horns sticking out on top!

Pat completed his first Middle East run in 1972, an experience that rocked him to the core, as he decided this was the only way to live from then on. By 2002, Pat had managed to complete an astounding 150 full round trips to the Middle East, of which the majority involved his well-recognised F88 that was painted in light blue with white stripes on the cab doors and the front panel.

After retiring from the Middle East run long after most of his contemporaries of the seventies era, Pat rebuilt the Volvo once more as a hobby, and he bought a Seddon-Atkinson tipper to do some local work in his home county of Lancashire. This was a job that he did until 29 January 2010. On the evening of that day, Pat was out with his truck on a resurfacing job on the M62 motorway, and as he shovelled the last of the hot tar out of the back, he suffered a massive heart attack and he died shortly afterwards.

Born to a middle-class family, Pat attended the local grammar school in Lancaster, although securing a white-collar professional career definitely didn't rock Pat's boat at all, as his brother Des, who accompanied Pat on three Middle East trips, went on to explain:

'Pat was mechanically minded; he loved making things, such as motorbikes. As for example, he made a motorcycle from a Triumph frame to which he then added a Norton engine, so we could go out riding on this across the sands of Morecambe Bay near where we lived. He was good with his hands, and he also liked working on guitars. Pat was very bright at school, but he just couldn't get on well with authority at all, so he fell afoul of the school system. It didn't help that Pat had a nervous laugh as this didn't go down well when he was reprimanded by the teachers. So Pat rebelled. He left school and negotiated an apprenticeship with the Reyrolle Parsons engineering firm in Newcastle-upon-Tyne. Then he dipped out of that job and began working as a mechanic at a number of garages in his home town of Lancaster before

Pat Seal always enjoyed a full head of hair and a bushy beard. DS (Picture slightly damaged)

he got his HGV licence. His first lorry driving job was with a bloke called Jack Chippendale of Garstang. And from this, he soon developed a romantic notion of being out on the road as some kind of latter-day cowboy.'

After passing his Class 1 test at the age of 21, Pat drove an Albion Reiver for Jack Chippendale of Garstang. However, Pat's real break into the role he saw for himself occurred when he secured a job with the firm of Simon International, Brick Lane, London, and he set off on his first Middle East run in 1972, a trip that took him to Tehran, probably driving a Leyland Marathon or maybe a Guy Big J.

The entries in Pat's passport then started to fill up any available space very swiftly, with exotic-looking stamps for the likes of Syria, Iraq and Saudi Arabia now featuring in addition to those for Turkey and Iran, by which time he was driving for Tug Transit which was followed by a spell driving for Whittle Freight.

Following on from his rebellious schooldays, Pat had a mindset that did not take well to doing as he was told; so even if any bosses expected him to follow their instructions to the letter, this was not someone who was going to bow to convention by toeing the company line!

'He always wanted to do things exactly his own way,' said Des. 'So becoming an owner driver and making all his own decisions was his main objective in life. The breakthrough came for Pat after he had been working for a Dutch firm called Altrex for some time on the Middle East run as the pay which he earned with this firm gave him the cash to do up a 290 Volvo F88 which he then drove for many years until he gave up driving abroad. The Dutch firms paid their employees well for doing Middle East work, much more than any British firm would have done at the time.'

David Miller was working as a driver for the Dutch Altrex firm at the time when he took Pat round to their offices to introduce him as a possible new employee for this company:

'I remember talking to Pat once when he was driving an F89 for Alan Altug. Pat had already purchased an old F88 and his next step was to try and get some money together so this truck could be put back into working condition, but he was not having a lot of luck: Pat was skint and therefore he didn't have the money to finish off the truck. Working for the Dutch Altrex firm was a good way of getting round the cash problem of building his own truck as they were always fantastic payers. So I decided to introduce Pat to Altrex, as they were looking to take on a new driver. I said I knew someone who was the best driver they could ever find. So Pat and I arrived at Altrex's really smart offices in Holland, just after Pat had come home from a trip to Tehran, so he was still wearing one of his famous T-shirts; these were always covered in fag burns and also showed off the legacy of the many breakfasts which Pat had eaten over the several preceding days. You could see the heads of the girls turning in amazement as he walked through the offices! The bosses were not convinced at first, but they took him on after I had added: "Do you want a male model or do you want the very best driver on the road?" So they agreed to give him a job after adding a comment directed at me that if this appointment didn't work out, then both Pat and myself would be in for the sack! Fortunately, it worked out fine, and this eventually gave Pat all the money which he needed to finish off the Volvo. He also obtained some

Pat Seal doing his best to make a positive impression! DS

Pat Seal and his cherished Volvo F88 which he later rebuilt. DS

Volvo parts for free, as when he was travelling back from one of the runs he made for Altrex driving one of their trucks, he spotted a wrecked F88 that had been abandoned in a region of the desert known as the TAP line, and as these parts were just what he needed for his truck, they were lifted aboard the now empty Altrex trailer to be taken home!'

Pat eventually completed work on his treasured Volvo. This truck was seven years old at the time; a left-hand drive model, registration HFA137N that was found in a Birmingham scrapyard. Pat added a sleeper cab that was to become his home from home for many years, and also a lifting third axle for the tractor unit's chassis which was allowable under the regulations as a way of increasing a lorry's maximum load weight. The twin-axle trailer was also modified to improve the maximum load capacity by converting the axles to a three-axle layout. Further adaptations for desert driving included a larger capacity oil system and an improved oil filter.

The Volvo was ready for the road by 1980, and this old stager went on to cover many hundreds of thousands of miles, and as a result, the TD100A engine was rebuilt on a number of occasions, sometimes by the roadside, with Pat making good use of his cherished set of spanners!

Des recalled:

'Pat loved working with his hands so much – he was much happier when his truck broke down so that he could then fix it. If he saw an abandoned truck on the side of the road, of which there were many in those days, he would collect any promising-looking spares for future use. He would always carry a lot of spares in the F88, such as a turbo, a cylinder head or a differential assembly.'

Always the perfectionist when it came to anything mechanical concerning his beloved F88, Pat never had the radio on when he was driving along, Des recalled, as he constantly monitored the sound of the engine so that he was instantly aware if anything had started to go wrong.

Just like in the old days when the Seal brothers drove their motorbikes out on Morecambe Bay's sands, Des was drawn into the wake of his elder brother and he followed Pat's example when they signed up for a drive with Tug Transit that took them to Tehran. Trouble wasn't long in arriving, as after Pat and Des had spent all the cash they had with them in an Istanbul nightclub of the decidedly less reputable kind, Pat was absolutely comatose with all the booze that had passed his lips. This left Des with the unenviable task of driving Pat's F88 back to their overnight accommodation at the Londra Mocamp. That journey was never going to be

Pat Seal made over 150 trips to the Middle East, the majority in his Volvo F88. DS

Pat stopped to assist when he came across this F88 with a badly twisted trailer. If anyone could fix it, he could! DS

easy, as Des did not have a clue which direction he needed to follow in order to return to the Mocamp, and getting any sense out of Pat was impossible: he remained dead to the world, lying in the passenger-side footwell of the truck!

Des set off in the wrong direction for the Mocamp, and after trying to bluff his way across the Bosphorus bridge, as he had no money to pay the toll fee, he was arrested by the Istanbul police and promptly hauled off to jail. Des reported what happened next on an evening that seemed to go from bad to worse:

'I was charged with driving under the influence of drink, but then I managed to get off the charge with the help of a lawyer; although this then cost five times what I would have paid if I'd simply owned up to the offence and then pleaded guilty. All the while, Pat was still lying fast asleep in his F88, completely oblivious to what had being going on!'

Travelling in the company of Pat usually entailed a degree of risk by way of becoming involved in situations that could turn out rather badly; however, Des threw caution to the wind by taking another Middle East trip with his devil-may-care brother, the destination this time being Iraq. So began their innocent involvement, together with some other drivers, in a financial scam organised by a firm that had promised to supply some items of construction plant equipment for a housing development to be built near Baghdad in the early eighties.

'Our job was to deliver some of the plant equipment required for the project,' Des explained. *'All the prefabricated sections of the buildings were assembled in the UK and the job of transporting everything to Iraq had been won by Tug Transit. I drove an F88 that was carrying some JCB diggers – these were really old and they had only been re-painted – they looked good, but they were knackered really! Pat and the three other drivers were given some Leyland and Bedford water bowsers to drive that were all about thirty years old. It was fortunate we managed to get out of Iraq without being arrested, as unbeknown to us, the development firm behind the deal, which was really nothing but a scam, promptly disappeared with a sum amounting to several million pounds which had been transferred to their bank account, although all the promised construction equipment never did arrive!'*

Surprisingly for someone who was so adventurous, going up in an aeroplane was definitely outside Pat's comfort zone; he didn't like the idea at all of trusting life and limb to the crew of an aircraft that flew at 30,000 feet and travelled at close to the speed of sound! So after Pat and Des boarded the plane that was to take them back from Baghdad to the UK, this form of transport didn't go down well with Pat, and the only recourse he had to relieve his fear of flying was to single-handedly empty the drinks trolley! As the flight took a few hours to complete, getting Pat off the aircraft was somewhat difficult, being very much the worse for wear, so he was carted away in a wheelchair. This was something which Pat took grave exception to,

Pat Seal and two other drivers transporting old Leyland and Bedford water bowsers to Iraq. DS

Pat takes a ride at the pyramids on a rather subdued looking camel! DS

firmly closed on both sides. His rather shallow excuse for this was that he wanted to keep all of the heat and dust that had been churned up by the truck's wheels out of the cab interior. But this wasn't true at all, and if Richard had been paying more attention, he would have noticed that Pat was resolutely munching his way through a large jar of pickled onions, so the cab became full of the tangy smell of vinegar, not to mention the even less appealing whiff that was about to make its odious presence felt. It was this particular example of Pat's raw humour which now explained why he had insisted on the windows remaining closed all the while!

As well as this onslaught on Richard's nasal senses, he was on the point of collapse as he was so hungry, so Pat promised to pull over at a roadside café in the middle of a desert. After they had sat down at a table made of an old door supported by a pair of breeze blocks on and his predictable reaction then earned him a spell in the airport prison cell before he was allowed to go home!

Pat's somewhat schoolboy sense of humour came to the fore when the cab of the F88 was being shared with a mate, Richard Baxter, who was targeted as the butt of a long drawn out joke as they sped along miles and miles of empty, extremely hot Iraqi desert. Pat kept on insisting the cab windows in the truck should remain

Pat and unknown driver, presumably Dutch according to the truck's number plate. DS

Pat Seal wearing Arab head gear. A true Son of the Desert when it came to having a laugh! DS

each side, Pat ordered a coke, rather than a meal, which should have suggested to Richard that maybe something was decidedly wrong with this establishment! The chef explained to Richard the dish of the day was meat kebab and rice, and after Richard gave his approval, the meal was prepared by first of all cutting up the ingredients for the kebab using a meat cleaver. This was when the chef noticed an opportunistic mouse was in the process of attempting to grab a mouthful of rice off the table. Quick as a flash, down came the cleaver, slicing the mouse in two parts, which the chef flicked to one side before continuing to cut up the meat using the bloody, unwashed meat cleaver. Richard was no longer interested in what the chef had on offer, which amused Pat no end! But recognising Richard's need to assuage his hunger, Pat took pity and handed over a tin of beans from the food locker before they had climbed back into the truck to continue the journey!

Des had the following comments to relate about his non-conformist brother who's now sorely missed by the Seal family and all who knew him so well out on the Middle East run:

'There was only one way of doing things according to Pat, and that was his way and only his way, which is something that made him unemployable, so the only way he could make a living was to become an owner driver. He was only answerable to himself, and as such, he lived life to the full. Pat was always so self-contained, and whatever he did, he always made sure that he did it well. This included working as a driver for himself and doing all of his own paperwork, also keeping his old Volvo F88 running all those years, which became such a familiar sight to any other drivers out doing the Middle East runs.'

RIP Pat Seal, a legend in his own time who's sorely missed today. DS

Jeff Kedward remembers Pat Seal as a very good friend and also as someone who was always good for a laugh:

'We were at a party, and Pat said, "Come and see my new car." He was always an unknown quantity, so we all went out to take a look, and there was this bright blue Reliant Robin, so we all had a good laugh!'

The only time when Pat was guaranteed to be absolutely unapproachable was before he chose to wake up each morning, as Chris Stephenson recalled:

'Pat Seal was a gentleman who didn't ever start work until it was at least nine o'clock, and you knew not to try and wake him up before then!'

CHAPTER 5

How Different Trucks Performed

Spending so much time driving a truck and then having to spend a good deal more either resting or sleeping in the cab could make for a claustrophobic experience, rather like living in a goldfish bowl, some might say. Looking at this situation from an alternative perspective, however, it would also be true to say that the physically tight confines of a truck's cab did in fact provide a welcome degree of sanctuary from the larger, and often difficult to comprehend, world that was outside!

Any Middle East drivers who had been given a traditional British truck of sixties design to drive out to the Middle East could well have had a few issues that they may have wished to complain about. These trucks often lacked refinements such as power steering, and the power output from the engines could be meagre. Imagine driving a truck with a 150 Gardner while trying to maintain a decent cruising speed on the flat, never mind when any hills of even the shallowest gradient came in sight! And as for using a crash gearbox with the intention of stirring some life into the proceedings, these were a relic from another age of commercial vehicle development!

Often built round a wooden framework, the cabs of this older breed of trucks were usually very noisy and also rattle prone; the poor design could leave a driver half-deaf by the time they tumbled out of the cab after a long, uncomfortable day on the road. Although trucks such as Atkinson Borderers, Guy Big J and various Leyland models of older design were still in production during the seventies, the manufacturing technology employed was more in tune with truck designs of earlier decades, the fifties or the sixties.

Maybe the suitability of using trucks such as these models for this type of work had been encouraged by Bob Paul and Michael Woodman, successfully using a 1962 Guy Warrior to make that very first trip to Afghanistan. But the times were changing by the seventies, so driving an outdated, uncomfortable

Picked clean of any useful parts, this 'Mickey Mouse' Foden S21 is a long way from home! FT

A couple of old British trucks that must have made for a long, hard drive. Guy and Atkie arctic units. COPYRIGHT UNKNOWN

This old Foden probably never made it back to the UK. RW

Atkie Borderer and fighting it all the way by grappling with the heavy steering was a real trial of stamina and unyielding determination.

It was also nigh on impossible to get a good night's sleep in a non-sleeper cab – sleeping across the front seats was uncomfortable – so drivers began to demand a sleeper cab as a fundamental right if they were going to be travelling so far, and who could blame them!

But there were a few drivers who were not quite so scathing about these tough old British trucks. David Miller was always enthusiastic in his praise for the Scammell Crusader which he drove when he worked for the Eileen Ellingham haulage firm out of the firm's depot in Isleworth. David's partnership with the Scammell served him well, even though its design was so outdated, and it earned his approval for steadfast reliability on many long overland trips, with a record that remained unsurpassed, prompting the following dry comment from David: 'It was always so depressingly reliable.'

This was praise indeed as the other trucks that Ellingham's operated on the Middle East run were Volvo F88s that David also drove from time to time, trucks that were considered to be the benchmark for long-distance work according to a good many truck drivers!

David recalled coming to his Scammell's defence when it was under fire from a salvo of witheringly mocking comments from a group of German truckers:

'They were saying, "Ha-ha, Englischer antique truck" among other things that weren't all that nice, so I swung open the side-hinged fibreglass panel on the front of the truck, which allowed the radiator on my truck to swing outwards just like a barn door. This provided excellent access for checking over the Scammell's Rolls-Royce 280 engine. I wasn't having any insults about my truck from all those Germans! So my reply to them was: "How long would it take you to change the fan belt on that piece of Mercedes junk?" So this immediately shut them all up! I loved that old Scammell, it was a damn good lorry.'

Given the historical significance of the Holy Land, journeying there in a truck with such an evocative name as 'Crusader' may potentially have caused problems for David and any other drivers with the same model, although this was never an issue for David.

David also drove a German-registered Büssing for a short while when he was working for Ellingham's,

This 1968-registered Mercedes lay abandoned in a customs yard. FT

and this truck was also much admired. Firstly for the powerful engine, and secondly for the almost complete absence of engine noise, which was all down to the way the engine had been positioned in the chassis frame. The designers turned the engine on its side for a lower profile, so it could be mounted further back than usual, and the engine sat behind the cab rather than the more normal position directly underneath. Consequently, any engine noise was barely discernible from inside the cab. David also praised the quality of the ride, which was down to this lorry being of the drawbar type, a rigid six-wheeler towing a four-wheel trailer; a combination that has always been a popular choice with many European haulage firms, although British companies favoured a tractor unit hauling a full length trailer, of the articulated tractor and trailer design.

Admirable though the Scammell was in David's estimation, a parting of the ways came a couple of years later when he was pulled over to the side of the road by the police after arriving back on home soil at the end of a Middle East trip. David felt quite confident that he hadn't done anything wrong after he climbed out of the cab to see what the police wanted, although the situation became less friendly when one of the two policemen asked why such a large truck carried the same registration number as a Puch moped that had been stolen in London! This was something that David couldn't answer, and he was in no position to do so, which was accepted by the boys in blue, and he was free to go without further questioning on the theft of a moped. This incident may have been connected in some way with Ellingham ceasing trading shortly afterwards, thereby ending David's association with his reliable old Scammell.

In 1974, he then signed on with another Middle East firm, J and T International of Gravesend, a firm that operated half a dozen or so Scania 110 and 140s, trucks that David also took a liking to as these did so well in his hands, covering many thousands of miles without any serious problems.

J and T International were eventually taken over by the firm's main customer, Muhammad Bahar, who held the position of import agent for Caterpillar and Volvo products throughout the whole of Saudi Arabia and also the Gulf States of Kuwait, Qatar and the Emirates. Owing to his pre-established connection with the Swedish truck firm, he added thirty new Volvo F89s to the Scanias, together with a new trailer for each of the new trucks. These were then put out to work with the

Oryx advertising material. DB

sole task of delivering Caterpillar and Volvo spare parts to the Arab owner's businesses, which were scattered across the Arabian Peninsula. The trucks were then painted up in a new livery that took the name of Oryx Freight Lines, the first part of this title referring to a breed of antelope found in the deserts of Arabia.

This firm became a very significant player on the Middle East run, and the advertised journey times from the UK were 21 days to reach Dubai, 20 days to Abu Dhabi, 18 days to Doha and 14 days to Kuwait.

Simplicity has a virtue all of its own when you are working far away from home and far beyond the reach of any truck manufacturer's service and repair depots or dealer network. This explains why Peter Bamford was keen to emphasise the value of driving less sophisticated trucks that were so easy to maintain at the time – notably the Volvo F12 model introduced in 1977, and he also sang the praises of later versions of the Scania 141 that he drove at one time in his career. The defining reason why Peter praised these particular

David Miller and his Oryx Volvo F89. DM

Establishing good contacts in the Arabian Peninsula underlined the success of the Oryx Freight Lines company. OR

models from the two competing Swedish manufacturers was all down to how easy these trucks were to repair by the roadside using just a few basic hand tools, such that it was usually possible to see the repair job through in next to no time allowing him to be on his way again. As long as the engine of an F12 or a 141 could be coaxed back into life, Peter always knew he had every chance of making it back as far as the English Channel without having to sort out any further problems.

Jeff Kedward expressed a preference for Volvo's imposing-looking F88:

'This was a very good truck as far as I was concerned. I had two over the years and both trucks worked really well for me. I did try out a Ford Transcontinental some time later on, and the advantage of the Ford was the excellent cab design as this was so roomy. The cabs were all supplied to the Ford company by the French truck firm, Berliet. I remember there was a problem with the Transcontinental if you wanted to travel through Syria. This was because the Ford name wasn't liked at all in that country, due to some belief that the firm had supported the Israelis in some way or other in the past. However, you could easily get round this problem by changing the position of the first and last letters that were displayed on the front of the cab so they no longer spelt out "FORD" but rather "DORF". You also had to make sure your wagon wasn't referred to as a "Ford" on any of the paperwork – you would simply record "Transcontinental" as the name, and this was never questioned in my experience.'

Some Transcontinentals had the name of the engine, 'CUMMINS' spelt out on the front of the cab for the very same reason.

Martyn Moulsdale also admired Ford's Transcontinental model, first of all for the quality of the ride when rolling over any bumps or potholes in the road. And secondly for the powerful Cummins engine that

David Miller with his Fridco DAF 2800. DM

Radclive Volvo F12 driven across the Saudi desert to Doha by Kenny Dormer. MD

Bob Thompson's DAF with spread axle trailer. Courtesy of DAF Used Trucks ©

was fitted in the one he drove. The Cummins motor seemed to be unbreakable; the only occasion when it didn't look as if this statement was true occurred when Martyn's Transconti was left crawling along a motorway hard shoulder at a snail's pace on a journey which seemed interminable:

'I was coming back through Belgium when I heard a funny noise, so I turned the radio off first of all so that I could hear if the engine was running properly. I knew exactly what that rumbling noise was: I had run one of the big-ends on the crank. After managing to carry on through Belgium I caught the ferry at Zeebrugge. I decided to leave my trailer behind after the ship had docked in the port of Dover. Uncoupling the trailer from my truck made it much easier to continue on my way home. I could pick my trailer up later on. There wasn't an M25 circular motorway in those days, so I had to drive right through the centre of London! After reaching the motorway, there was so little power produced by the damaged engine, I only managed about 10 mph all the way to South Wales, and that was only achieved by driving along the motorway's hard shoulder! By the time I had finally managed to arrive back at home, a section of the crank where the set of big-end bearings had gone west was worn down to an inch when it should have been about three inches in width!'

To be issued with a lorry that was a lot better than most to drive was an important part of the job for many drivers, and Les Higgins recalled taking over a DAF 2800 which he had really coveted when he worked for Jenkinson's of Salford.

'This truck had been featured on the front cover of Commercial Motor *magazine,' said Les. 'It was given the registration GND 600N although it was only actually taxed for the road with a tax disc on the windscreen when it was*

Chevalier Brothers changed from MANs to Ford Transcontinentals after deciding a more powerful engine was needed for climbing steep hills. MC

First introduced in 1962 as the DAF 2600, this truck upstaged even the Swedish manufacturers in terms of driver comforts. RW

a trip with a much slower Guy Big J. This would have involved (following his suggestion) the driver of the faster Volvo pulling over at regular intervals throughout the day so as to allow the driver of the slower Guy to catch up with him. While the driver of the Volvo awaited the arrival of his slower running mate in the Guy, the Volvo driver could make good use of his standing time by cooking up a meal for the both of them. Imagine how well this lamebrained idea would have gone down with either party given the unpredictability of when

featured in the magazine. That was because this lorry spent most of its time working outside the country. What interested me about this truck was that although it had been badged as a DAF 2800, a more powerful 310 motor had been fitted, so it could really motor on! The gearbox was a 13-speed Fuller, and Jenkinson's bought an identical DAF 2800 with the same uprated engine and the Fuller gearbox, which was driven by a mate of mine, Graham Cartmail.'

Jenkinson's bought both trucks at the same time off the DAF stand at the Commercial Motor Show in 1976, and Graham's DAF carried the consecutive registration number, GND 601N.

'Everyone wanted to drive a Mercedes-Benz, a Volvo or a Scania in those days,' said Graham. 'So no-one seemed to be interested in driving a DAF 2800 when these became available, although I would say the DAF benefited from having such a large, roomy cab. What also impressed me was you would never see any DAF trucks broken down by the roadside.'

It made sense to match trucks of similar performance that were going out on a run, although this wasn't always possible, and Les recalled that a transport manager whom he knew had set himself up for a fall when he suggested a Volvo F88 could be paired up for

Ian Tyler with his Chapman & Ball Volvo F88. ITY

Mike Dunstan's Volvo F89, his pride and joy when he worked for Radclive. MD

the driver of the slower Guy was about to arrive! Cold camion stew, anyone?

As well as the DAF 2800, Les also had lots of praise for Fiat's 619/21 model like the one he took on three Middle East trips. It also proved to be very reliable, with no mechanical problems along the way, although Les was wary about the tendency of the clutch plates on a Fiat to wear out suddenly, something that could occur without prior warning, instead of being evidenced by a slipping clutch that became progressively worse!

Later on, Les swapped over to a Volvo F88 which he admired for its gutsy engine performance, although there was a downside to this: having so much horsepower on tap was all very well, but this meant racing at full revs and going flat out all the time was a real temptation. Les found he could cover a lot of ground very quickly in an F88, but travelling at speed could so easily cause the brakes to be overworked when slowing down, resulting in overheating followed by brake fade, which could have dire consequences when descending the precipitously steep slopes in the mountainous regions of Turkey.

Les drove a Volvo F10 as well, which he mildly criticised, as the engine was not as powerful as Volvo's earlier F88 model. This truck was followed by a Scania 141 which was in fantastic condition, as previously owned by Robert Dods-Brown.

Gordon Summers drove a Volvo F88, although his impressions were not as favourable, which could have a lot to do with the one that he drove being past its best so that this example no longer represented the forefront of Swedish truck design by the time he drove one:

'The Volvo F88/F89 was a good truck in its day, but the one I was driving on a trip to Saudi wasn't in good condition at all, and so it let me down, and it had to be fixed. But it was getting on and well past its best by then. I liked the later Volvo F12 model that replaced the earlier F88/F89 models. To my mind the F12 was a much better truck to drive. I remember the windscreen wipers on my F89 were air operated, so every time you slowed down, or when you had to touch your brakes in order to lose some speed, there would be a loss of air pressure and the windscreen wipers would start to slow down as the air pressure all bled away. So imagine if it was snowing heavily; in this sort of conditions there was never enough air pressure to operate the wipers properly!'

Chris Stephenson drove for Dayson's of Carlisle, and he recalled that this firm's Scania 111 and 112 trucks were well matched to the job, as he encountered very few problems along the way over many thousands of miles, although he had a sneaking admiration for a DAF 2800 he drove for a short while for another Middle East haulier, Bob Blaylock of Kirkbride Transport Services. The only drawback of the DAF that Chris can remember was the poor cold starting:

'The DAF was a real pig to start on any cold winter morning. I remember having to mix some petrol in with the diesel in the fuel tank to improve the starting. The petrol could make up as much as ten per cent of the contents of the tank, which would then be topped up to the brim with diesel

Trans UK Volvos setting off on the long haul from Felixstowe. BC

Dayson's were a one-make firm when it came to Middle East runs with Scania's 110 and 111 being the trucks of choice! DAY

before attempting to start the engine on a mixture of petrol and diesel fuel. But you always had to remember there was a big disadvantage in putting any petrol in the tank first of all. If this method of starting the engine failed to work, you didn't dare use the other accepted way of getting your engine to fire up. This involved heating the fuel up by lighting a fire underneath the fuel tank, and if any petrol fumes had been lingering about, this could have a bad result once the fire under the fuel tank had been lit, with every possibility the tank would have exploded!'

Chris had a few further comments on the fleet of Scanias operated during his time working for Dayson's:

'Scania trucks were what you could call idiot-proof because there wasn't a lot that could possibly go wrong with them. They were a damn good wagon with nothing sophisticated about them at all compared to any of the much more complicated wagons which are built nowadays. This sort of simplicity was what you needed to get them fixed when you had so little in the way of resources or back-up when you were out in the middle of nowhere. My Scania only broke down once and this occurred when it was being driven along in hot desert conditions. The reason for the breakdown was very simple: the plastic air intake pipe had broken into two pieces, which had serious consequences later on. The break in the pipe allowed fine particles of sand to enter the truck's engine, causing the motor to be very badly damaged so it wouldn't work properly at all. Dennis Cook, another Dayson's driver, towed me all the way from Baghdad in Iraq to Ankara in Turkey, where we made some temporary repairs so the engine was running again and I had some chance of driving this truck home. Or at least I would have done, but a further problem occurred shortly afterwards as the layshaft in the gearbox gave way when I was driving through Hungary. So I arranged with another driver I had met for my damaged Scania to be transported back to Dover, and my trailer was taken home by another driver who had kindly agreed to help me out as well.'

Gerry Holmes was given a job with the firm of H.J. Atlas of Avonmouth after the company had bought DAF 2800s for Middle East work. Gerry was excited by the prospect of travelling all over the Middle East and the opportunity of driving a DAF 2800, a truck he admired for getting the job done without any drama. The spacious cab made life on the road very pleasant, whether he was on the move or had stopped so he could take a kip or enjoy a brew in the cab.

'They were good workhorses in their day,' said Gerry. 'Mine had a 280-hp engine, which is nothing at all by today's standards of course! The only problem I can recall with these DAFs was that the air filters were always getting dirty in any desert conditions, so they would always be choking up if they were not attended to. Otherwise, the build-up of dust and sand in the engine caused it to splutter and lose some of its power. But I suppose this problem may have applied to many other trucks that were working out in the sandy, desert conditions, as found throughout the Middle East. Other than that, there wasn't any Achilles' heel type of fault which you needed to constantly watch out for when

H J Atlas of Avonmouth bought eleven DAF 2800s which attracted Gerry Holmes to work for the company. The spacious cab was well appreciated. GH

you were driving a DAF 2800. The ones operated by H.J. Atlas made life even more comfortable out on the road as they were fitted with twin bunks, a cooker and a fridge.'

It was a lucky man who was allocated a brand-new truck to drive. Plenty others weren't so lucky, which is something Frank White mentioned, as there were many drivers who gamely soldiered on in trucks such as AEC Mandators, Ford D-Type A2818s and Leyland Marathons, with even the occasional Dodge or Bedford to be seen out there which were not up to the job at all! Frank did not envy them one bit as he drove along in one of the Volvo F86 trucks that he operated at the time. The only drawback he encountered with the F86 concerned the tendency for the clutch plates to wear out prematurely.

Dave Jamieson drove a Volvo F12 for Frank, and he recalls the White fleet was very new and well maintained at the time. After returning from each trip abroad, the truck in question would be temporarily withdrawn from service so it could be overhauled and serviced in the workshop. And the brake drums would all be removed for close inspection to sort out any present or future problems.

'I had no problems at all driving any of Frank's trucks,' said Dave. *'They were so well looked after. I also drove other trucks later on, for Don Hubbard as an owner driver initially, and then I drove an F89 Volvo on Middle East jobs, which was followed by a Scania 111, then a Scania 141.'*

It didn't take long for Mark Chevalier to become seriously disenchanted with the performance of the first truck he took out on the Middle East run, a MAN 16.232, due to the lack of performance from its 232-hp motor, which soon came to the fore when Mark was climbing any steep hills with a full load on board:

'Going so slowly over the Tahir Pass showed up the problem of my truck's lack of power. I thought the engine in my MAN lorry was powerful enough at the time I bought it, but then I started to notice that the V8-engined Scanias were making my truck look really silly – they would come rushing past and leave me as if I was standing still! So we swapped over to Ford Transcontinentals, trucks that were a lot more powerful than the MAN trucks we had owned. The only disadvantage we came across was that the Fords cost a lot more to repair than any of the MAN trucks we had operated earlier on. In particular, the brakes on a Transconti required frequent attention and readjustment, and we found it far more difficult to get these trucks through their MOT

Chevalier Brothers' Ford Transcontinentals on the move. MC

test so they were roadworthy. One useful tip I remember with the Transcontinental concerned the batteries. These were fitted with open, exposed terminals so that the cells were interconnected by sets of steel bars fitted to the poles. If the battery was damaged and one of the cells then became inoperative, you could use any piece of metal of the right size to bypass a dead cell and bridge two of the active cells together, so this meant the battery worked just fine again, with only a slight reduction in voltage owing to one of the cells being missing. More seriously, a crankshaft snapped on one of our Transcontinentals, so I remember this truck having to be transported home on a trailer.'

Chevalier Brothers took on a DAF 2800 at one time, and although Mark's first impressions were not all that favourable, this truck's qualities soon became apparent as the miles rolled by:

'One of the drivers had a problem when the engine of a brand-new DAF 2800 blew up en route in Austria. This truck had only just been serviced by a DAF dealership in Graz, but they had forgotten something really important, but I can't remember what the fault actually was now after all this time. Anyway, the engine was completely wrecked. So we contacted DAF headquarters in Holland, and they flew out a replacement engine to Austria, at no cost to ourselves. So this was some really good service from the DAF company,

Chevalier Brothers' first Volvo F12 model. MC

Chevalier Brothers' Volvo F12 travelling through Turkey. BR

with no quibbles at all. Flying that replacement engine out to us must have cost the firm a fortune.

'There was one regular problem we found with the DAF 2800, and this came to our attention when these lorries were being driven along at a steady speed of just over 52 mph. The engine seemed to use considerably more oil than normal at this sort of speed. This led us on to a suspicion maybe the engine oil was being blown under pressure from out of the engine breather pipe? If you kept below a speed of 52 mph, then the engine never used any oil at all. We also ran a couple of Volvo F12s for a while, and they were also good motors which did really well.'

Brian Robertson bought a second-hand and well-used Scania 110 to start off his Middle East career as an owner driver and this lorry delivered a full year's service before finally giving up the ghost when the crankshaft failed so the engine was badly damaged.

'I was working with the Davies Turner firm as an owner driver at the time the engine in my Scania broke. I was already thinking of giving up and packing the Middle East job in, but the Davies Turner people then told me that Chevalier Brothers, Mark and Andy Chevalier, were looking for new drivers, and my first trip for them was in one of their MAN 232s. These trucks were extremely underpowered when you were carrying a load of up to sixty tonnes along with you! But after I had done a couple of trips for Chevalier Brothers, they gave me a new Transcontinental, and this always worked like a dream as far as I was concerned. The only problems I ever had with that Ford truck concerned a few minor electrical problems.'

Brian worked for Chevalier Brothers for the next two years, although as he wanted to resume the independence of going it alone as an owner driver, he bought a DAF 2800 that he used on trips for the Davies Turner firm as before. The DAF did extremely well, so that when it needed to be replaced, Brian bought another 2800, an ex-PIE truck, which was all kitted out to full Middle East spec with a sleeper cab, cooker and freezer.

Brian Robertson's Transcontinental in Greece after he became an owner driver. BR

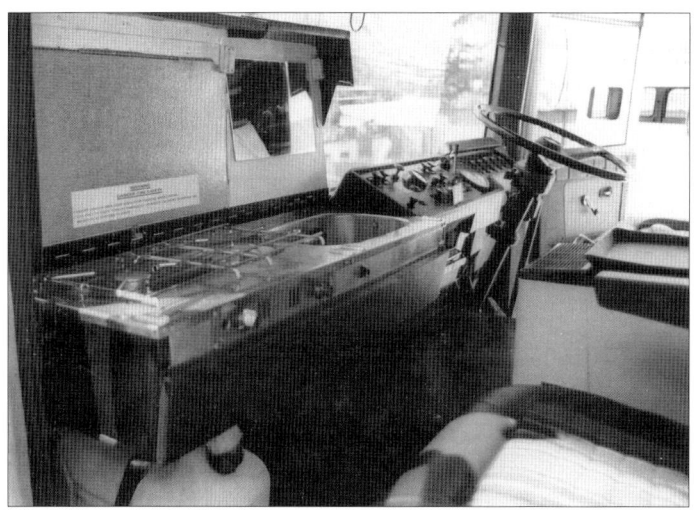

Ford Transcontinental with Middle East mod cons – cooker, etc. EW

Air-conditioning, a fridge and a small cooker soon became must-haves, and DAF and Volvo were at the forefront of updating their model line-up with the Middle East in mind. Ford made a serious attempt at stepping into this market with their appropriately named Transcontinental; Leyland also had a go with their heavyweight Marathon and this firm provided a demonstrator to Astran which Dick Snow drove in the BBC's *Destination Doha* television documentary. Leyland went as far as setting up a parts and repair facility for their trucks in Tehran in a bid to attract new sales. And when Volvo introduced their new F10/F12

Eric Wilson of the Birdale company picking up the keys of a brand new Ford Transcontinental. EW

Everything including a freezer box and the kitchen sink in this Transcontinental! EW

models, the service interval was extended to 15,000 kilometres which allowed for a return trip from the Middle East to be conducted without the need for any servicing partway.

When it was noticed that the Middle East offered a new sales venture, in addition to what truck manufacturers could provide, there was also the need for a few home-made improvements and adaptations; such as fitting belly tanks to the trailers, which then allowed for an extended fuel range that permitted diesel to be bought where it was cheapest. A typical scenario would involve filling the belly tank with 'red diesel', which was taxed at a lower rate on account of being classed for off-road agricultural use rather than for on-road use. This fuel would then remain in the auxiliary belly tank until a truck sent out to the Middle East had reached a country where using this type of fuel

Travelling open TIR this Transcontinental owned by Birdale is loaded with sealed cases and a front loader. EW

'I drove an ERF European that had the steel panel cab, it was powered by a 350-hp Cummins, and this truck was something out of this world in my estimation. My ERF was quite capable of keeping up with the best of the rest, such as Volvo's powerful F89. We had four ERF 220s running together at one time. The only serious mechanical problem concerned the dual pump for the power steering which had a habit of leaking hydraulic fluid, so that some of the oil for the power steering then managed to get into the truck's cooling system. We always carried lots of spare parts along with us, and this always included some gasket material so that we could carry out any roadside engine repairs.'

Mike Dunstan summed up his appraisals of the various trucks that he had the pleasure of driving all that way eastwards:

'When I started work with Radcliffe Transport of Faringdon, they gave me a Volvo F88 first of all, and later on I was given a more powerful F89, which was about a year old. I recall this F89 was a brilliant truck; it never let me down at all. Later on I worked for Dow Freight of Stockport, although they also had a depot in Swindon, and this was nearer to where I lived, so I worked from there. I was

was permissible, and the truck's main fuel tank would then be recharged from the belly tank on the trailer, which could hold up to 500 gallons. Fitting a belly tank also came in handy to reduce fuel costs as the price of diesel fuel was as low as two or three pence a gallon in oil-rich Saudi Arabia.

Trailers were also kitted out with large locker boxes as a secure and safe means of storing any supplies, such as food and water, tools and vehicle spare parts.

At one time, British-built ERF trucks were a strong player for use in the Middle East as they were popular with a number of UK operators, with a fair few of these trucks being sent to do internal work in Saudi Arabia as well as doing overland trips from the UK. Keith Burson was an enthusiastic fan of this type of truck and he recalled his experiences of how well these performed in the desert lands of the Middle East when he was employed on internal runs in Saudi Arabia:

Volvo F89 offered more power than the F88, and as only available in left-hand drive, this was also a bonus for Middle East use. Courtesy of Volvo. COPYRIGHT UNKNOWN

Mike Dunstan's first truck with DOW was a MAN with a column gearchange. Note the belly tank on the trailer. MD

This pair of Fiat 619 T1s joined the fleet of Chapman & Ball of Stoke-on-Trent. CB

driving a MAN initially, which we called the "Bullworker" after the muscle-building appliance of that name that you could buy in those days. Working the truck's stiff, column gearchange did much to build up all your muscles. All the effort of changing gear involved just the one arm, leaving you wondering whether the other arm was now a lot weaker by comparison! I was glad when they gave me a Scania 111 to drive as this had a normal floor-mounted gearchange. I did drive a newer MAN later on, and I was very pleased to find this truck had a normal gearchange rather than the column change I had experienced to my cost with the other MAN truck earlier on!'

Volvo N12 as specified for use in hot countries with a normal control cab. RR

Although never a strong seller with British haulage firms operating in the UK, the Fiat 619 really came into its own with some Middle East operators and drivers, and Paul Rowlands was a strong advocate of this Italian-built truck:

'I was a Fiat man through and through, and I drove a Fiat 619 when I was working with Bob Carter for his Trans UK firm. Bob was always a really nice guy to work for, and my interest in working for him concerned doing some continental work first of all, although I was also desperate to have a go at doing a trip out to the Middle East. I wanted to drive as far as I could possibly go, the farther the better in those days. I also drove for Mitchell Rowlands, although he wasn't any relative of mine even though we have the same surnames. Mitchell had a Fiat truck franchise and he gave me a 619 non-sleeper to drive which was completely trouble-free. The Fiat trucks were a lot heavier than any British trucks of those times, and they sat on a taller set of wheels of the Trilex type. The Fiat 619 was certainly man enough for the job, and I never had any mechanical problems at all driving one of these trucks. The Fiat engines had not been turbo'd to produce more power, but they went very well and I had no complaints about these trucks being too slow. I swore by these trucks as the ideal tool for doing the Middle East run. I once kept a Fiat's engine running for a solid 11 days nonstop as I didn't ever dare turn it off because the weather was so bad – the temperatures were dropping way below zero.'

Steve Stephenson's Trans-UK Fiat. He later came off the road and worked for Bob Carter in the Trans UK offices. BC

HG Brown Mack F700 truck; some drivers swore by them, others viewed them as too old fashioned. HG Brown

Ian Taylor was also keen to recount his impressions of the big Ford Transcontinentals which were mainly built in Amsterdam, with a smaller number built at the Foden factory in Sandbach.

'I drove a Transcontinental for Carmans, and I have to say this was a brilliant truck. Although the Volvo F88 with the big, powerful 290 engine was thought to be the dog's bollocks until then (well at least according to some drivers) a Ford Transconti with a 270 Cummins engine and a 9-speed Fuller 'box also did very well when I took one of these out on a Middle East run. These trucks were so fast, I wouldn't have ever dared drive one flat out at top speed; and they were a really comfortable truck. Some didn't like the Transconti at all, but as is often the case with any kind of truck, you have to take account of the way that someone took to driving it along.'

American trucks have always had a certain appeal in this country, but Ian was not at all keen when he was given a Mack F700-Series to drive one day when he was working for the firm of Chapman & Ball. Ian was sent out by plane to recover a Mack F700 after the original driver slipped in the snow when he was transiting through Bulgaria, and as he needed medical treatment, he couldn't drive his truck home. A load of urgently needed military aircraft spares were still on board the Mack, so after picking up the truck, Ian then had to complete the other man's delivery to a military base in Saudi Arabia.

Terry Tott's MAN which he drove for Redcliffe Roadways. TT

This didn't go well, as the Mack was woefully lacking in creature comforts according to Ian's estimation, and although he did respect this truck's powerful, lusty Maxidyne engine, the two-stick splitter gearbox was tricky and awkward to operate. It allowed up to 13 speeds but was extremely difficult to use as it required a high level of physical and manual dexterity. Ian summed up the experience of driving the Mack as follows:

'You can keep the Mack. No thanks, being my own opinion. And I don't think these trucks were highly rated at that time back in the United States, either. The driver of this one may have thought it was the very best thing since sliced bread for all I know, but when my boss offered this truck to me after I got back – the original driver who had injured himself had to leave the firm because of his back problem – I said he could keep it. I wasn't going to drive this Mack F700. This was the only one that Chapman & Ball ran to the Middle East and I didn't like it at all.'

After a spell driving a Scania when he worked for Astran, Terry Tott decided to have a go working alone as an owner driver, and a Leyland Marathon was bought for him by the Knights of Old haulage firm, although it didn't do him proud, as this truck seemed to relish every opportunity to breakdown:

'I don't know why I kept that lorry for so long. I had it for two years before I finally got rid of it. I suppose the reason

Terry Tott and his Leyland Marathon – buying this was not one of his better decisions! TT

it was bought was because it was so cheap. But as well as breaking down all the time, it wasn't made for this sort of job at all. One day when I was driving with the missus through Jordan, the truck was rattling around badly; the cab was on the point of falling apart, with the top of the roof coming away along the join line where it should have been firmly welded to the top of the cab. This Jordanian bloke asked me if this was how we were making trucks in the UK! One time when I got back to Dover, with the wheels wobbling about so badly from side to side, this policeman pulled me over and said to me, "You're not going anywhere with a truck in that state." So I had to leave it where it was and then arrange for some repairs before I could drive it home.'

Big John Ward's Volvo F88 beside Robert Dods-Brown's Scania 110 – Scandinavian rivals that were on a par! RDB

Jimmy Cadwallader with his Scania Vabis 76 – pioneers of the Middle East routes! DM

BMC Boxer that failed to make it there – most probably a one-way export truck. FT

Glen Harley's Transcontinental and Bob Hedley's Scania 142 in the desert near Nasirya, Iraq. GH

Burt Reid stands beside his M&P Transport International F88. ITY

Martyn Moulsdale's DAF and Ron Slater's Ford parked in Ankara. MM

How Different Trucks Performed

A smartly turned out Anglo Continental AEC Mandator disembarks at the start of the long haul eastwards. AG

Trans UK Volvos became one of the most familiar British trucks on the Middle East runs. BC

CHAPTER 6

Mechanical Mishaps

Breakdowns of the mechanical or any other kind had more significance to anyone who was stranded out somewhere in the Middle East than to someone working in the UK, as they would be so far away from the normal support services that could be relied on to assist. Whether by means of the firm that they worked for, or by utilizing an external repair and recovery agency, in the UK or indeed anywhere in Western Europe those services could be contacted quite easily.

To put the issue in the simplest terms, taking a walk to a phone box and then making a call to arrange for a breakdown truck or for a mechanic to come out and wave his magic wand so a truck was operational again, wasn't an option if your truck had crawled to a halt on a desolate mountainside in the middle of Turkey or some other remote spot elsewhere!

So from the moment an engine started to splutter out its warning message of discontent, or should the brakes remain locked so that the truck wasn't going anywhere for the foreseeable future, the burden of responsibility for sorting out any repair work usually fell quite squarely on the shoulders of the guy who happened to be sitting in the cab.

The best approach to carrying out any repairs singlehanded was always to appraise the situation as calmly as possible and try and establish the nature of the fault, and then assess what would be needed to put things right again. And if the fault could in fact be repaired without calling for any outside help, then all was well and good! But if this wasn't the case and help from an extra pair of hands was needed, or advice from someone who had a greater technical appreciation of what was needed, then the best approach was to request assistance from any other drivers who happened to be passing by or had also called in to an overnight stopping place. Helping out others was a well-accepted code of duty which most drivers did their utmost to adhere to in the spirit of comradeship!

It also helped to have acquired extensive knowledge of the technical ins and outs of how to carry out repairs to mend trucks, and many Middle East haulage operators sought confirmation of such skills when they were interviewing any prospective new drivers.

Taking along a useful store of tools and spare parts was also something of importance that could ultimately save the day. And if the tools chest frustratingly lacked the part that was needed to affect a repair, skills at begging, borrowing, or in fact stealing any spare parts from abandoned trucks were also necessary accomplishments!

Peter Bamford drew attention to the point that even when there was no common language between those who needed help and those who answered the call, it was a matter of basic respect for drivers to pull over and help as best they could, regardless of nationality:

'Someone would have a spanner, someone else provided the part that was needed for the repair, and if the only contribution you could make was to put on the kettle and make a brew, then that's what you did.'

Assistance from other drivers was easy enough to obtain in those days, as no-one felt under any pressure to get anywhere to meet a fixed schedule. Pulling over to help someone out with repairs for a few hours, or even for a couple of days, became a fairly

Scania engine being repaired at a roadside garage where new spares would be hard to obtain. FT

Micky Prigg mending a starter motor – a fantastic mechanic as well as a very experienced driver! BC

common occurrence, not only with owner drivers who had the option of travelling at their chosen pace, but also company employees. What the boss couldn't see couldn't hurt them, as there were no mobile phones that drivers were obliged to answer in those times!

Peter Bamford continued with his thoughts on breakdowns, both with regard to his own particular experiences and also to the general need for making sure trucks were properly prepared for the journey that lay ahead:

'I had quite a lot of breakdowns, which was often down to simple things, such as alternators that failed, and in particular, I remember the propshafts on Volvos had a habit of failing. Many faults were down to plain old wear and tear; although it's also true to say, many trucks weren't properly maintained by their owners back at home. Press on regardless was the mantra for some operators, and also some of the drivers, so everything was fine for them until they came to a sudden halt when something finally went bust!'

The facility to think through a problem and come up with an innovative solution was an important attribute, as well as the will not to give in too easily under external pressure, as Peter demonstrated with the following account:

'On one occasion, the fuel supply from the fuel tank to the engine wasn't getting through as it should, with the result my engine wasn't running properly at all. I tried the usual tricks to draw some fuel from the tank to the engine, but these were not working at all. This breakdown occurred when I was driving through Bulgaria as it was going dark. A policeman turned up as I was working on the truck and he wanted me to abandon it where it stood and come away with him, so that it could be driven away. I didn't want to go at all, as thieves could have arrived later on and stripped my truck down of whatever load I was carrying at the time and also of any parts from the truck that could be removed. I tried everything I could to draw some fuel through to the engine. Later on, I finally found the cause of the fault after I had withdrawn the pickup pipe from inside the fuel tank. One of the baffle plates fitted inside the fuel tank to stop the fuel from swilling about had managed to come loose so that it had started swinging about from side to side, and it had been continuously hitting the fuel pickup pipe that was inside the fuel tank. The motion of the loose baffle plate had eventually worn away a section of the fuel pickup pipe so that it was holed, and this explained why fuel wasn't being drawn down the pipe. The pump was only drawing air through the hole in the pipe rather than any fuel from inside the tank. So how was I going to mend this? If you look around a truck carefully then there's always something non-essential which you can use to improvise a repair somewhere else. I removed a rubber seal from the chassis first of all, and then I found a Jubilee clip that I used as a clamp to put a seal around the broken section of pipe. This repair worked, and the engine started …'

It didn't take long for Jeff Kedward to assemble a willing gang of volunteers to help out after he came close to scalping the top of the cab on his Volvo F88 when he collided with an overhead gantry sign as he was passing through Istanbul on his way to make a delivery at Baghdad University with a strongly constructed heavy metal container on his trailer:

'I didn't notice the height of this overhead gantry over the road. The gantry was then knocked over by the steel container I was carrying on my trailer, so the gantry was thrust forward, and this landed right on top of my cab, causing a lot of damage which needed fixing before I could continue on with my journey to Iraq. All the boys from the Mocamp came out to help me by getting my truck back to the Mocamp so it could then be mended as best we could. We used some oil drums to stand on while we repaired the shape of the cab, and we used a set of hydraulic jacks to raise the cab roof upwards while we managed to force it back into approximately the correct shape. We then popped the windscreen back into place, which luckily hadn't broken, and this was secured around all the edges using many strips of gaffer tape. I had no problems with the repaired cab travelling all the way to Baghdad and then all the way back home. I was expecting a problem when I saw this old police sergeant who was taking the time to examine my lorry after I had stopped at the motorway services station near Wolverhampton, but I was lucky as he decided to make no more of the situation!'

Perhaps that policeman had the common sense to realise that as Jeff had managed to travel so far with the cab in its present damaged condition, then surely he could travel just a bit further down the road without causing any incident or threat to other road users?

The various routes that were taken across the Middle East passed through regions where living in poverty was a way of life compared to the far more affluent standards of Western Europe. These were regions where a culture of make do and mend was deeply ingrained as an established way of life, which may suggest a negative attribute, as how could a village blacksmith be expected to repair a modern truck when using very basic repair facilities and elementary metal-working skills? To the surprise and immense relief of many stranded drivers, the blokes with the Zapata moustaches, whose overalls bore the burn marks from stray welding sparks, were surprisingly accomplished at mending lorries as well as knowing how to shoe horses! They could achieve amazingly sophisticated results using a blacksmith's forge, some welding gear and a few basic tools, but none of the facilities that would normally be found in a modern garage in Europe.

David Miller recalled an incident when the propshaft on his Scania 140 road train snapped as he was climbing towards the summit of the Tahir Pass. Finding someone who had the know-how and also the equipment to mend the propshaft did seem to be extremely unlikely. Nevertheless, the repair to the propshaft was done by a local blacksmith, who tackled the job with admirable skill and enthusiasm:

'I ripped off the truck's propshaft after I had changed down a gear rather too quickly. This was because the truck had lost traction with the ground momentarily, so I had to change down a gear, and the extra strain on the drive line caused the propshaft to snap into two pieces, so there was no longer any drive taken to the rear wheels. My first move was to uncouple the broken propshaft from the gearbox at one end and the rear axle at the other end. After this was done, a tractor and trailer happened to turn up. I asked the driver to take the two detached pieces of the propshaft to a local blacksmith in the hope a repair could be done by welding the parts back together again. The blacksmith sized up the welding repair job by putting the two sections of the propshaft together in a sandpit so they were perfectly aligned, one to each other. He then skilfully fabricated a repair section over the join to bring the two pieces of propshaft back together again, and then he welded the repair section into place. He was some clever bloke, as once the repaired propshaft had been refitted there was less vibration in it than the one which Scania originally made for my truck: absolutely brilliant, intuitive engineering.'

Peter Bamford had a similar experience in Bulgaria when the fuel tank on his truck developed a split

Repairing Peter Bamford's alloy fuel tank – safety goggles optional! PB

along one side so it was useless unless the split could be repaired. Mending the fuel tank was more difficult than it normally should have been as the tank had been made of stainless steel, so it was far more difficult to weld the surfaces back together than it would have been if the tank had been made of steel. Consequently, everyone who was asked to take on the job had declined, although Peter eventually tracked someone down who was equal to this difficult task, but Peter felt rather queasy watching this guy at work with his welding torch; there were sparks flying about in all directions but the local mechanic had not taken the precaution of wearing protective goggles!

Dave Jamieson remembers when a simple mistake resulted in the wrong spare part being sent out from Britain for John McClung's Volvo F89 which then caused further delay before John could resume his journey. A stub axle pin had broken as the Volvo was travelling through Saudi Arabia, so the answer was simply to send out a replacement part by air from Heathrow. But when the pin arrived, the diameter of the replacement stub pin was found to be too small, so it was back to square one! After giving the matter some thought, it was decided that any further delay by sending out the correct substitute part from the UK would be unacceptable, so a workable solution was agreed that involved fitting the undersized stub pin and then packing out the surfaces so that it was a really snug fit against the stub axle and the wheel hub. The material used to pack out the stub axle pin was obtained by cutting it out from the sides of a used baked bean can, and plenty of grease was then added as a lubricant to keep everything turning as it should, a repair that was good enough to get this truck up and running again!

Dave employed the same spirit of innovative engineering when the spring that held the gearstick in place on his DAF 2800 suddenly broke free, so he was no longer able to change gear, a problem he managed to fix with the following solution:

'I was going over the Taurus Mountains at the time, and when I went to change gear, there were no gears I could find to select: the gear lever wasn't where it should have been any more! I managed to solve the problem by instinctively pulling the gear stick lever up using one of my hands to hold on to the shaft, and with my other hand that was holding on to the top of the gear lever, I managed to change gear by moving the lever into the correct position. Taking this action allowed me to drive the truck for a while so it could be taken off the road and repaired. And all was well after I had managed to reinsert and reposition the spring so the gear lever was secure and I could use it once more.'

So it was fortunate that when Dave was using two hands to change gear the truck's course was straight ahead, as with both hands removed from the steering wheel, this could have turned out to be very tricky if he was negotiating a bend in the road at the same time!

It was reassuring to know that the firm that had sent a driver out over many thousands of miles had an efficient service and repair facility so that a truck was properly prepared for each long intercontinental journey. The quality of the work was all down to the mechanics and fitters who took on this most important task, a topic that Ken Ward was keen to comment on:

'Grangewood's employed an ex-Polish national who arrived in this country after the Second World War. George Wieczorek was his name, and he was rated very highly in my estimation for the way he set about preparing the Grangewood firm's Volvo F88s and F89s as well as the Scania 110s which we drove later on. There was also a fitter who was not as skilled as George and I remember an occasion when he prepared my truck for me that didn't go all that well. This was brought to mind a few days later when I arrived at the Mocamp in Istanbul only to discover that the brake drums on my truck were so overheated, they were glowing red hot! It was then I discovered the brakes had not been properly prepared, so this was causing them to heat up. After removing the brake drums, I noticed some

Herbert 'George' Wieczorek, a Polish émigré who became Grangewood's star mechanic. KW

damage to the surfaces of the brake drums: the steel had started to split apart round the entire circumference of the drums, as a result of the excessive heat build-up. This was due to the mechanic using a smaller size of rivets than he should have done when he relined all the brake shoes, so this meant the brake shoes were working loose each time that I had applied the brakes; the rivets finally broke, throwing the brake shoe loose and one of these was floating around inside the brake drum, causing the brake drum to overheat and crack open, reducing the efficiency of the braking system. I appreciated George's skills a lot more after that incident and I always made sure he was the one to prepare my truck from then on.'

Chris Stephenson maintained absolute faith in the mechanic employed by Dayson's. In recognition of the mechanic's dedication to always carrying out any job properly and to the best of his abilities, Chris would hand over a few packets of duty-free cigarettes to him whenever he returned home, all the while kidding him that this free fags bonus would be withdrawn should Chris's truck suffer any breakdown when he was far from home!

Jeff Kedward's drive in a Transcontinental came to an abrupt halt when the water pump failed after reaching Istanbul on the outward leg of the journey:

'Dai Blunt helped me repair the original water pump as we couldn't find a replacement anywhere. This was because we were in Turkey and this type of spare part was not available to buy. My Transcontinental truck had the Cummins 290 engine, the same engine as fitted to many Seddon-Atkinsons and ERFs at the time, so finding any spares such as this would have been easy enough back at home in England. But not so in Turkey as they only stocked spares for the larger Cummins 350 engine, as fitted to their own trucks. So we had no alternative but to try and repair the broken water pump. After stripping all the parts down, we did manage to find some replacement parts that we could use to rebuild the pump again with a set of seals and bearings of the correct type, which were intended for some other use.'

Finding spare parts was often assisted by the large numbers of abandoned, broken-down or crashed trucks be found just about everywhere by the roadside or at most overnight stopping places. In circumstances of dire need, which was often the case, robbing any parts was thought to be fair game by many drivers as a way of getting them out of a tight spot. But not so according to the police in Turkey, as one luckless driver from Manchester found out to his painful cost. He was apprehended lifting the spare wheel from an abandoned truck in Ankara, a crime that was to earn him the sort of punishment that he possibly remembered from his schooldays, as after he was taken away to a police station, a sound thrashing with a cane was delivered to his backside!

Ken Ward reflected on the differences of operating and driving a heavy goods vehicle within the narrow constraints of the laws applicable in the UK and most of the continent, compared to driving on the less-well-governed roads encountered on the Middle East routes where looser rules and codes applied:

'You lived with your lorry all the way there and back, and you always had to keep it in the best roadworthy condition that you could possibly manage. So you had to do whatever repair or servicing work was needed on your own if you wanted to get home in your truck! This was always an important guiding principle for any Middle East drivers. Of course, keeping your truck going could often make a complete nonsense of the VOSA [Vehicle and Operator Services Agency] inspections and all the other business that has more to do today with making sure that you precisely follow their rules the whole time rather than what it should be directed towards at all times – road safety! I seemed to have developed a sixth sense concerning any mechanical breakdowns arising on a trip. This came to my attention one night when I was actually asleep at the time. This was when I was working for Grangewood's. I woke up suddenly after noticing in my sleep that I could no longer hear whether the fridge unit was working. It had stopped in fact. To sort out the fault on the fridge unit, I climbed out of the cab, all the while wearing just my underpants and nothing else, and I managed to get the fridge unit working properly again by fitting a new alternator drive belt. Carrying a spare alternator along with us was essential for a refrigerator truck or trailer, as otherwise, the whole load could be lost if the food could no longer be kept cold. Grangewood's encouraged us to take along as many spare parts as we could carry, within what was reasonable. These included items such as engine oil, anti-freeze, wheel bearings, and Hardy-Spicer universal joints. We also took along a good supply of fuel filters, as this was particularly important if we were travelling through Eastern Europe: because the quality of the diesel fuel was so poor it could prevent the engine from running well if the fuel filters were all gummed up.'

Not everyone was a whizz kid at always knowing what to do with a set of spanners and a screwdriver in order to get going again, and Les Higgins freely admitted that just the thought of any mechanical breakdown filled him with dread and foreboding:

'I was never a mechanic, and my first instinct was always to panic, but then you instantly realised that this sort of behaviour was not going to do you any good at all. Graham Cartmail gave me a piece of good advice one day when he suggested that I should never chuck anything away which may turn out to be useful some time in the future. So I kept this box of bits and pieces in my cab just in case these parts ever came in handy. And this definitely worked in my favour one day when a front shock absorber broke free on my truck; this had swung outwards and snapped one of the brake lines, which caused an even more serious fault as my truck's brakes were effectively out of action. The broken shock absorber didn't really matter at all because my truck was still driveable in this sort of condition. But I did need to repair the brakes and get these working again before I could get going. So I decided the answer was to bend the brake pipe over in such a way that this sealed off the end of the pipe, preventing any leakage of the compressed air that worked the braking system on my truck. Using an old Jubilee clip that I was happy to find in my tin, I managed to seal off the end of the brake pipe which had been folded over to stop any air escaping. I then did the same job to the pipe on the other side of the truck. Although this brake pipe hadn't been broken, the braking action needed to be balanced on both sides of the truck. This worked perfectly, albeit my brakes weren't as effective as there was no braking action at all on the front axle.

'I was a bit worried about this reduction in braking efficiency when I was travelling through Germany as my truck could have been stopped and inspected to reveal the fault and the action I'd taken. So I drove all the way across Germany during the night hours to reduce any chance of my improvised repair being noticed by the police. This same fault with a snapped shock absorber that damaged a brake pipe occurred some time later when I was driving through Iran. So I used the same repair technique to bring my truck all the way home. Later on, I found out that my truck had been used in this condition to make a few trunk runs from Salford to Scotland and back before anyone noticed the need for a permanent repair that involved fitting new sections of brake pipe on both sides of the front axle.'

Les's faith in keeping a box of spare parts for emergency repairs was further vindicated one day when he pulled off a desert road to take a photograph, and then after climbing back in the cab, the engine could not be restarted as the plastic switch had fallen apart in his hand, and piecing this back together was clearly impossible. Help was at hand, however, from an Arab driver who kindly approached to offer his assistance:

'He helped me to get the engine going again by handing over a large, very old-fashioned, brass switch that he had with him. This looked so old, it may have come off some ancient steam engine at some time in the past, but it worked just fine once it was fitted. My engine fired up, and I was on my way!'

On another occasion, Les had not gone very far at all when he discovered the mechanic who had serviced his truck for an 8000-mile round trip had not tightened up the drain plug on his truck's radiator properly, so all the coolant had run out, and the radiator was now empty. This was brought to Les's attention when he noticed clouds of steam appearing because the engine was overheating. Les made a brief search for the plug, but this was abandoned as the plug could have been lost at a fair distance further back down the road. Help then arrived from an unexpected quarter, as Les spotted one of his mates driving along in a Ford Capri. This person came up with the novel solution of extracting something from his car boot as a workable substitute for the missing drain plug. Les's friend handed over a second-hand spark plug, and after checking whether the spark plug thread pattern matched the one on the drain plug hole, the spark plug was screwed into place, and Les could then resume his long journey to Saudi Arabia:

'I went all the way there and back with that Ford Capri spark plug sticking out of the bottom of the radiator as it was such a perfect fit. And I did many more miles after that before the spark plug was removed and replaced with the correct item!'

Many of the trailers that went to the Middle East were hired out by specialist firms such as Willhire, and when Les was towing one of their trailers through Yugoslavia, a wheel bearing wore out, so he contacted the trailer hire firm to advise them that this had happened and also to obtain information on what he should do next:

'They desperately wanted me to stay with the trailer throughout so it wouldn't go missing for good. Many of their trailers and those of other hire firms were lost altogether in this way, or they were stripped down of any parts and became useless. So they sent a mechanic all the way from Graz in Austria who had a replacement wheel bearing with him, but this turned out to be of the wrong type, so he had to go back to Graz to pick up a replacement, and he returned

again, this time with the correct item, so I could be on my way again.'

This incident provided Les an insight on how grievances can linger on after one country has been militarily dominated by another nation, as occurred in Yugoslavia when occupied by the Nazis during the Second World War:

'The mechanic was very efficient at doing the job as quickly as he could. I remember that he spoke with an Austrian or German accent, which explained why he was so keen to finish the job and get moving. He was scared stiff about leaving the side of the road for any length of time after he had started work on the trailer. This was all because of what the Nazis had done, making the locals suffer so badly in Yugoslavia during the years of the Second World War. People have long memories, and his presence could well have sparked off an act of revenge if any locals had decided to get hold of him with those memories in mind.'

Ron Slater always took the precaution of having a spare half-shaft with him and this worked well for him when the one in his Guy Big J snapped as he drove through mountainous terrain near Mardin in southeastern Turkey on his way to Baghdad in 1975. Ron was accompanied by another Big J driver, Lennie Venables, who worked for the same firm, British Crane Hire. The Big J trucks were unusual as they were built as part of a special batch of twelve, and these had 220 Cummins engines and 9-speed Fuller gearboxes, a Far East export order which then failed; so British Crane Hire bought all twelve at the Commercial Vehicle Motor Show, to be used on the Middle East run.

Brian Robertson heaped praise on the skills that many Turkish mechanics and blacksmiths demonstrated with metalwork repairs and also fabrication, particularly as it would have been unlikely that they would have received the sort of apprenticeships and training that would have been available to them here in the UK or elsewhere in Europe:

'I broke a spring on my Scania 110 – there was no air suspension in those days, only old-fashioned steel springs! The Turks would simply make any replacement parts that you might need by working away inside a small hut beside the road. First of all, we jacked up the axle to remove the broken spring, and it was taken away on a horse and cart. When the men doing the job came back a short time afterwards, they had brought along a replacement spring that was an exact copy of the original, to the very last detail of the one I'd asked them to copy. This leaf spring had been forged so recently, it was still extremely hot, and it was burning a hole in the bottom of the horse-drawn trailer! Maybe the repair would have cost me £20–£30, but this was nothing if it got me going once more with only a short delay between asking those Turks for some help and the new spring being made and delivered so it could be fitted to my truck!'

Brian reported a similar incident when the balance pipe that distributes fuel between the two fuel tanks on his truck broke when he was near the town of Biriack in Eastern Turkey:

'The mechanic removed the pipe so this could be repaired while he asked a kid to put a finger in each end of the broken pipe so as to stop any of the diesel fuel running away!'

Most trucks travelling back to Europe would not be carrying a return load, which proved to be very convenient to those who had a broken-down lorry that needed to be transported back to the UK or elsewhere in Europe; this was often achieved by the method known as 'topping' which involved a broken-down truck being transported on the back of another truck. The only problem with this arrangement was the overall height of one truck sitting on top of the trailer of another truck could so easily result in problems passing under low bridges or low hanging wires, etc. For this reason, the broken-down truck was loaded onto the back of the one that was to carry it home with a few modifications to reduce the overall height. These involved removing the front wheels, and if a tilt trailer needed to be carried as well, the tilts from both trailers were stripped down and stored away on one of the two available trailers. Brian Robertson recalled the occasion when he found himself helping out another Chevalier Brothers' driver in this very manner:

'My mate Peter Robinson, who we called "Bootsie", was driving an old MAN truck through Eastern Turkey when the engine seized, so we "topped" his truck onto the back of my truck. Getting his truck onto the back of mine seemed to be a huge problem at the time, as there we were, somewhere out in the middle of nowhere. But this issue was answered by asking a Turkish bloke who was driving this bulldozer if he would dig a large hole in a field for us so that we could first of all drive my truck and trailer into the hole. So this then enabled Bootsie to drive his truck straight onto the back of my truck, which now had its trailer at ground level after the trailer had been reversed into the hole dug by the bulldozer. Although the engine was damaged on Bootsie's truck, it was still driveable; the engine was still working at ticking over speed, so he drove his truck onto the back of mine. We then

Bob Thompson's DAF loaded on its trailer and then recovered to the UK by John Buffham. JB

set off back to England with one truck stuck on top of the other one, and we managed to get all the way to Ankara, where a low bridge then blocked our way due to the extra height of one truck sitting on top of the other. So we had no option but to find an alternative route to avoid this bridge.

'This route then passed under some live power lines for running the city's electric trams. In order to get under the electrically charged wires, Bootsie stood on the back of his truck and used a tilt board to lift the electric power lines, so I could then drive my truck underneath the cables that were hanging down above the tramlines. He managed to avoid getting himself electrocuted as the wooden tilt boards were non-conductive – he was isolated from the high voltage of electricity that was still running through the wires. But things went seriously wrong when two of the cables touched causing the electricity to be shorted out – so none of the trams were running in that particular part of the city! Our next move was to clear off as fast as possible before anyone found out … !

'We went all the way across Turkey, which occasionally involved ripping down any hanging wires and some of the street lighting we came across. Later on we took the precaution of cutting the top section of the headboard off Bootsie's truck to stop this sort of incident happening, but this decision didn't really make much difference at all with his truck sitting so tall above the top of mine.'

Later on, Peter stopped to pick up a pair of British Z-platers, (cars bearing German export Z-plates that were being exported to countries such as Turkey or Iran), who were about to endure a most frightening ordeal later on that day:

'We had no room in the cab of my truck for the two of them, so they both climbed up onto Bootsie's truck while we took our place back in my truck's cab. We picked up these two delivery drivers somewhere near the border where we had crossed from Yugoslavia into Austria, and after coming down the long, winding road, which was known to us all as the "Ho Chi Minh Trail", we came across a low bridge outside Salzburg which was something we hadn't expected to come across in this part of Austria. We could see that this bridge looked as if was too low for us to pass under, but we didn't have time to come to a stop owing to the speed we were going at the time. Luckily, we just scraped through without tearing the roof off Peter's truck that was sitting on top of mine, which still had the two delivery guys sitting in it! We pulled over to see if there was any damage and to check out whether our "upstairs" passengers were still OK, which they were, but they refused to travel any further on with us!'

John Buffham became an artful dodger at 'recycling' spare parts from an abandoned truck when a running mate of his discovered he wasn't going anywhere unless a set of replacement batteries could be found

Bob's DAF shunting a trailer into position. JB

to replace those stolen from his lorry at Kapıkule just after crossing the border into Turkey:

'Someone pinched the batteries off Bob Thompson's DAF truck on the first trip that either of us ever made. This took place when we were away from the border as we had to go to Istanbul to pick up some papers that we needed for the rest of the journey. When we arrived back, the two batteries on Bob's DAF were missing as these had been stolen, so the answer was to go out and find ourselves a set of suitable replacements. We began to take an interest in a compound at the border post as this was full of many confiscated vehicles of all types. Obtaining a set of batteries from one of the trucks in the compound seemed to be the best answer to Bob's problem, but the compound was guarded by some armed soldiers. Their job was to watch what was going on from this Volkswagen van all the while, so there was the real possibility of being shot by these soldiers if we were caught stealing those batteries! Under cover of darkness, we managed to find a hole through the wire surrounding the compound, and we removed the batteries from a truck that had been left there standing for who knows how long. We managed this task OK without being seen by any of the guards or having some shots fired in our direction, and this was assisted by a curtain of thick fog which came down and hid us from view, but this also meant you could hardly see your hand in front of your face. We had to take just one battery at a time, as a task we had to share, as the batteries weighed so much. But after retrieving the first one from the compound, going back and finding where we had left the other one was very difficult in all that thick fog. Fortunately, we managed to find the second battery in the early hours of the morning, just before it was light once more, as by then it would have been impossible to pick up the second battery without being seen.'

It wasn't always convenient to recover a broken-down or accident-damaged truck and the accompanying trailer by the process of 'topping' onto the back of another truck. This was only possible if the trailer body of the 'recovery' vehicle was of the removable tilt design that could be stripped down to the level of the loadbed so that a broken-down vehicle could then be carried. It was not possible at all if the trailer of either truck was of solid box construction, in which case an alternative solution had to be adopted to get a stricken vehicle home.

The usual method in such circumstances was for the broken-down or accident-damaged truck to be towed by another one to the nearest repair workshop. This solution would have been easy enough to adopt if the distance involved amounted to ten or twenty miles, but how about towing an artic behind another one over a journey lasting hundreds of miles!

Graham Cartmail explained the routine they followed when he towed Karl Nowotarski's truck over a huge distance with the tow rope stretched taut all the way:

'After disconnecting the propshaft to avoid winding up the gearbox, we put a twelve-foot chain on to tow Karl's truck along. He still had the full use of the truck's brakes, as the engine was still working. It had to be towed because the fuel tank had split wide open, but we managed to rig up an alternative fuel supply to get the truck moving. We managed to cross halfway through Damascus in Syria with Karl's truck on tow, but then the driver of a three-wheeled van tried to get between our two trucks, forcing Karl to slam on his brakes and avoid colliding with the small van. This caused the tow chain between the two trucks to snap just where the chain was attached to the back of my trailer. The shock generated caused the long length of chain to fly backwards through the air on the recoil and straight through Karl's windscreen. Luckily, the end of the chain shot through the passenger side of the windscreen, so Karl wasn't injured at all, although he well might have been! I eventually managed to tow Karl's truck for about 1500 miles before it was repaired after both trucks crossed the border into Turkey.'

There had been an earlier attempt to repair the split in Karl's fuel tank, and a pair of Syrian mechanics had been asked to do this work, although this had gone

George Brooke's DAF being repaired following the failure of the wheel hub. GB

seriously wrong! Although they had been told to fill the fuel tank with water before they began doing any of the welding repair with a flaming torch, this advice had been ignored, so that when a hot gas flame ignited the residue of diesel lying at the bottom of the tank, the tank exploded and split apart so it was now utterly useless!

Throughout Turkey the quality of road repair work was fairly basic, and Graham Cartmail remembers he wasn't at all impressed when the underside of his truck received a coating of hot tarmac when he went by some road works where resurfacing was taking place:

'They would just put the tar down on the road surface when this was still hot and wet, so that you would then have to travel on this surface for a few miles before they came along later to put down any chipping stones. This meant the underside of the truck's chassis, the axles and the brakes would soon be completely smothered in a coating of hot, wet tar thrown up by your truck's tyres, which then hardened, and the tar would become a real problem if you needed to change a wheel, or work on anything else under the truck or the trailer, which was now encrusted with thick deposits of tar from the unfinished, tar-coated road surfaces.'

Beyond repair! ERF abandoned at Bazargan, Iranian border. BC

Graham was pleased with the quality of service he eventually received from DAF after the radiator on his 2800 was dramatically destroyed as he approached the city of Plovdiv in central Bulgaria:

'Before setting off, the DAF dealer had done some work on my truck, which required the guard on the radiator fan to be removed. But this hadn't been put back on properly by the mechanic, and it came off, hitting the fan blades and removing two of the blades, which then smashed the radiator to bits so it was finished. DAF Aid were the best, as they delivered a new radiator and fan by air into Belgrade where a van was sent out to deliver the parts and repair my truck on the spot. Everyone who originally wanted a Scania or a Volvo was getting wise that in fact driving a DAF was best as the DAF Aid set-up was so effective if you needed to be helped out. The Dutch had the Middle East job sewn up for many years, and their trucks were always so well built for the job.'

Ian Taylor used a straight bar to tow a DAF 2300 behind his Scania 111 for almost 300 miles on one occasion, a favour that was repaid when his Volvo F88 broke down as the engine had dropped a valve just after he had completed his delivery, which was unloaded at Riyadh, Saudi Arabia:

'This bloke, although I can't remember his name, towed me halfway along the desert TAP line through Saudi, and then onwards all the way through to southern Turkey, but we were only using an eight-foot straight bar, which meant there was not much in the way of any forward visibility for me at all! We covered a distance of almost a thousand miles, and all the while I had to concentrate like mad in order to make the correct steering inputs so my truck could exactly follow the one in front. The steering had to be adjusted with such immediacy, even though I had no idea at all of what the driving conditions were like ahead of us, either immediately or further on down the road. After arriving at the Oryx Garage in Turkey, we discovered my truck couldn't be repaired out there for some reason, so a more convenient arrangement was worked out for the rest of the journey back to the UK, and my Volvo was piggy-backed on to another bloke's truck.'

This breakdown was an unusual occasion, as Ian normally managed to fix any mechanical problems for himself. He also enjoyed working on other people's trucks, as for example, a Fiat 619 that had cooked its clutch in Ankara:

'The gearbox on the Fiat sat further back on the chassis than is usual on most trucks, and was then connected to

the engine by a short propshaft that was easy to remove, so getting the clutch in and out wasn't a problem. Unlike some other truck manufacturers, Fiat spares were easy to obtain anywhere you went throughout Turkey.'

Running a truck through harsh desert conditions would result in sand particles being ingested by the engine and then causing lots of damage, although this can take months to manifest, as Ian Taylor went on to discover when he was given a Volvo F12 to drive which had really been put through the mill:

'I was driving through Germany in this Volvo F12 when I noticed the engine was looking dicey because it had started to blow out clouds of thick, black smoke from the exhaust. So I stopped at a service area and proceeded to strip down the engine to find out what was wrong. This truck had been used out in Saudi Arabia for a long while, and as a result, lots of desert sand had found its way into the engine, so this explained why the engine's pistons and the piston rings were all so badly worn.'

Martyn Moulsdale took on a fair number of roadside repairs, for example when a leaf spring on his twin-axle trailer broke. To get home again, he chained up the one axle so the wheels to each side of the trailer were lifted off the ground. The weight of the trailer would now be resting on the remaining axle that was still in contact with the ground. And he then drove off with the axle suspended thus, until he located someone who knew how to mend or fabricate leaves to repair the spring.

Similarly Martyn soon found an answer when the windscreen wipers on his truck packed up. He found a piece of rope and cut it to the right length so it could be tied to one of the wipers, and after passing the other end of the rope through the open cab window, the rope could be hauled by hand to clear away any rain from the windscreen. To the wiper blade on the other side of the truck, the offside, he attached a length of elastic bungee cord, which was secured to the far side of the cab, opposite the driver's seat. After the set of wipers had been drawn in one direction by hand to sweep across the windscreen from one direction, the bungee cord would automatically draw the set of wiper blades back the other way to sweep the windscreen, and the whole process was then repeated as needed!

When the fuel lift pump failed on Martyn's truck, his solution followed the usual practice of securing an empty five-gallon oil can on to the roof of his cab, and after this had been filled with diesel, a siphon tube was added from the can to the engine's injector pump, the fuel then being supplied by gravity action.

Andy Chevalier's truck once broke all the studs on one of the drive wheels; however, knowing where to obtain a set of replacements was easy enough: Andy simply removed one nut from each of the other wheels to transfer over, so each of the wheels was missing just the one securing nut, which made driving the truck almost as safe as if it still had a full set of twenty or so nuts securing each of the wheels.

Bob Carter's commitment to sorting out breakdown issues by himself extended to driving halfway across Europe to rescue one of his drivers on one occasion after their Trans UK truck had broken down. The problem was simple to resolve: an air leak was preventing the operation of the gearbox, a repair job that took Bob all of ten minutes to complete. Imagine travelling all that way to Yugoslavia to carry out a repair which turned out to be so straightforward!

Checking the oil on a Bromilow's Scammell Crusader, as the Rolls engine was prone to using much oil. Hungary 1976. KP

Dougie Fry changing a spring – Jeddah workshops of Trans Arabia. JC

Repairing the brakes on Gordon Summers' truck. GS

Mike Dunstan's Volvo at Radclive's depot, Faringdon. Brian Winfield – left, Pete Posey – right. MD

Oliver Watson changing an air filter, a regular task when operating trucks in hot desert climates. GS

Ted Hannant sorting out an engine problem. COPYRIGHT UNKNOWN

CHAPTER 7

Different Loads

It would be logical to assume the majority of freight that was transported out to the Middle East would be of the 'heavy' sort, essential items such as materials for building projects and roads, or airports and port facilities, items that were vital to the development of a country's infrastructure in the future. Some typical loads of this nature might include prefabricated buildings, precast or steel bridge sections, diggers and excavators; cranes used for unloading of shipping were in particularly great demand. All the equipment needed for oil and gas exploration and extraction, and all the refining equipment would also fit into this same category. The vast sums of wealth generated by the reserves of oil in the Middle East funded all the above developments, and also encouraged an affluent lifestyle for the citizens of these oil-rich lands. In later years these riches were channelled into the towering high-rise developments that crowd the skylines of many Middle East cities today, such as Riyadh in Saudi Arabia, and the principal cities of the smaller Gulf States, notably Abu Dhabi, Qatar and Kuwait.

However, once the viability of overland deliveries from Europe had been established in respect of the 'heavy' items and equipment, this left the door open for a whole range of consumer products to be transported by the truckload to many Middle East destinations.

Western food items became popular, both with the local inhabitants of all these countries as well as the growing number of ex-pats who came here to take well-paid jobs on the back of the surging oil boom.

Thanks to the thermal efficiency of refrigerated vans, perishables such as chocolate bars, eggs, meat and even loads of ice cream could successfully make the journey and arrive as fresh as they were when the van had been packed and the doors slammed shut back in the UK, and these consumables were on their way across deserts where a temperature of over 100°F/38°C was considered quite normal!

Unbelievable as this may seem in view of the distance that was involved, a load of men's aftershave was sent out all the way to Karachi in Pakistan. And gourmet delights such as grouse, pheasants and frogs' legs were sent out all that way in reefer (refrigerated) vans to a luxury hotel in Tehran.

Stepframe trailer maximised load carrying capacity although smaller tyres could overheat and burst. CB

These cement-mixing silos were used to build runways for the Saudi air force. ITY

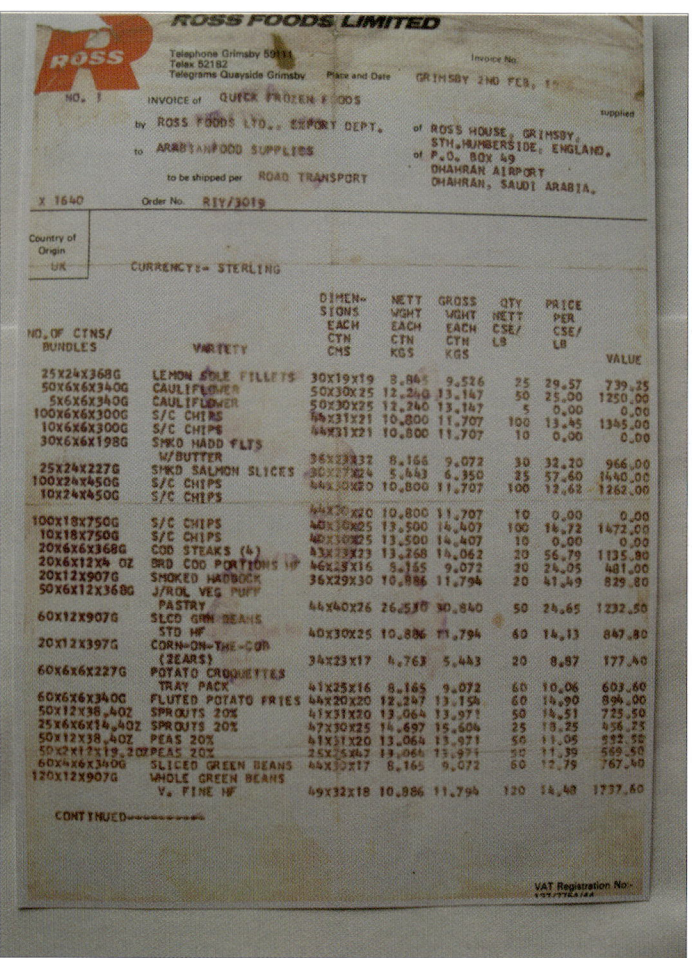

A typical refrigerated load for Ross Foods delivered to Dhahran airport. DB

The sorts of return loads available from Middle East destinations included fabrics and carpets, fruit and vegetable produce in season, and donkey meat for the tinned dog food market.

So maybe it was best to refuse the offer of any backloads? The situation did improve, however, after getting a lot closer to home, as some firms instructed their drivers to arrange for pickups of new loads in Yugoslavia, Austria or Germany, which worked out well by improving profitability, and requiring perhaps only a day or two to reload, so the driver was soon home again at the end of the trip.

Frank White expressed the thoughts of most drivers when it came to picking up a return load for the journey home:

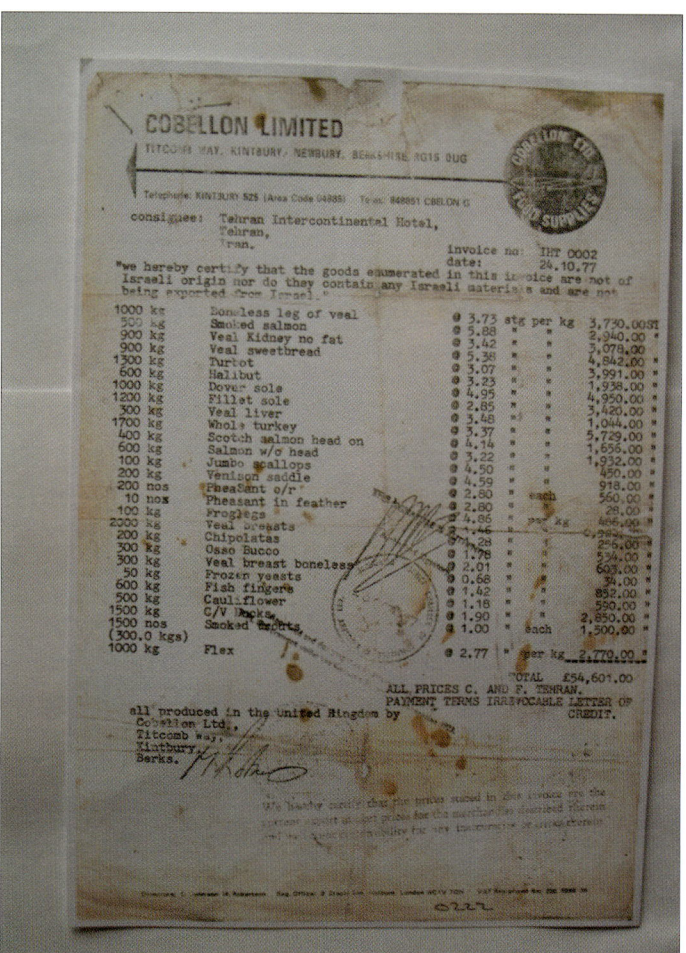

Invoice for frozen foods supplied by Cobellon provides a disclaimer that none of the items is of Israeli origin. DB

Although an outward trip could turn a nice profit, it didn't take long for Middle East hauliers to consider that maybe a backload could be found out there to make the trip home profitable, even if this was on a much smaller scale. There was a further incentive for picking up a backload as this would weigh down the suspension, making for a much more pleasant ride home. But taking on a return load required the extra burden of taking on all the extra paperwork and documentation, and yet more hassle when going through customs at each border post, and the need for extra care and security so the goods reached the final destination still intact. As a further disincentive, the going rates from the Middle East to Europe made it difficult to turn a profit, they were so poor! In 1976, taking a load to Tehran could earn £4000 whereas a return load from Tehran to the UK only attracted a fee of about £1000.

Outside the old customs warehouse in Tehran. BC

'I only ever took one backload from the Middle East. This was a load of furniture from Tehran. Taking a backload through any borders was never worth the hassle. It was far easier to pick up a load in Europe and take it home with you. You wouldn't get much cash for such a short-haul trip, but this was a lot better than getting nothing at all.'

Mark Chevalier had a few problems at the Turkish border with a return load of tea dust which he had picked up in Iran:

'The trouble started when I rolled my MAN truck over onto its side coming into Turkey from Iran. The road ahead was blocked by trucks coming the other way; I had a set of snow chains fitted at the time, and I was loaded with twenty tons of tea dust, which was all contained in heavy sacks. After I had been stuck standing where I was for three hours, I decided I would try to move my truck forwards, but suddenly, just after I had started this, the surface of the earth road which I was driving on collapsed under me, so my truck and trailer rolled over onto their sides. Eventually, the military came to help me and they sorted the traffic out so all the other trucks could get past. They brought a large American crane to lift my tractor and trailer up and get both of these back onto their wheels. I lied to them about the weight of my truck and the load carried on the trailer, otherwise they would have wanted me to unload all the tea dust first of all so as not to overstrain the crane, which would have delayed matters even further for me. The extra weight of all that tea did cause the crane's jib to bend as the heavy trailer was lifted, but at last we managed to extricate the truck and trailer so they were back on their wheels. The tilt and the frame of my trailer had been badly damaged when it had tipped over sideways, so I found an English bloke who was prepared to take on my job of delivering the load of tea dust. I paid some Turkish lads to unload the sacks of tea dust onto the other bloke's trailer; those Turks were so strong, they had impressive stamina, like those Turkish wrestlers! The tea dust was probably sold off cheaply as you could smell the diesel which had been spilt out of my fuel tank. The tilt was repaired when I got back to the UK, and the tractor was none the worse after a new cab had been fitted by our local MAN dealer.'

Mike Dunstan was more fortunate when it came to finding a backload which paid a fair return:

'I often came back from Turkey carrying lots of hanging garments. This was the other side of the coin to me taking

Trucks parked up at the new customs compound, Tehran. BC

John Buffham's Volvo on the train through Germany with a backload of two Zetor tractors picked up in Austria. JB

the way it had been unloaded from the truck. Geoff Morgan recalled the occasion when he encountered this sort of 'couldn't care less' approach when he arrived at a warehouse in Iraq in order to unload some expensive electrical power generators:

'A crew of labourers came along, and after the side curtains on my trailer had been drawn back to allow access, a JCB arrived, and this was used to push each of the generators off the trailer so that they struck the ground with a bump after dropping from a height of about a few feet, which meant the generators were all damaged from this fall. The only explanation I could come up with for this sort of behaviour was possibly the customs duty on imported equipment being a lot lower if any items had been damaged: perhaps so they could then be described as broken and the out the loads of yarn, which was manufactured by Courtaulds in the UK, so that clothing could be made over there!'

Mike also did well taking loads of Massey Ferguson tractors in disassembled, knockdown form to a tractor factory in Turkey; he also took loads of Perkins engines to another tractor factory in Belgrade, Yugoslavia.

Drivers were responsible for making sure what they carried was protected from accidental damage or theft, so it was very frustrating to discover that a load that had been transported over many thousands of miles with everything intact and undamaged then became ruined through sheer carelessness by

Volvo F12 loaded with ventilation plant equipment for the Sheraton Hotel, Jeddah. MD

Dave Mayer's DOW Volvo, Frankie Andrews' MAN, and Mike Dunstan's Scania, that's loaded with Massey-Ferguson tractors bound for Istanbul. MD

parts considered as "spares" rather than equipment which was in full working condition?'

Brian Robertson observed a double whammy of needless destruction when he took some food supplies out to the British embassy in Tehran as well as some fragile X-ray tubes made of glass that were for the city hospital. The food was unloaded so roughly and carelessly, Brian watched in disbelief as he saw some of the liquid items leak out and run along a gutter. Then to cap it all, the customs men began to unload the precious X-ray tubes by also throwing these items off from the back of his trailer, so his attention was then alerted by the sound of breaking glass as the X-ray tubes shattered into tiny pieces:

'You tried your utmost to take care of what you were carrying, only to see it all destroyed as soon as you had arrived, which was a real shame. I did my best and I was never held responsible for any damaged goods in any insurance claims made against me. And in fact any such claims that were made were all dismissed as completely unfounded.'

Chris Stephenson was passing through Saudi customs when he watched the unloading of sides of beef from a refrigerated truck which was being inspected for contraband by border officials. The driver began expressing concern that the meat would soon start to go off quickly if exposed to the extremes of heat found in this part of the world. But the customs officials ignored his pleas, and the meat remained outside the trailer's refrigerated interior for a good while before it was eventually reloaded when the customs men had completed their inspection. So this left the driver worrying that maybe the meat would have gone off so it would then be condemned by the customer when he reached its final destination. But speaking with a wealth of experience behind him, Chris advised the driver to relax so he could take a more rounded view of the situation: everything was bound to turn out fine providing the meat was approved and signed to this effect by a chit that confirmed it was fit to eat. And who could conclude otherwise after the meat had been refrozen to the same hardness and density as a piece of granite rock!

Misconceptions over the nature of a particular type of cargo could result in long delays at border crossings, as Jeff Kedward found out when he arrived with some items that looked very suspicious to officials at the old customs house in Tehran:

Keith Tabernacle picks up the paperwork for another Middle East delivery for Redcliffe Roadways. RR

Handballing a load of Oxford University Press dictionaries in Amman, Jordan. MD

'I was delayed for nearly two weeks as the customs men decided that maybe the oxygen cylinders I was carrying to a hospital were in fact a type of bomb which they thought I was trying to smuggle into their country; so they wouldn't let me unload until they'd finally decided otherwise!'

Brian Robertson took a load of brake drums out to a car factory in Tehran, where the Paykan was produced, the local version of the Hillman Hunter. He then came across a pile of brake drums that had been left outside so they were all rusty – brake drums he had delivered there over two months previously. Clearly an oversupply problem which made a mockery of any forward product planning!

Dave Jamieson took a job driving for Frank White in July 1977, and the first load he carried was in one of Frank's DAF 2800s to Dammam, Saudi Arabia, as part of a three-truck convoy. The load carried on all the trucks was a set of three cable reels each, but when the journey was only part done, a cable on one of the trailers started shifting sideways, which brought all three trucks to a temporary halt. Dave explained how this problem came about:

'The wooden cable drums had to stand upright on their ends to avoid the overall weight of each drum from damaging the plastic insulation on the lengths of cable. With three of these big reels sitting on each trailer, it was important the large reels were properly chained and chocked down. On the trailer that was towed by Tom Smith's truck, one of the cable drums had started to buckle under its own weight as we drove over bumpy road surfaces on the Taurus Mountain range. This drum started pushing sideways through the sides of the trailer's tilt canvas, so it was threatening to fall off sideways from the loadbed. We managed to reposition the drum reel so it was standing where it should on the back of the trailer once again, and away from the side of the tilt. We also needed to patch up a tear in the side of the tilt where the loose reel had forced its way sideways through the fabric. Sealing up the tilt and hiding the repair work was important, as we needed to hide the fact that this trailer's load had been exposed, which could have resulted in problems with the customs at the next border crossing.'

But all went well in fact, and Dave and his mates crossed the borders into Syria, Jordan and then Saudi Arabia without any problems.

As for anywhere else in the world, carrying any unusually large loads has its attendant risks, not only concerning the need to avoid hitting low bridges and any overhead wires, but also complying with exacting bureaucratic requirements, which often seem to have little relevance to the task in hand. This was something that concerned Dave Jamieson as well as his running mates when they were delivering a batch of Ruston and Hornsby turbine pumps to a distant location in Iran. To further complicate matters, the pumps had to be dropped off at a number of locations where they would be installed at intervals alongside the oil pipeline:

'We used a set of low-loader, "super-cube" trailers to take the pumps to wherever they were needed along the pipeline. Iranian rules required us to have a special wide load permit for each of our oversized trailers. This was something we only found out about some time after we had crossed the Iranian border and had arrived at one of those police inspection places that you came across in that country. The police ordered us to go back to the border post in a taxi so we could then obtain permits to carry our wide loads. This was done, although we were fined by the authorities for taking

Butrako Fiat loaded with steel bridge sections in Belgium for a temporary flyover at Riyadh airport. MD

our trailers into the country without having any of these special permits in the first place! The conditions attached to our permits indicated our top speed had to be restricted to an average of about 30 mph. To enforce this, we were supposed to report to every police inspection checkpoint along the way. The idea behind this was, by referring back to the time we had left the last police checkpoint, and by how long it had taken to reach the next checkpoint, they could then calculate the speed we had been travelling at, and a fine could be imposed if we had gone any faster than about 30 mph between the two police checkpoints. But after realising it was going to take at least two and a half days to get to where we were to begin delivering the turbines, we decided to ignore this rule about having to stop at any police posts we came across, and pressed on as fast as we could go after we had reached the city of Tabriz, which wasn't all that far from the border after entering Iran. We had no further problems with the police over this matter. The only other cause for delay was all the blow-outs on the trailer tyres meaning the spare wheels had to be fitted.'

The reason for the unusually high number of blow-outs was that the wheels fitted to low-loaders required a smaller type of tyre and these were more susceptible to the sort of heat and friction that were generated when driving in hot climates.

One of the golden rules of international trucking was for drivers to be hypervigilant when it came to taking any return loads, in view of the risk of smuggled contraband being hidden away on a truck. The implication being that the driver must surely have been aware of what he was carrying when and if prohibited items were uncovered by customs officials later on. Brian Robertson recalled the day he let his guard down; with hindsight, he could see that getting involved in some business that had started looking shady could have had serious repercussions. This was something that gave him a cold sweat beneath his collar for a good long while afterwards:

'I had been told the return load I had been offered and had then accepted was some farm machinery which I carried all the way across Turkey with my truck and trailer. I first became aware that maybe something was not right after I had noticed I was being followed by someone in a Turkish-registered car. When I stopped to go to bed at night, the driver in the car would park up behind me, and he would stay there all night until I had set off next morning, when he would begin following me again. The mysterious driver of the car that was always following me never revealed who he was, and I never found out what I was actually carrying, as I hadn't seen it when loaded on the back of my trailer. It certainly looked as if the man in the car was guarding something that was in my trailer the whole time. This made me very nervous, and I made a promise to myself that I would never do anything like this ever again!'

Graham Cartmail provided an account of a return load that kept him busy for weeks, driving back to the

After suffering one more tyre burst, Ian Taylor settled down to making some repairs out in the desert. IT

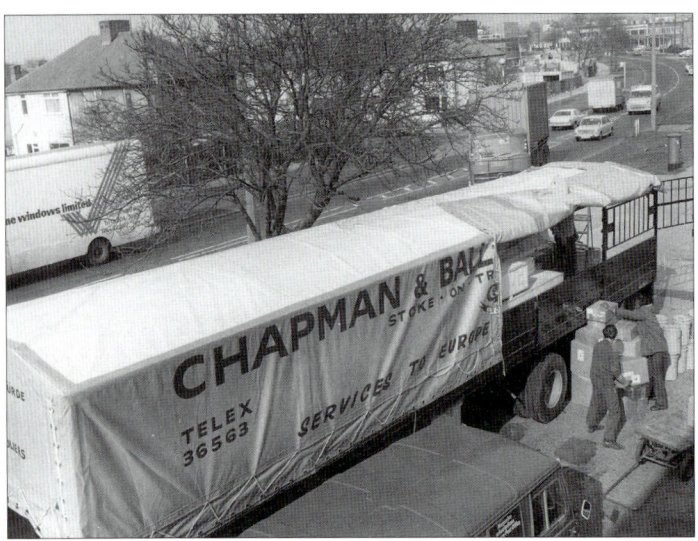

Loading up almost completed at Chapman & Ball depot premises. CB

Such was the demand for all sorts of goods from Europe, carrying a mixed load of goods that were ultimately delivered to many different customers became an alternative source of revenue to taking on dedicated loads that were to be delivered to just the one customer at the end of a trip. Groupage loads then attracted a higher rate of pay although the rewards needed to be balanced against the possibility of any delays occurring due to the recipient failing to turn up on time to collect their goods, which needed to be signed off to clear import procedures before the driver could start their return journey. Brian suffered such a delay on one occasion:

'I put in my customs papers at the Davies Turner offices in Tehran, and there was just the one unclaimed package left that weighed about 30 kilos and it contained some oxidising materials. The customer was away in America, so I then had to wait for three weeks before the owner turned up and claimed the package. Every day I would ask the customs agent if he had arrived. Not that I was too bothered as I spent all day beside the Davies Turner swimming pool and I was paid £100 a day for demurrage, which was just fine by me!'

One of the most frequently discussed stories about a load that almost reached its intended destination but Gulf with an extra load, and then reloading the trailers with oranges that were brought home to the UK:

'When I was returning from Qatar, I had come back as far as Cologne when I was asked to turn round and go back to Turkey, which I then agreed to do. This was just before Christmas, but I didn't mind being away from home, I was the only bloke out of the other four of us out there who didn't have any family commitments.

'Jenkinson's had shipped six unaccompanied trailers from Felixstowe docks to Turkey, and my first job wasn't a return load, it was to deliver the trailers to various destinations in the Gulf where they would be unloaded. I collected each of the trailers from somewhere outside Antalya in Turkey, and after returning from the Gulf to Turkey with each of the trailers, which were now empty, the next job was to load these up with hundreds of crates of oranges and take these loads back to the UK. So I would set off with each trailer in turn and I would then arrive at a particular orange orchard which I had been instructed to find. It was clear I was in for a long delay, as after arriving at any of the orchards I then found the oranges hadn't been picked or sorted. The idea was to keep the fruit on the trees for as long as possible until I had arrived with my truck and trailer so that the oranges were kept nice and fresh. But I would be waiting for a day and a half while the local women and children picked the fruit off the trees, a process that was delayed by having to put each individual orange through a riddle so as to make sure the size conformed with the agreed contract requirements!'

Ray Scutts with his Anglo Continental AEC Mandator at the Tehran trade fair circa 1970. Exhibition materials were a popular choice of work. RS

was then destroyed concerned a full refrigerated trailer of ice cream that Stevie Swaine was carrying when he was working for Jenkinson's. The temperature gauges on the freezer unit suggested everything was OK, although in fact the freezer had already malfunctioned, so when a customs inspection required the doors of the refrigerated trailer to be opened, out slopped eight tons of melted ice-cream onto the tarmac in a wallowing, slow-motion wave!

Sometimes there were problems when unusual cargoes were unloaded that could result in long delays. However, John Buffham managed to work this sort of situation to his advantage after arriving at an American military base in Turkey with an oversized Portakabin on his trailer. This had already caused a few problems for him on the way when he was travelling through Yugoslavia:

'This prefabricated building was so long and so tall, I was really worried when it was being transported through the low, narrow tunnels, which I liked to call "rat holes", which you travelled through on your way towards the Yugoslavia/Bulgaria border. I was surprised to emerge from these tunnels with the large Portakabin still in one piece. After crossing into Turkey, I got to the military base without any problems, but there wasn't any lifting equipment to take the Portakabin off my trailer, it was so large and heavy. So I spent a whole week waiting for the right size of crane to arrive, during which time I ate very well in the military cafeteria used by the soldiers and drank plenty of Budweiser beer!'

Taking loads into Saudi Arabia could be particularly awkward as the customs searches were very detailed, sometimes extending into cutting holes into the chassis or fuel tanks in their search for banned goods, such as alcohol. But Gordon Summers knew that he was not going to have any such problems when he picked up a Volvo F12 truck bound for Saudi which was owned by the Butomus company. The reason being, this truck was carrying liquefied gas for refilling an air-conditioning plant, so the tank was sealed tight and pressurised! The only problem Gordon had was that the tank had not been fitted with any baffles to prevent the liquid gas from sloshing about, so any corners had to be taken with extreme caution to avoid the tanker tipping over!

Transporting military aircraft spare parts always worked out well for Ian Taylor as these sensitive and valuable loads were exempt from the exhaustive and time-consuming searches that were normally carried

Butomus Volvo F12 gas tanker driven by Gordon Summers to Saudi Arabia. GS

out at Saudi border crossings. The officials would simply add an extra customs seal before ushering Ian and his truck on its way, the final destination being Dammam air force base.

Drivers who delivered military uniforms to both of the warring countries during the Iran–Iraq War of 1980 to 1988 were entitled to feel nervous making a delivery to one country after having previously made a delivery to the other side carrying a different style of uniform!

Archie Bowden parked up in Germany as an abnormal load could only be taken at night between 8 pm and 6 am. MM

Archie Bowden in the red Transcontinental leads Martyn Mouldsdale's, carrying two separate halves of an electrical substation to Iraq. MM

When Martyn Moulsdale took a job with CVH Transport Services of Bedwas, South Wales, he partnered the late Archie Bowden on a trip which involved each of them taking an electrical substation out to Iraq on a job that had been arranged for the Schenkers electrical firm. At seventy-foot long and sticking out by a couple of feet on each side of the trailer, these substations that housed electrical generators may well have been one of the largest loads to be transported out to the Middle East. Martyn found that travelling through Germany with an oversized load was far easier than he had imagined. Good forward planning and valuable assistance from the authorities in Germany made light work of this task, with explicit instructions on which direction to take and what to watch out for explained down to the last detail:

'Doing this job took months of planning, and after we arrived at the German border, we were directed to the nearest transport bureau, where they then told us which way to go for the entire route across Germany. They told us what to expect along the way down to the finest details, such as whether to go under a bridge to the left- or the right-hand side or through the centre. It took us only three weeks to get to Basra, where the electrical substations were used to power all the pumps that transported crude oil out to the tanker ships that were moored offshore.'

Martyn Moulsdale delivering a mobile electrical generator for Schenkers. MM

This was one of the larger loads taken out to the Middle East. MM

Trucks were often abandoned after their loads were transshipped following mechanical breakdowns. Kapıkule, Turkish border. BC

Scania 140 broken down and dumped at an old customs yard in Tehran. BC

MAN truck being coupled to an abandoned trailer. RW

CHAPTER 8

Perils of Winter

In an age when package holidays and jet travel can so easily whisk holidaymakers to resorts along the Turkish coastline in just a few hours it may come as a surprise for those pleasure-seekers to learn that beyond the sunny beaches of the Aegean lies a country that has a far less agreeable climate during the winter months. Travelling north-eastwards reveals the open steppe lands of eastern Anatolia, where temperatures plummet to well below zero, snow can build up in piles as deep as a few metres, and roads become impassable when thickly coated with layers of treacherous, rock-hard ice!

Those who drove across Turkey in the seventies had more than adequate grounds to fear the arrival of winter. Roads would disappear beneath deep falls of snow that could bury a truck up to its roof so that it became almost invisible within this featureless landscape. With temperatures dropping as low as –40°C, traffic could often remain trapped and snowbound for periods of up to a fortnight before conditions improved, allowing the snowploughs to emerge so that the roads could be made passable once more, freeing any vehicles that had been half-buried along the way. It was so cold that by the time a truck driver had been rescued by the snow ploughs, most of the tilt boards would have been burnt up to supply firewood in order to keep warm.

In response to such intense cold, diesel fuel would start to solidify into a waxy substance that could not be fed along the fuel lines to power an engine. Peter Bamford described a method he employed to keep the diesel fuel in his tank flowing so the engine kept on running. This was not only for the immediate purpose of keeping the truck moving if the road ahead was still clear, but also as a matter of life and death, as a driver who became snowbound when a road was blocked had to rely on a truck's heater to keep warm, which in turn relied on the engine working when powered by diesel from the fuel tank:

'In the wintertime, driving across Europe and the Middle East could be a really serious business. One of the main problems was deciding how to prevent the diesel from going waxy due to the cold in the fuel tanks. Do you put some petrol in the diesel in order to stop the diesel fuel from gelling up? I would only do this as the very last resort. There was a better method in my opinion and this involved soaking a rag in diesel, and when this had been nicely set alight, I would place the blazing rag beneath the fuel tank so the flames would slowly thaw out the diesel fuel. One point that always had to be remembered was, if the other method, of putting petrol in the tank, had been tried out already, but this hadn't worked, some of the petrol fumes could have been left hanging about, either on the tank or as fumes circulating nearby in the air, which could then make for an explosive situation when the fumes were exposed to a bare flame!'

Adding petrol to a tank of diesel could work out rather expensive, so many Turkish filling stations took

Iranian refrigerated truck operated by TBT slid into the back of a Tonka. GP

Roger Pierce dressed for temperatures well below freezing. SN

'Whenever I stopped overnight in any freezing, icy weather, I would have my meal first of all, and after I had finished eating, I would move my truck along by just a few feet. If you had been running all day long, the tyres on your truck would be quite warm by the time you came to a stop to take a night's rest. So the tyres would start to melt any ice which was already underneath the tyres, and after everything had cooled down, the melted water would start to refreeze later on. So if a truck was left standing for any length of time, by the time it was started up on the following morning, all the tyres could be frozen solid to the ground! This could be easily avoided by moving the truck a short while after you had pulled over, by which time the tyres had already cooled down, and the problem couldn't occur then. We also used to put ethanol down the brake lines to stop any water moisture from building up and freezing as this would then block the pipes.'

Brakes could also become frozen so that the shoes stuck to the drums, and a truck then became immovable. In February 1976 a Scammell Crusader operated by H J Victor Limited became snowbound after it had slid off the road near İmranlı in Turkey. Perhaps not realising the brakes had now become locked on solid, an attempt was made to free the truck and trailer using a six-wheeler grader as used on road construction jobs, although this was to make the situation far worse. Such was the power of the grader, this tore off the Scammell's front axle.

on a stock of paraffin to sell at a much cheaper price, and this worked just as well as petrol!

There was a further problem that could occur when diesel fuel took on a waxy consistency. It was also important to also ensure there were no blockages of the fuel lines that delivered diesel to the engine. The narrow diameter of the pipes meant these were very susceptible to blockages when the fuel went waxy, and Peter's approach to this problem involved lagging the pipes using some insulation material, exactly the same precautionary measure taken to protect domestic water pipes in cold weather conditions.

Peter recalled another useful tip that he employed when it was time to call a halt for the night when travelling in freezing weather during the winter months:

It was a cold day when this picture of Roger's White Freightliner in the snow was captured. RP

Grader station on Tiere, Eastern Turkey. MD

Les Rivett encountered a similar winter problem when the wheels of his truck froze to the ground on a winter's night in Czechoslovakia. This affected both front wheels, so by engaging first gear and employing full revs, he managed to snatch the wheels free of the ice's grip, without any damage to the clutch. But this was not the end of his troubles, as the weight of the front end of the truck had caused the bottom section of the tyres to take on a flattened shape overnight, which was quite normal. As the truck moved forwards, the area of the tyres which had become flattened should have resumed their normal shape as the front wheels had moved round. But they still retained the flattened shape, even when the sections of the tyres which had become flattened were no longer being pressed down by the truck's weight. This made the truck impossible to drive for any distance, with a jolting response at each rotation! So driving for just a few miles at a very low speed would have been a very flat-footed experience for Les!

It was fortunate Les had the foresight to bring a couple of spare wheels and tyres along with him that allowed him to continue the journey without incurring a further delay searching out a set to buy. He later discovered the reason why these tyres had failed to resume their original shape: this was traced to a manufacturing fault after these duff items had been returned to the supplying manufacturer. Les took a lot of care to make sure his boss had got the message that only quality tyres should be bought in future, such as the more costly but much better-performing set of Michelins!

David Miller remembered a trip across Yugoslavia through bitterly cold weather when he was running along with Pat Seal:

'We managed not to fall off the side of the road on what turned out to be a terrible trip after we had left Zagreb behind and we were driving along in conditions of freezing fog. We were making only about ten miles an hour on

Come winter the Turkish mountain roads soon become hazardous. COPYRIGHT UNKNOWN

with their snow chains still in place after covering 732 miles in just the one, long-drawn-out hop! All the while they were travelling over poorly maintained roads which were sheeted over with treacherous layers of black ice or partly blocked by deep snow drifts that made their trucks slide alarmingly close to banks of snow, or more alarmingly, the deep ravines running alongside the road!

David kept to the following advice when driving on treacherous snow- and ice-covered road surfaces:

'I would always keep my side window open if I could so that I could listen to the sound of the wheels. As long as you could hear the swish of any spray of snow or water coming off the tyres, then all was well. But as soon as the tyres fell silent, then you knew you were now in trouble. The best thing to do at that point was to remove both feet from the foot pedals, and also take both hands away from the steering wheel. You might as well have put your hands together and prayed there wasn't going to be any need to brake suddenly or make any changes of course or direction with the steering. The correct technique to follow in these circumstances was to allow any speed to gently bleed off so the truck became more controllable. You could of course fit a set of snow chains, although putting these on and taking them off again would get to be very annoying when they only needed to be used for a short period of time. Trying though this process was, it often had to be repeated time after time.'

David added the following humorous story concerning the alternative which the East Germans adopted instead

İmranlı, Turkey, February 1976. When towed out by a six-wheel grader, this pulled off the front axle as the rest of the truck was frozen solid to the ground. COPYRIGHT UNKNOWN

average for much of the way, covering a distance of about 400 kilometres, and during all that time, we couldn't find a single place where we could stop until we finally reached the National Hotel in Belgrade some fourteen hours later.'

On a return trip from Iran, David was accompanying Alan Hobbs in the worst sort of winter weather conditions after setting off from Tabriz towards the Iranian border. They then crossed into Turkey to commence the long, difficult run that took them through Erzurum, Erzincan and Sivas, which was generally accepted as the worst section of road to follow in many ways throughout the Middle East road network. Physically and mentally exhausted, they finally arrived in the city of Ankara

Hicks of South Wales' drivers have piled into the cab of this DAF 3300 to keep warm! Courtesy of B & T Hicks of South Wales

Butrako Ford Transcontinental in Eastern Turkey en route to Tehran. MD

of putting salt down on their roads in winter to melt any ice. They came up with a more economical practice that involved collecting up cow urine from farms, which was then sprayed on to the surfaces of any main roads:

'This had the same effect as spreading salt on a road to melt any ice, but it smelt pretty bad, and it was so corrosive, this could then play hell with a truck's bodywork. And it also made parking in lay-bys hazardous if this was near a field that had a bull in it, as they would soon pick up the scent of any female cows from the urine!'

Jeff Kedward was asked to make a delivery to the small town of Bitlis, which was far off the usual beaten track from Turkey to Iran. His instructions then took him to an out-of-the-way town in Eastern Turkey near Lake Van. The load carried in the box van he was towing contained a bulk consignment of loose tobacco which the Rothmans tobacco firm had sent to this remote region of Turkey to set up a cigarette factory:

'This delivery took place in the winter months, so I had to use my snow chains for long distances on many occasions, which made life very difficult as I had lots of trouble putting the snow chains on the tyres fitted to my truck's driven axle. This was due to the design of box vans as there wasn't enough space between the lower edge of the box van and the truck tyres to fit the snow chains in the usual way from the front, over the top of the tyres. So I had to put the snow chains on backwards, fitting them over the top of the wheels first of all and then pulling them forwards; this was like fitting a set of caterpillar tracks on a tank.

'I spent ten days sitting around at the tobacco factory, which was stuck out in the middle of nowhere. I had to wait that long before I could unload as a customs man had to be flown out from Istanbul to Diyarbakir airport in order to check over my paperwork against the load of tobacco I was carrying. I wasn't even allowed out of the factory due to the local political situation; there were Kurdish people living here, and there had been a lot of trouble with the authorities.'

Mark Chevalier recounted the rigours of travelling across Eastern Turkey in the winter months:

'I remember parking up in Ankara one night, and when I woke up in morning, the fall of snow overnight was so deep, it had drifted over the trailer and up on one side of my truck's cab to the full height of the roof. It could take six weeks rather than a couple of weeks to reach Tehran in these awful snowy conditions. I had bought a job lot of snow chains from a firm called Evans in Glasgow before I had set off, which was a good move which allowed me to keep on going. Keeping warm was my main problem then, as there were no night heaters in the cab in those days. So I would keep the truck's engine running, both by day and also throughout the night. One morning, I woke up to find the temperature had dropped to −17 in the cab, even though I had taken the necessary precaution of keeping my truck's engine running all night.'

Keeping the roads open in the Turkish mountains was always very difficult, and following the first falls of snow, gangs of local council highway workers, who were known as the *karayollari*, would be based at grader stations, where a hut would be built to provide cooking and sleeping accommodation, as going home at night was not an option during the winter months. The grader station name was derived from the machines based at these remote, highland locations, and the graders that were normally used to plane down and smooth out any damage to road surfaces also came in handy as snowploughs, a role shared with bulldozers that carried large blades at the front. Many stranded European truck drivers were welcomed by the charitable road menders, as after seeking sanctuary, the grader stations were a place to sit and warm up beside a pot-bellied stove while drinking scalding *çay* and chatting about this or that in broken English and German with a few Turkish words thrown into the mix! A sublime experience that many drivers will never forget!

Under instructions to keep the roads open at whatever the cost, the grader and bulldozer drivers

Passengers crossing an area of road that had been destroyed by a landslide, in order to reach buses parked on the far side of the blockage. GP

Roads could be blocked for days by this sort of destruction from landslides. GP

would shove any vehicles that had become snowbound into the ditch or down into a ravine.

This was something the drivers of two brand-new Ford D-Series experienced first-hand when they had to abandon their trucks together with another two they were carrying along piggy-back style. The drivers had wandered off to get help in one direction, although in the meantime a bulldozer had arrived from the opposite direction, and the four new Fords that had been sent out as demonstrators to Iran, were then bulldozed off the road and were reduced to much scrap metal!

This Boxhill Haulage Scania 110 skidded off the road in Eastern Turkey in 1976. MC

The driver was lucky when a Chevalier's Transcontinental affected a rescue as Barry White and John Arnold watched the proceedings. MC

Roger Pierce getting to grips with removing a spare wheel in the snow. SN

all the while by sitting in our cabs and spending our time drinking coffee, playing cards and chatting away with each other.

'We had to keep our engines running, both day and night. It was so cold out on that high, open plateau at about 3000–4000 feet above sea level. We had to make footway paths through the snow so we could get from one truck to the next one, the snow was that high. Then one night, one of the drivers came banging on our doors saying would we help him out as the engine on his Scania, which he had left on all night, had stopped running. So we all piled on layers of clothes to see if we could help out by getting the engine on his Scania restarted. If an engine was left frozen for too long, you would never manage to get it going, and you would have to wait a very long while before the temperature became more normal and the engine became unfrozen.

'Like many other drivers, I had tended to look down on the Romanian drivers who travelled everywhere double-manned, and they never seemed to be going all that fast as they went along. We referred to them as the "F-Troop" after that American television programme about some bungling squaddies in the days of the Wild West. But they managed to save the day for us, as these guys had been doing Middle East trips for many more years than we had, and they knew all there was to know about bad weather after all the experience they had all gained driving their trucks as far away as Russia, also further on to Siberia, during the winter months.

Paul Rowlands recalled travelling through Turkey in the winter of 1975–76 when the roads were suddenly closed following the onset of bad weather, leaving him stranded with some other drivers at an isolated garage somewhere beyond the city of Erzurum:

'There were a couple of Romtrans lads with me at the time, also a bloke called Taffy Dinwiddy, and some Romanian drivers. There wasn't anything for us at this garage, it only had a couple of fuel pumps standing outside, and that was that! I remember the weather being so bad that the temperature was often down to about thirty below.

'The garage attendant left us because of the bad weather after he had been offered a lift on a road grader machine to the nearest village, which I remember was a place called Pasinler. We had been told some really bad weather was coming our way, so we decided to sit out the storm and wait

A bad day for Graham Ryan when it was clear his journey had come to an end in a most dramatic fashion. GR

Trucks owned by Ford sent out for an exhibition but destroyed by a road grader that was sent out to clear the snow. GR

The second Ford was carried piggy-back fashion on the chassis of the one beneath. GR

'In all truth, I don't think we would have survived without their knowledge of what we needed to do in those bad winter conditions. They got out some sawn-off oil drums from underneath their trailers, and they then lit a fire under the Scania truck's engine, which was then successfully restarted in next to no time at all. They certainly knew what they were doing, and I had a much higher opinion of any of the Romanian drivers I came across from then on!

'Keeping your engine running was essential to keep you alive, and for this reason, you could never get to sleep properly in this sort of severe weather, as you were always listening to check out whether your engine had in fact stalled. After that frightening experience I made a point of making regular stops to find out what the weather was like ahead when I was driving in the winter months. And if it looked bad, then I would hold off for a couple of days until things had improved. It always paid to ask any drivers who were coming the other way what the weather was like ahead of you. Some reports had to be taken with a pinch of salt of course, but then it was for you to decide on whether or not to be careful.'

Martyn Moulsdale made a similar observation:

'During the winter in Turkey, you needed to be able to read what conditions lay ahead of you before starting out each morning. If any trucks arrived from the direction that you wanted to go in all covered over in snow, then it paid to hold off for a while and not go on any further until the next day when conditions might have improved. These sorts of conditions could get so bad you might have to use your snow chains for two days on the trot when pressing ahead into some bad weather conditions.'

Graham Cartmail recalled an occasion when he was travelling with Les Higgins somewhere near Plovdiv in Bulgaria, and after waking up one morning, it was discovered a foot of snow had fallen overnight, a situation that all and sundry accepted as a task that could only be resolved by everyone clubbing together to clear away the snow with shovels and whatever else fell to hand:

Snow chain weather! GP

Snow chains were essential when the weather got rough. Here is Mike Dunstan chaining up in anticipation of poor conditions further down the road. MD

'Everyone in Bulgaria seemed to be so used to living with the snow, that clearing it off the road was never a problem. If you got stuck in, then you would notice everyone came forward to help out. No-one was going anywhere until the road was cleared of the snow, which applied to all of us, of course!'

Getting stranded in the days leading up to Christmas could mean Santa wasn't coming on this particular year, as Gordon Summers discovered after he agreed to pick up a return load in Yugoslavia:

'I was held up over Christmas in Ljubljana waiting to be reloaded with enamel pots and pans on my way back to the UK. There were no engine heaters in those days, so as it was about –25 to –30, I had to keep the engine running non-stop for twenty-four hours a day.'

Making it back home in time for Christmas was something Geoff Morgan was determined to achieve on his third Middle East trip, but after getting as far as Austria on the way back, this plan came unstuck when he ran into some terrible wintry conditions. Realising there was no way he could get back home for Christmas while at the same time matching his promise to pick up a return load along the way, something had to give if Geoff wanted to avoid a cheerless Christmas sitting all alone and miserable in his cab. So he decided to leave his truck and trailer temporarily in Austria, where it could take on a return load when the holiday season had ended, and he then cadged a lift back to the UK in an old Leyland lorry which had seen much better days. Geoff recalled what happened next:

'The main fuel tank on the Leyland had frozen up, so to get round this problem, the driver had placed an oil drum containing a reserve supply of diesel which was sitting in front of my seat. It was my job throughout the journey to be the fuel delivery man, which involved gravity feeding the diesel fuel into the engine by means of a tube fitted to the injector pump. As it was so cold, an additive had been added to stop any of the fuel from freezing up, which told me how cold it was sitting in that cab!

'I live in Hereford, and it was lucky I saw a Lloyd's of Ludlow Scania 111 after we arrived in the port at Calais where its driver was just about to board his truck onto the boat for Dover. As Ludlow is fairly close to my home in Hereford, I swapped lorries after asking the Lloyd's driver if he would take me on to Hereford. The only problem was, the Lloyd's driver had not slept for the last three days because he was also in a rush to get home for Christmas. So I ended up driving his lorry all the way while he was sleeping beside me in the passenger seat! I arrived at the bottom of Dinmore Hill on the A40, which is just outside Hereford, where I had previously arranged for a mate to pick me up, although he drove straight by me first of all: I looked such a complete mess, he'd mistaken me for a tramp of the road!'

The haste with which someone like Geoff begged a lift halfway across Europe, only to return just a few days later to pick up his truck, left behind for reloading, suggests a certain degree of desperation. Imagine spending Christmas with nothing to open but a tin of beans followed by a few spoonfuls of tinned pears as your meagre festive repast!

Spring brought its own problems with the snow melting. GP

Fording rivers was hazardous, as depicted by this Iranian Mercedes. GP

CHAPTER 9

Hazards of the High Ground

Middle East drivers faced many mountain roads that were awkward to negotiate and dangerous. This applied not only to the ascent but also the descent as the latter was often more dangerous than the former, because the sudden influence of gravity could easily catch a driver out so that their truck was plunging headlong down a hill at a speed that was impossible to control.

TAHIR PASS

Of all the upland routes that the drivers had to take, the Tahir Pass was the one that was renowned for its twisting, serpentine bends that coiled all the way up and down the mountainsides. This route was taken by drivers travelling towards Iran, so climbing the Tahir did not affect those travelling south-east towards Iraq and the Arabian Peninsula, although they did have the Taurus Mountains to contend with!

The Tahir route gained the sort of notoriety that was credited to the rounding of Cape Horn between the Atlantic and the Pacific by seafarers in the days of wooden ships and iron men.

Rising to 8122 feet at the summit, and often attracting bad weather conditions, the Tahir Pass demanded strong nerves to surmount its steep inclines and loose dirt track roads that had only been casually maintained. Periodically a grader machine would run over any uneven surfaces that had formed; or a bulldozer would be brought along to correct the ravages of winter after torrential rainstorms had caused mountain streams to overflow and the surfaces of the road to be eroded and washed away.

All it took was a moment of indecision, or a failure to get the steering set right, to result in a driver failing to maintain any traction at all between the wheels of his truck and any snow or ice-coated surfaces that passed for a road. Tahir was where so many trucks came to grief, leaving their drivers to face the difficult task of recovering the vehicle so it was back on a full set of wheels once again to resume the journey, maybe a week or even a month behind schedule!

On a summer's day in July 1976, any Middle East drivers passing nearby the summit of Tahir could have stopped to notice an arctic tractor unit and trailer forlornly lying down on its side, but with no-one in attendance. The nature of the load it was carrying was immediately noticeable, as from the side of the split

A one-in-four hill on the approach to Sivas in Eastern Turkey gained a certain notoriety: a foretaste of what Tahir had on offer! COPYRIGHT UNKNOWN

Bob Crofton-Sleigh's Trans UK Fiat eating dust climbing Tahir. BC

Crossing Tahir in the spring when the snow was melting, adding to any other existing problems. GP

Abandoned Guy truck on the Tahir Pass. FH

canvas tilt which had been torn open when the trailer had tipped over, thousands of Lego bricks had spilt out into the mud in a huge multi-coloured heap. Someone had risked life and limb taking this journey which had come to a sudden and untimely end, just to deliver some toys for children to play with!

In winter, freezing temperatures and deep snow falls made the Tahir route impassable for days at a time, whereas in the summer months, choking clouds of dust thrown up by any vehicles travelling in front shrouded any bends that lay ahead from view as well as any traffic coming from that direction.

One well-recognised hazard concerned the village boys of all ages who were enrolled as shepherds at a very young age to look after each of their family's flocks of sheep and goats that roamed the uplands of Tahir. Gangs of these shepherd boys would gather in twos and threes by the roadside with malicious intent gleaming in their eyes and facial expressions: they would then imitate

Crossing Tahir was a real rite of passage for Middle East drivers. BC

Smashed windscreen caused by a stone flung up from the road or maybe the hand of a shepherd boy! RW

Bulgarian SOMAT truck come to grief on Tahir. GP

the up and down hand movements of smoking a cigarette with one hand while holding a hefty stone in the other hand; a threatening motion that made it easy to see what might happen next … If the driver of an oncoming truck had then failed to throw a few Benson and Hedges or Rothman's cigarettes out of their cab's open window, then a fusillade of stones would be hurled at full force with the cruel intention of smashing a truck's windscreen as a penalty for not coming up with the goods in this juvenile version of highway robbery!

There was also the possibility of more serious banditry as armed Kurdish rebels were active in the area, desperate men who were prepared to take on the Turkish army in the occasional firefight with pistols and rifles, as well as steal from any travellers they held up by the roadside. This was the reason why vehicles were forbidden from travelling over the Tahir Pass during the hours of darkness, and in the daylight it was preferable to travel as a group in a convoy, although a police or army escort wasn't usually required in normal circumstances.

Many drivers had just cause to question why they were sent over the top of a mountain by way of the Tahir Pass when there was a perfectly serviceable low-level route that would have been much easier to drive along. The alternative route that drivers were barred from using was known as the military road. The Turkish armed forces maintained exclusive rights over this road as it had strategic military importance: as Turkey was a member of the NATO pact, and bearing in mind the close proximity of this country's border with the USSR in those pre-Perestroika days, this road was closed to civilian traffic for a long while until it was finally opened to all and sundry in 1977. From the Turkish side of the border with Iran at Bazargan, the snow-capped peak of Mount Arafat, of the Holy Bible's Noah's Ark fame, could be seen, and beyond the summit the not-so-distant state of Armenia could be seen as a reminder

This view of a Chapman & Ball truck demonstrates the steep gradient of the hillside. FH

Overtaking the truck on the right-hand side of the road paid little heed to any possible oncoming traffic! FH

'Tahir wasn't a proper road at all; this was the old route of the Silk Road to the Far East from the past. It was just a camel track which we had no alternative but to use until things improved some time in 1977 when we were finally allowed to use the military road instead.'

Crossing Tahir in the winter months always required a good set of snow chains, and woe betide any driver who wasn't properly prepared in this respect, as Les Higgins and a running mate discovered to their cost one day in the depths of winter:

'I remember driving over the Tahir Pass one winter when I was travelling with someone else but we only had one set of snow chains between the two of us. So after getting one of the trucks moving for a while, we would then have to remove the set of snow chains from the wheels of the first truck and drag them back down the hill before chaining up the other wagon. We never went up Tahir in the dark as it was always closed by three o'clock in the afternoon during the winter months.'

As someone who had already become involved with road transport for musical gigs and events, Des Seal brought along many of the old-style music cassettes which had been donated to him by pop groups when he delivered all their musical instruments, props and

that the considerable might of the Soviet armed forces were not all that far away.

Crossing the Tahir Pass was an invitation for things to go wrong as it was so easy for trucks to skid off the road and become irretrievably stuck down an embankment where any hope of recovery soon had to be abandoned. It is also true to say that although the Tahir Pass could frequently entrap a truck so that it was lost together with the load it was carrying, there wasn't the same threat to life and limb that other upland routes could impose throughout Turkey, namely the Taurus Mountains and the steep ascent or descent of the Bolu Pass, which was followed later on by another long ascent/descent that the drivers knew by the ominous name of 'Death Valley'.

Travelling over the Tahir Pass could be said to be a safer route as the unsurfaced roads and sharp bends enforced slower running speeds; and using the lower set of gears was necessary to maintain any forward traction! The volume of traffic crossing Tahir was also substantially less than elsewhere, which could not be said for the more intensely travelled routes that went over the Bolu Pass or the Taurus Mountains.

Ivor Whittall remarked on the fact that the route over Tahir had ancient origins dating back to the days when this was a single-lane track used by pack animals:

Paul Rowlands looks as if he is about to bail out! BC

stage equipment to destinations throughout Britain and Europe. His method of tackling the Tahir when driving a noisy, but powerful, Volvo F88 truck was to turn up the right sort of music to full blast:

'I had previously been working with the Tangerine Dream pop group by shifting all their gear from one musical gig to the next, so I had plenty of their chilled-out, avant-garde music that I had taken along with me. The group's music made a strange contrast to the noise of my truck engine and the sounds of all the gear changes as I wrestled with the steering on my way towards the summit of the mountain. Driving over the Tahir was rather like doing thirty rounds with Muhammad Ali in terms of the high standard of physical fitness that was required of you when you were at the steering wheel!'

Paul Rowlands leading the initial Bob Carter-organised convoy over the Tahir. BC

Ken Ward remembered showing a novice driver the beginnings of the road over the Tahir a short while after the military road had finally been opened:

'This bloke wanted to see the route that we had taken in the old days, which began shortly after the main road went over a railway level crossing. He couldn't believe this was the way we had to go, as the road was so steep! If the wheels on your truck started slipping, this could then induce lots of wheel spin, so you would then need to go up a gear in order to maintain forward traction. But this meant you were going slower, and almost stalling the engine. So you would then have to engage a lower gear to maintain any good traction. I chose to ignore any instructions I had once been told about the need to evenly load my truck as a means of improving traction by balancing out the weight distribution along the length of the trailer: I thought it was always a good idea to put as much weight as you possibly could over your truck's driven axles when you were climbing steep mountain roads, rather than spreading all the weight out. If you had a problem with maintaining traction when running empty, then it was possible to apply more weight to your truck's driven axle by sliding the fifth-wheel forward as far as it would go, as this would alter the weight loading and make the trailer sit as close as it possibly could to the back of the cab.'

Ken recommended fitting a pair of Austrian spec and supplied double chains to both of the drive axles first of all, with a single chain fitted to the nearside front wheel of the tractor unit, and a pair of chains attached round the trailer's rearmost set of wheels, one on the nearside front wheel of the pair, the other chain on the offside rearmost of the other set of wheels.

One day when Les Rivett was coming back over the Tahir on his way back from Karachi in Pakistan, he was watching an overloaded Bedford TK tipper truck struggling uphill when the driver finally gave up the uneven struggle and came to a standstill in the middle of the road. As Les looked on with increasing disbelief, the driver came up with a solution to his dilemma of not being able to go on any further. Untroubled by the consequences for anyone else who came that way from then on, he operated the truck's tipper mechanism and dumped about ten tons of mud and rubble that blocked the middle of the road before merrily continuing on his way again! This left everyone else to scrape by on what little of the road the Tonka driver had left as free passage!

As previously mentioned, the local shepherd boys excelled at scrounging cigarettes from any drivers crossing over the Tahir Pass, which no doubt made their lonely vigils over the sheep and goats a bit more exciting. Being young in age and fleet of foot, they

Rescue of an Atkinson Borderer by the locals who jumped at the chance of a photo session. COPYRIGHT UNKNOWN

Trans UK trucks following two Greek trucks crossing Tahir. BC

were also at a distinct advantage, as after threatening a driver with what might happen if they didn't throw some cigarettes out of the cab, as the truck in question slowly rounded an uphill corner, they would race ahead uphill to intercept the truck as it rounded the next tight corner, where the implied threat would be carried out as a shower of rocks aimed with unerring accuracy at the more easily breakable parts of the cab, notably the windscreen or the front set of headlights! The prospect of driving huge distances after removing a smashed windscreen, or having the truck's headlights put out of order, was always enough to convince most drivers that chucking a handful of fags out of the window was a very small price to pay! Some drivers guarded against these stone-throwing activities and also accidental breakages by fitting stone guards over the cab windows, which Gerry Holmes found to be an effective deterrent in both respects. Any drivers who lost their windscreen in this way faced a long journey home while covered from head to foot in dust and dodging any insects that had flown into the cab at an injuring rate of knots!

A driver by the name 'Geordie' who was driving an AEC Mandator for the Wakefield Haulage Company over the Tahir decided he would put an immediate stop to the local shepherd boys demanding cigarettes and then throwing stones when none were forthcoming by using a starting pistol which he had brought along for this express purpose. He used the pistol to fire off a few blanks from the safety of his cab, which sounded authentic enough, as far as the raggedly dressed youths were concerned, as they sensibly ran away. But this driver's comeuppance came very swiftly: just a few miles further on down the road, his truck was overtaken by a police car, and Geordie came face to face with an irate policeman who immediately confiscated the starting pistol, and after checking this over and verifying it was in fact safe, the policeman commented in English: 'In Turkey we always fight with our fists, and not with a gun!'

Unsurfaced roads made for dusty driving conditions that took ages to settle after a truck passed by. BC

Still a newcomer as he was only on his second trip, Fred Hodgkins almost ran into some trouble with the authorities, and maybe a lot more would have been in store, when he attempted to break the rules by crossing over the Tahir Pass rather late in the day, as he was in a hurry to cross the border between Turkey and Iran before the frontier was closed overnight and it wouldn't be reopened until the following dawn:

'I was already running late, and the light was fading, but my plan to make it to the border looked as if it was now hopeless after I was stopped by a couple of Turkish soldiers, who were standing in the centre of the road so they could stop any traffic from getting through. They made me pull off the road by their command post as they kept on repeating the same word "Bandits, Bandits" the whole time. This was frightening as far as I was concerned, particularly as I was the only one now standing out there on my own in the dark. But I had no choice but to do exactly what they said. I tried conversing with the soldiers, who were friendly enough, but our conversation was broken off by a single rifle shot that came from a fair distance away. I could hear the sound of the bullet striking the roof of the command post before I then heard the sound of the gunshot that had been fired from a long way away. Thankfully, this was a one-off event. Shortly afterwards, a pair of headlights appeared as a Turkish taxi approached from behind my truck. The taxi driver was also ordered off the road, and then some local Turkish trucks came along, so I felt a bit more comfortable as I now had some company with me. We had to wait there all night, and there were no more incidents during that time before we were allowed to leave and continue on our way the next morning. This was when we came across an abandoned truck which had been operated by the French firm, Stouff. This Berliet truck had been attacked by someone out there who had thrown a hand grenade at it, destroying the cab.'

BOLU PASS

Travelling eastwards, the Bolu Pass made a steady ascent to 6000 feet by way of a series of twisting bends which ran alongside steep, plunging valleys. Situated roughly halfway along the main road from Istanbul to Ankara, this route is much safer today as it has been upgraded to a motorway; this road now passes through a tunnel for some of the distance, which has helped in avoiding most of the steeper gradients.

In the old days it was the easiest thing in the world for a truck to lose all its overheated brakes so it became a runaway and it would then plunge over the edge of the road into a rock-filled ravine with unavoidably fatal consequences for anyone on board.

Bolu is where many drivers came to grief in the old days when their downhill rate of progress exceeded the capacity of the brakes to hold in check a vehicle's weight and the rapidly rotating wheels. David Miller suggested the following approach on the basis of his hard-won experience over many years:

'Even in those days, the road from Istanbul to Ankara was a good quality, single-track highway, although it did have some startlingly long and steep rises and falls. To survive driving along this particular road, you had to acquire a full understanding of how to control the speed of a heavy vehicle as it began descending any long, steep hills. This would involve using the truck's engine and the gearbox by going down through the gears as well as using the brakes. If you didn't manage this, then Mum was due for some bad

Lenny Baylam in a Trans UK Volvo F88 climbing Bolu, 1975. BC

news very shortly. I remember watching a Bulgarian driver deliver himself to the Great Commissar in the Sky because he had not learnt this most important lesson of using both the gears and also the brakes to slow his lorry down. But if you thought that by the time you'd crossed Bolu and reached Ankara you had seen it all – brother, you were now in for some real surprises, as from then on the journey was going to get a lot worse!'

David described the technique he adopted when crossing Bolu or any other high ground where steep drops promised to ruin his day if he lost control of his truck:

'There was an advantage in the early days if you were driving a lower powered truck when descending steep hills with sharp bends that were an extra hazard. The advice from the older driver who taught me to drive was, go down any hills in the same gear that you would have selected to go up them, which provided perfect control of a truck's speed on any descent, and this often meant you never had to touch the brakes at all. So there was plenty of braking power still held in reserve. But imagine a young kid in a much more powerful Scania 142, with the engine engaged five gears higher than the driver should have selected in these sorts of circumstances, which meant he was relying on just the braking system on his truck to slow him down. There were no disc brakes available on trucks at the time, and drum brakes didn't like that sort of treatment at all, as they would soon overheat, so the brakes would fade and then fail to work at all in the worst cases.'

The spectacular scenery of Bolu could leave a crashed lorry and its trailer in a startling position and Chris Stephenson recalled travelling through the area of Bolu known as Death Valley on an occasion when he came across a lorry which was suspended by the drawbar of its trailer, dangling vertically over an alarmingly deep precipice.

TAURUS MOUNTAINS

Located down in the south-east of Turkey, the Taurus Mountains posed many difficulties for those travelling from Ankara and the town of Adana before proceeding onwards through Syria to destinations in Iraq or then down through Jordan to Saudi Arabia and the Gulf States.

Crossing the Taurus Mountains was often characterised by long processions of slow-moving trucks which constantly jockeyed for road space where the road narrowed or at any suitable passing places. The narrow roads running alongside the mountain gorges were so deep that sunlight failed to reach as far as the bottom, where turbulent streams raged over well-polished rocks.

As far as David Miller was concerned, Bolu and Tahir were challenging, but crossing the Taurus stood out as always the real, true test of both man and machine:

'The route over the Taurus was something else. In those days it was like a rural B-road that climbed and climbed taking a path through the middle of villages which didn't look as if they had changed all that much since the Crusaders passed by this way travelling towards the Holy Land in the eleventh century. You would come across hairpin bends that you could not get round without hanging one of your trailer wheels off the side of a cliff edge. There was also the opposition to contend with, which came in the form of the backbone of Turkish road transport, locally built Ford D1000 four-wheelers, which were always overloaded by at least a hundred percent. These would be driven by identically moustached drivers, for whom the word fear had no meaning whatsoever!'

On David's first trip over the Taurus Mountains hauling oil drill pipes to Basra in Iraq, the lethality of this road with its sharp bends and precipitous drops became ingrained in his memory as something to predict and watch out for on future trips:

'A Dutch driver warned me that the narrow country road through pine forests which I was about to come across was

Archie Bowden taking it slow and easy on a long descent. Small trailer tyres were easily subject to blow outs in hot conditions. MM

really dangerous. The Scammell was towing a York trailer with spread axles, and the corners were so sharp, the back axle of the trailer was hanging out over thin air at times before I reached flatter ground! This took place in February, and I remember the abiding smell of wood smoke everywhere I went. Luckily, there wasn't any snow about to add to my problems, but I suddenly realised I was a very long way from home. This impression was further reinforced when I went past a butcher's shop where I saw great chunks of cows and goats hanging from the branches of a pine tree which was next to the roadside. This tree served as the butcher's shop window, and he was sawing off pieces of meat for his customers! I also recall stopping in Adana after crossing the Taurus, and without realising the consequences for the next morning, I unfortunately parked beside the tower of a mosque. What a noise there was very early on when I was awoken by someone who came along and climbed the minaret to call the faithful to prayer through a microphone!'

As a general suggestion, which extended to travelling anywhere on dangerous Turkish mountain roads, Ken Ward advised any rookie drivers to make sure they always made full use of any road surface, as using the full breadth of the road from side to side could provide just that little bit more space to control a truck that had started skidding sideways; but all the while making adequate provision to avoid any oncoming traffic approaching on what was still indisputably their side of the road rather than his! Ken found this technique to be particularly worthwhile when the camber was slanted towards the edge of the road where there was a drop into open space that should be avoided at all cost, as the camber of the road surface tended to encourage a crab-like sideways motion, which greatly added to the attendant danger of tipping a truck over the edge!

Ken also made a point of using any rocks and loose pebbles that may have rolled down the side of a mountain to good effect, as driving over any stony lumps and bumps then provided the tyres with improved traction and better grip when compared to a dirt road surface or any glazed tarmac that had been worn smooth by heavy traffic passing by over the years.

Ian Taylor recalled an incident when his Volvo F88 was nearly lost as he came very close to falling off the side of a mountain road near Mardin in southeastern Turkey:

'This was because the differential lock on the rear axle had broken up, which left one of the drive wheels spinning wildly. I was rapidly losing traction and had started to head sideways towards the drop at the edge of the road, but I managed to regain control by easing off on the throttle. The truck was an ex-shunter which I was using on my first trip. I wasn't prepared to take out that old truck again, so Carmans Transport then gave me a new Volvo F88 with a more powerful 290 engine.'

Whether the route involved crossing Tahir, Bolu or the Taurus mountains, having a good appreciation of what to expect along the way could make the difference between an easy run and one that was soon fraught with many difficulties. After making deliveries to Tehran on a number of occasions, which required crossing the Tahir Pass, Brian Robertson was getting itchy feet to try his hand at taking a new route, so one of the bosses at Davies Turner's suggested trying out a trip that took him beyond the Turkey/Iraq border to Baghdad:

'You had the right to choose where you went on the Middle East run in those days, so when I got back from Tehran, they asked me if I would like to take a trip to Iraq. This I didn't enjoy at all to be honest, as unlike the Tahir, which I had crossed on a number of occasions, I didn't know what to expect when it came to crossing the Taurus for that very first time. I had not realised this important basic fact before – there always was a strong advantage in following any route which you had already got to know. You knew every bump in the road before you reached any of them, and also how to deal with the customs officials you came across again and any paperwork. But if you went to another country by a different route, everything was different, and this added to the workload.'

M S White Volvo F12 after the brakes failed to stop it when coming down a military road in Turkey. MM

Martyn Moulsdale recalled a particular hazard that applied whenever he was following any Turkish oil tanker lorries up a steep gradient in the Taurus mountains:

'There was a big mountain you had to cross near Mosul in Syria. This was where you would come across many overloaded Turkish tankers which would be driving along with gallons and gallons of raw, unrefined oil gushing out of the top of the tanker body as they travelled along, whether they were going uphill or downhill. We called it "Oil Hill". Once you started skidding on any oil which had spilled out of a tanker, your heart would soon be in your mouth as the trailer you were towing would start to travel sideways, for up to 90° away from the direction you were supposed to be taking in your truck! The answer was to put one set of wheels on the dirt rather than on the tarmac which had become so slippery. The dirt was a better surface to drive on as this would have already soaked up the oil and there wasn't as much of a problem.'

CHAPTER 10

Desert Travel

Middle East drivers were often so well suntanned it would have been easy to come to the conclusion that they had recently enjoyed exceptionally good weather while sunbathing on a beach down on the Costa del Sol during a sun-drenched fortnight. But closer scrutiny of these sun-bronzed figures often revealed that one arm was far more suntanned than the other one was. This was something that was determined by whether the person under review had been driving a left- or a right-hand drive truck with one of their arms propped on the driver's door window frame, fully exposed to the rays of the sun!

Middle East driving involved many miles of desert travel and maybe taking quite naturally to driving across deserts is a characteristic British trait? Something that may have been reinforced for this generation of drivers after they had enthusiastically watched that cinema epic of the First World War, *Lawrence of Arabia,* starring Peter O'Toole as the enigmatic officer, Captain T E Lawrence. So who could blame any novice Middle East driver from laying it on a bit thick with a few stirring stories of how they had gloriously battled against adversity through a hostile sea of burning sand! To the victor should go the spoils!

At one time it wasn't at all unusual to see trucks such as a Volvo F88 heading up the M1 or the M6 motorway with the paintwork still coated in a thin patina of ochre-coloured desert sand, the lettering on the tilt emblazoned with the names of distant foreign countries, which suggested a roll of battle honours, along both sides of the trailer. With maybe a motto printed in flowing Arabic script across the front of the cab. And a pair of windswept, battered palm fronds secured across the radiator grille that would immediately convey the message to other road users that this truck and its driver had travelled far and wide!

Coming across a truck that had so obviously returned from the deserts of the Middle East would have surely stirred many other drivers to appraise what they were doing with their lives. They may have previously thought that driving from Birmingham to Glasgow and back was a long way to go. Maybe now they felt motivated to rethink their present work situation so they would demand their employment cards and seek a more adventurous career than the workaday, hum-drum existence of identical, multi-drop, supermarket runs, conducted time after time!

Miles and miles stretching to the horizon! KW

A White Freightliner puts out plenty of smoke hauling a double container load. GF

Numbers in Arabic and Roman script on numberplates. Most European drivers picked up the Arabic numbering from road signs. DB

Ian Taylor carrying a container across H4. IT

David Miller recalled his initiation into desert driving which occurred when he ventured onto a dirt track over open desert known as 'H4' after an oil pumping station; it covered a distance of about seventy miles across Jordan towards the Saudi border, which provided David with the sort of driving experience he now needed as an intro to desert driving, and ultimately, desert survival:

'There were quite a few initial difficulties; the first time I drove across H4 was an experience that frightened the

View through the windscreen as Glen Harley runs across H4 in March 1978. GH

Kelvin Parfitt's Foden S28 in Saudi on the way to connect with the H4 desert route. KP

Crossing the desert wastes of H4 in convoy. RW

Terry Tott crossing H4, a route that caused the cab to fall apart. TT

Bob Thompson driving across H4. JB

Kenworth sand tractors as developed for desert operation with large wheels and sand tyres. JC

living daylights out of me. It wasn't what you would call a traditional sand desert as it was a stone desert. There were old tyre tracks that had been laid down many years ago, and these went off in every possible direction which added to the confusion of choosing which way to go. As I had been to sea as a sailor in the years before I took up driving trucks, I was confident that, wherever I was, I already knew which direction faced south, and having established this information, I knew I had to go to the east of south in order make my way and cross H4. Choosing the route to take became easier after I'd noticed a series of rusty old barrels which had been provided as a guide to help drivers select the right course to take. You had to continually watch out for any potholes, which were not easy to see as these were full of "bull dust", very fine particles of sand that filled up any holes. Drop a wheel in one of these potholes, and if you weren't quick enough to get your truck free by shifting down through the gears as quickly as you could to escape, you would be bogged down, where you would remain stuck in the same spot for many hours before you'd managed to dig yourself out.

'Lots of dust was thrown up into the air by the trucks as they moved along across a desert, and for this reason you couldn't drive nose to tail, as any forward visibility would be obscured but for the first truck. So you would have to travel with any other trucks all spread out in a chevron pattern, in a vee shape, as this allowed everyone to see the way ahead.'

Most of the trucks driven by Europeans on any of the Middle East routes were designed for European roads, the exceptions being of American origin, such as Kenworths, Whites and Macks. It would be fair to say that all the European makes had been designed and built with the emphasis on highway running and performance in fairly moderate climatic conditions as opposed to churning away across the endless tracks of sandy deserts which gave the suspension and chassis components a fair old hammering; and the type of tyres fitted were well-suited to the driving conditions at home, not the far worse hot conditions where punctures from sharp pieces of splintered rocks were a very common occurrence. And of course the hot temperature during

The back of Robert Hackford's lorry on the TAP-line in Saudi. Wandering camels were a serious hazard when negotiating desert lands. RH

Easy to see in the daylight, but you wouldn't want a camel through the windscreen at 60 mph in the dark! Taken on the TAP-line near Niyariya. RH

the day posed an additional strain on a truck's cooling system, which was soon overworked, so that overheating became a problem, and clouds of boiling hot steam would finally erupt from a radiator with unstoppable geyser-like force!

The suitability of operating with trucks designed for European conditions could raise a few issues. Most trucks taken out to the Middle East were of the forward control, cab over design, which had the engine sitting directly underneath the cab, although most locally operated trucks were of the normal control design, which had the engine sitting out in front of the cab, which aided engine cooling as well as improving access to the engine for repair work. The downside of the normal control set-up was that the extra bonnet length made these trucks less manoeuvrable in tight spaces, which of course was a high priority for anyone driving a truck through the congested streets of towns and villages in non-desert regions.

Mark Chevalier noted that most locally operated trucks in desert lands had 24" wheels rather than the smaller 20" wheels fitted to European trucks; this then provided a few extra inches of axle height which came in handy for clearing obstructions, although there was a downside, as when loaded to the maximum height with a tall load, these trucks precariously swayed along from side to side in much the same way as an overloaded camel!

David Miller expanded on the unsuitability of using any European-designed trucks in the roughest desert environments where heavy-duty Oshkosh and Kenworths had been brought in that had been specifically designed with this type of use in mind, notably for oil exploration. However, there was a

Camels along the roadside may have initially been a novelty for the driver of this Redcliffe MAN truck, but not for long as they would soon lose their novelty status! RR

This Oshkosh tractor unit on sand tyres had the power to haul heavy loads without getting bogged down. DM

to carry the loads on across tricky sections of open desert, Oryx could lay claim to being the first firm that managed to arrange point-to-point deliveries to many Gulf destinations without arranging for transshipments – other than by their own trucks of course!

As time went by, operators adapted their trucks for the comfort and safety of drivers by fitting air-conditioning so the interior of the cabs didn't become a cauldron of stifling heat throughout the daylight hours. And to take care of the cold in winter, night heaters were provided so that drivers could keep warm, an asset that was just as important when crossing deserts where temperatures immediately plunged downwards following sunset. These night heaters were also a vital asset to any drivers who had the misfortune to be stuck in snow drifts on a Turkish mountainside during the freezing winter months.

Truck manufacturers did not take long to latch on to the possibility that their sales of new vehicles could be improved by adding air-con and heaters, and making roomier cabs with double bunk beds, cookers and fridges. The advertising material described these vehicles in glowing terms as Middle East-spec trucks in the hope of obtaining more sales.

particular incident when one of these sand tractors had been called into play which did not turn out well at all:

'When I was working for Oryx and driving one of their F89s, the salt marsh desert between Doha and Dubai made it impossible for European wagons such as this to get through on this particular route. After going as far as we could go before we became bogged down in the loose sand, our trailers were detached from our trucks so they could be swapped over to be transported for the rest of the way behind huge Oshkosh six-wheeler tractor units, which were all driven by Pakistani drivers, drivers who really knew their stuff. With 800-hp engines, those Oshkosh trucks had some power. I remember seeing one of these towing along a trailer which had got bogged down in an area of salt marsh. With so much power, the truck and its trailer managed to keep going in these sorts of conditions, but on this occasion this was only after the entire suspension system and the wheel bogies had been ripped away from the bottom of the trailer, so the load and the loadbed were still surfing along on the trailer's chassis frame behind the tractor, leaving all the bogies and the torn-off suspension parts behind, half-buried in the salt marsh!'

By arranging for the desert-prepped Oshkosh trucks

Failing to take account of the many dangers to be found when driving through desert lands could have serious if not deadly consequences. David Miller went on to describe the sad fate of his close friend John Craig, who had been David's frequent companion from the beginning of their Middle East driving careers:

'One of my greatest experiences of sadness concerned John Craig, who was my best buddy. His problems began when he was snowed in on a mountain at Tarsus. He ran out of water to drink, so he drank some stream water. That simple mistake won him a month in the Hospital for Tropical Diseases which is in London. Although they never found out what was wrong with him, he was never completely well again. The doctors ordered him to give up the Middle East job because his illness left him susceptible to dehydration, which meant the extreme heat of a desert wasn't good news for him. He really did try to give up the job, but the bug had bitten too hard. In the summer of 1974, he was running on his own on the way to Kuwait with a J &T Scania when he had a blow-out on his trailer short of the Saudi/Kuwait border. This sort of incident happened often enough when you were travelling fully loaded in the summer months, so you would pull off the track and onto the desert, and then you would wait a while to allow time for the temperature to

Sid Carter suffered sunstroke crossing into Saudi and was hospitalised. Ian Tyler recovered his truck, requiring the tilts to be stripped. ITY

cool down rather than attempting to change a flat tyre in the heat of the day. On this occasion, John, for reasons that we'll never know, decided to change the wheel in the middle of the day when it was hottest. This he did manage to achieve, and he managed to make it all the way to the border, but this is where he collapsed. They got him an ambulance, but he died on the way to Kuwait City. The loss of my best friend hit me really hard, and I nearly gave up the job, but later on, when I was able to think about it more clearly, I realised John had died doing the only job he'd ever found which really fulfilled him. God bless you, mate!'

The rigours of enduring the heat at midday was brought home to Ivor Whittall when he arrived in Bandar Shahpur on the Persian Gulf, where the temperature was in the region of 40–45°C, so hot that touching the metal on his truck was always an extremely painful experience. The sheer effort required to work in those temperatures became apparent:

'I had already stripped down the tilt on my trailer so that I could unload, and after this had been done, I began putting the tilt on to the trailer, but then I found I was too exhausted to finish the job when working in that sort of heat. So an American who was working out there came along and ordered a work crew to put my tilt cover back together again on my trailer. I then went to a bar round the corner to buy myself a glass of German beer. Drinking that beer will be something which I'll always remember: it tasted just like honey! But of course, you had to be careful about drinking alcohol whenever it was so hot. An hour later, after I had taken a good long rest, I jumped back into the truck and drove on, leaving the heat of the coast behind me and driving up into the mountains where it was much cooler, and I parked up for the night in this peaceful spot.'

Ivor summed up the dangers of the section of open desert known as H4 in Jordan:

'Driving across H4 was rough, and although some will say there were some oil drums that pointed the way you needed to go across the desert, I only remember seeing about three of these drums, which you soon passed on your way out across the desert, but that was it from then on, there were no other points of reference to steer from later on, so you were on your own for the rest of the desert crossing! We would travel with one eye on the sun for navigation, although we did know whether or not we were travelling in roughly the right direction by following the tracks which had been left by other vehicles. The problem was, many of these tracks on the ground had been laid down by rigid, six-wheeler trucks with double drive which provided much improved traction on loose desert ground than the single-drive trucks many of us Middle East drivers drove back then. So if you followed these trucks, you could soon find yourself in trouble when driving an artic with a trailer that had a set of support

Robert Dods-Brown takes a rest beside his Scania 110. Note the goatskin water bag on the front bumper. RDB

legs hanging down underneath. Even when in the raised position, the legs would not be able to clear the ground if all the wheels of your truck were running in the deep ruts which had been created by the locally owned six-wheeler trucks.'

Dave 'Gypsy' Anslow arrived in November 1975 at the Trans Arabia compound in Jeddah where he was employed as a mechanic, a role he took on until 1978 servicing the firm's trucks which were used on internal services throughout the desert lands of the Arabian Peninsula. Driving trucks was also something that came his way, and one of the jobs he remembers most vividly is when he was asked to pick up a large Swedish diesel generator weighing fifty-eight tonnes which had arrived by ship at the docks in Jeddah. This generator had to be delivered to a power station 600 miles away, and although it may be easy to assume everywhere in Saudi Arabia was as flat as a large-scale map of the country may have suggested, this was far from the truth, as a tall mountain range cuts across the huge expanses of desert, a ridge of highland that ranges southwards as far as the Yemeni border. This obstruction came as a nasty surprise to Dave, particularly as this almost concluded with his American Mack R-Series truck ending up as a wreck when it looked as if his luck had run out.

On the way back to Jeddah, Dave suddenly noticed the brakes on the Mack were no longer working well at all as he began the descent of a long mountain pass. With the brake failure becoming more and more apparent, the truck started to increase its forward momentum, going faster and faster. Dave calmly informed his passenger that maybe the time was fast approaching to bail out of the runaway truck! But scared out of his wits, the passenger sitting beside Dave was unable to respond – he was totally transfixed – so bailing out of the truck was no longer an option for them according to Dave's code of behaviour. As quick as a flash, he racked his brains for an alternative solution:

'The only choice was to keep on going, and against all possible odds, try to maintain some semblance of control over my truck, which I did manage to achieve by making some swift, well-calculated steering responses so that the Mack did finally reach a patch of level ground at the base of the mountain, where the truck could then slow down and roll to a stop. However, there was yet another change of fortune for the both of us, as before the truck came to a stop, the front end struck a large pile of boulders. The force of the impact with the boulders was enough to push the front axle backwards, causing the front leaf spring to collapse so that the suspension was badly damaged. The individual leaves of the spring had run over each other, as the centre pins which had held the parts of the spring all together had broken and given way.'

Dave wasn't ready to call for any assistance by getting word of their plight back to the workshop in Jeddah; rather he managed to jury-rig a repair by first of all jacking up the truck's front corner and then rebuilding the damaged spring by reassembling the individual leaves of the spring together, which were resecured using the original U-bolts, which like the suspension leaves, were still in perfectly serviceable condition. The only issue that couldn't be solved was that the broken centre pins could not be repaired and put back into place, so the Mack had to be driven slowly all the way to Jeddah.

Dave continued with some further observations on desert travel:

'At times, you would notice the road hadn't been built at all, what you were driving on was simply a dirt-track surface. My firm had thought through the problem of how to get up the inclines with a heavy generator on board when driving on loose surfaces, and brought along a Caterpillar D8 bulldozer that could then give me a tow to the top of the steeper inclines! I was driving a heavy haulage Mack DM800, and this was towing a three-axle, low-loader trailer that was hired by my firm for this type of difficult job. This Mack truck did a fair job of work out there in the desert carrying the heavy generator, although the twin-stick transmission you had to use for splitting all the gears was regarded as a bit ancient by the mid-seventies.'

Sandstorms could bring a halt to any further progress shortly after being seen racing over the sands, and Dave remembered a sandstorm which seemed totally awesome as it swept over the desert, engulfing everything it came across in its twisting, billowing wake:

'I was caught in a sandstorm which was so strong it had the power to grind away the surface glaze on any windscreen glass and also ruined the glass on the headlights. I'd never seen anything like this particular sandstorm before. This storm had so much force that sand particles were being forced through the rubber seals of the cab doors. This storm only lasted for about a quarter of an hour, but it was really evil. The truck's bumpers were left looking all shiny: the sand had worn away the paint so that the steel looked like it had only just come out of a steelworks.'

Dave described a fault on Trans Arabia's fleet of ERFs which caused the hub reduction gears to

Ian Taylor lost a tyre after it burst, but kept the wheel to be reused, as depicted here. IT

Ian Taylor's F88 on the way out to Saudi. Note miniature flags on the windscreen so typical of a Middle East truck! IT

Ex-British-registered Mercedes out in remote desert country. FT

become prematurely worn due to lack of lubrication. The problem was traced to the use of hypoid 90 oil, as had been recommended by the truck's manufacturer, although a different type of oil was substituted which was more suitable when used in the sort of high temperatures to be found when driving in desert conditions:

'The oil took on the same viscosity as milk when our trucks were working out in the heat of the desert. So we needed to use a much thicker oil to prevent wear to the hub reduction gear parts, and this was answered by changing to a thicker, 140-grade oil.'

Tyres would also fail when subjected to high desert temperatures, and Dave made a firm point of always making sure he followed this sound advice:

'If you drove too fast, then the tyres would gradually start to heat up, and if the temperature became too high, they would blow out eventually. So you would need to slow down in order to save the tyres. But this also had a drawback, as your engine would soon start to overheat if the cooling system wasn't working as effectively as it should have been. You had to get the speed absolutely right so that both of these problems would be avoided.'

Other perils of the desert Dave learnt to deal with as a matter of course included negotiating deep wadis which became swift-running water courses following flash floods; also how to retrieve any trucks that had become bogged down in the sand or had sunk through the thin crust of any dried-out lakes that became a treacherous saltpan that was impossible to drive across.

Keith Burson was transiting through Syria when he was stopped and warned about an approaching sandstorm. He didn't think much of this at the time, but he changed his mind when he watched the sand starting to make its way into his lorry's cab as it stood stationary. On looking down at the dashboard a few moments later, he could have written his name in the sand that now lay all over the surface!

Ian Taylor on the way from Saudi after being asked to pick up a load in Cyprus. IT

Faced with hour after hour of desert driving and nothing coming the other way, Brian Robertson had lots of time to read a book while still moving! BR

Gordon Summers commented on the techniques he would employ when his truck was bogged down in loose sand:

'First of all, you would have to try digging yourself out as best as you could, and if that didn't work as well as it should, the next step was to let some of the air out of your tyres so as to improve traction. To avoid getting stuck in the first place, it was useful to learn the important skill of knowing how to read the sand which lay ahead of your truck. The trick was to identify where the sand was soft so that it needed to be avoided. I would always try to aim for any pebbly bits of ground which promised to provide a much harder surface that the wheels would not sink into at all. If you came across an area where the pebbles had not sunk down into the sand, this proved that the surface was solid and better to drive on than it was elsewhere which didn't have any pebbles on the surface.'

Paradoxically, a desert could also be a place of sanctuary, as when faced with such a harsh setting, there was a tendency for everyone to pull together and generally take a lot more interest in the welfare of others as a means of mutual support, as it was generally in the back of everyone's minds that the rescuer could soon turn out to be the one who now needed to be rescued as well, if there was a quick reversal of fortunes just down the road!

Gordon appreciated the isolation and safety of camping out miles from anywhere when he was crossing the desert lands of Saudi Arabia:

'You could stop anywhere that you liked in the middle of nowhere, as there was so little crime in that country. You had to be careful all the time in Syria, Jordan, Iraq, and especially when you were in Turkey, as the possibility of theft was always firmly on my mind.'

Gordon did however run into a long-term problem when a piston exited the side of his Volvo F89's engine, which left him immobilised somewhere along the TAP line, an oil pipeline in Saudi Arabia, for a full ten days:

'I was waiting for someone to come along who eventually towed me all the way back to Germany. My real problem wasn't so much that the engine had broken down but that this had occurred at the religious time of Ramadan, so getting any local help was difficult. The driver who was going to tow me back to Germany was delayed as he was stuck at the Saudi border owing to the religious festival. What made my situation much worse was that I couldn't get any food or water, as I was 200 miles away from the nearest town where I could have bought something to eat and to drink. Luckily, the rescue truck that had been sent to take me home did arrive on the very morning after I had finished the last of my water supply and when the only food which I had left was a single tin of creamed rice!'

Kenny Searle with his Oryx truck. He was accompanying Ian Taylor's F88 on H4. IT

Martyn Moulsdale pulling a couple of 40' containers in Dubai using an Astran Scania to make some pocket money doing a 'foreigner'. MM

Swantrans DAF and Robert Dods-Brown's Scania 110 on a desert crossing. RDB

CHAPTER 11

Working Internal Routes – Saudi Arabia

When the ports along the Red Sea coast of Saudi Arabia were open and operating efficiently once more, the cargoes that arrived by ship began piling up in the warehouses. The need to get this huge logjam of materials moving again was met by bringing in fleets of trucks which were then permanently based in the Arabian Peninsula for this purpose.

This created a new transport venture for many British and European haulage firms, such as Cunard, Trans Arabia and White Trux which set up transport facilities in Saudi Arabia, with many trucks and trailers specially imported to carry out internal deliveries that extended throughout the Arabian Peninsula. After making a trip from Europe while carrying a load all that way, many trucks and trailers would not be making a return journey, instead they were immediately pressed into service for urgent internal delivery work.

Indicating the growing interest that the internal transport business created in Saudi, the Cunard shipping firm set up their own transport operation to service their container freighters, *Saudi Crown*, *Jeddah Crown* and *Aqaba Crown*, with a fleet of ERF B-Series trucks powered by Cummins 335 and 350 engines providing onward transport from the docks to any final destinations.

Many trucks sent out with a load to Saudi were sold off at the end of the trip, as most probably occurred to this ex-Chapman & Ball Fiat. FT

Ex-UK Scania that was still working on Saudi number plates. FT

Ian Tyler standing beside the ERF B-Series he drove for CAMEL. ITY

Jerry Cooke and ERF A-Series shunter carrying a Caterpillar generator and radiators on the trailer. JC

As a twenty-one-year-old, Jerry Cooke was working as a mechanic in the Black Country for the haulage company of S. Jones of Aldridge when this firm decided to diversify its operations by setting up an internal delivery service based in Jeddah, known as Trans Arabia.

'I volunteered to go out to Saudi in 1977 as a relief mechanic for my firm. This was to be for a brief spell of six months initially, but I went on to do a number of twelve-month contracts between then and 1982. I didn't have much idea of what I had let myself in for when I arrived off the plane! I was met by one of the other mechanics and he took me to the place where all the accommodation had been laid on for as many as twenty-five blokes. After waking up on my first morning, the first job I was given was to repair a 335 Cummins engine; this required a new set of pistons and liners to be fitted. The damage to the engine resulted from all the wear caused by abrasion when sand had got inside the engine. This was a common problem of course when operating in desert conditions. I recall the repair facilities were basic to say the least. All the work was done out in the street because we didn't have a workshop at the time. So spending all day out in the sun involved applying plenty of suntan oil and always remembering to drink lots and lots of water. We wore a pair of shorts and a T-shirt all day, and I was amazed I had arrived in the cooler, winter season, as it didn't feel like it! Things improved, as later on, we had a covered yard that we used as a workshop which allowed us to work on the trucks in the shade, but even though you were not working in direct sunlight any more, it was still very hot for most of the time.'

There was an aspect to the job that Jerry was already thoroughly familiar with, in that he was working on ERF models for most of the time, as he had formerly done back at home in the Jones' workshop in Aldridge. These included Jerry's truck of choice, the ERF 5MW, and the ERF B-, C- and E-Series also arrived in the Jeddah-based workshop for repairs and routine servicing. The ERF trucks were supplemented by a

Dave Tickle's DAF shunting a trailer. DT

Dave 'Gypsy' Anslow and Jerry Cooke using a Trans Arabia Mack to recover an ERF 7MU that ran off the road. JC

Working Internal Routes – Saudi Arabia

This Trans Arabia ERF C-Series was built up from spare parts in Saudi Arabia. The Mack was one of six owned by the firm, the other truck is an ERF 5MW. JC

This ERF MW was brought to Jeddah by Eric Vick and bought by Trans Arabia. The second MW came from Holland and was wrecked in an accident. JC

number of bonneted Mack R-Series trucks that had been imported from the USA. This brand of trucks had been chosen by Trans Arabia's joint partner in this venture, a Saudi national with the surname Binlagr, who owned an import/warehouse business. Acquiring a Saudi business partner was the only officially approved way of doing business in this country.

So Jerry's loyalties remained true to the ERF trucks built in Sandbach, Cheshire rather than the Mack when it came to driving in desert conditions or climbing the high mountain ranges which he was surprised to find in the interior regions beyond the huge areas of desert plains:

'I drove both types of truck on normal delivery runs, as all of the mechanics would drive these on recovery jobs whenever a broken-down truck needed to be towed back to the workshop and then worked on. The Macks were fairly basic in my opinion; they were not as comfortable as any of the ERFs, and the ERFs benefited from being a bit faster as well, as the Macks were geared down to do only 50 mph at best. There was one advantage that earned my respect for those Mack trucks, and that was they were so ruggedly constructed. I also appreciated the large sleeper bed, as provided at the back of the cab.'

Trans Arabia ERF A-Series – ex-S Jones, ERF B-Series and Mack. Firm's trailer park – Jeddah. JC

Trans Arabia ERF with radiator removed and Kenworth K100, 1982. JC

Jerry Cooke out in the workshop's pickup used for recovery. JC

Jerry Cooke's Mack R-Series. JC

Jerry outlined his duties as a mechanic with the Trans Arabia company:

'I would drive the recovery truck to bring any trucks back to the workshop, although by our own choice, we would at least try to repair a broken-down truck where it stood out in the desert if we could do so. I would often drive out to the stranded truck in the workshop's pickup truck while carrying a few tools and spares I needed. On one occasion I drove a distance of 400 miles one way when the water pump on one of our ERF 7MWs needed replacing. There was never a dull moment, and I always found it was important not to let yourself become at all concerned by the task that lay ahead, as this would be sorted out in its own time.

'Our gaffer, Bill Smith, who came from Lichfield, would give me an instruction along the lines of, "One of our trucks has broken down about 300 miles that-a-way," as he pointed his finger in one direction of the compass before adding by way of reassurance that you wouldn't get lost, as there were not many roads to choose from out there in the desert! But of course, the consequences of getting lost out in a desert could be very severe … ! There were no mobile phones in those days, so sometimes it took a fair while before we got to know a truck had broken down if this had happened many miles away. But generally, word of a breakdown usually arrived when a driver called in to say he'd come across one of our trucks in need of a call out, whether they were employed by our own company or another firm. So this would set the alarm bells ringing, and off we would go!'

For recovery work, Jerry and the other mechanics would requisition whatever fleet vehicles happened to be available, and he remembers setting out in an ERF B-Series which still had its trailer attached, such was the urgency of getting the broken down truck repaired and back into service so another urgently needed load could be back on its way!

'We often used a dolly to tow a second trailer in the style of a road train, which was fine, as this was allowed by the traffic laws in Saudi. What's more, there weren't any weight restrictions on what you hauled along in those days. I would hitch the dolly onto the back of the trailer, this trailer being attached to the truck I was using for the recovery. After arriving at the scene where the broken-down truck was standing, I would hitch the dolly that was behind my trailer to the front of the damaged truck by using a straight bar. The broken-down truck may well have had a trailer of its own

Operating rules in Saudi allowed for Australian road train operations. RG

Dolly attached to trailer to tow a second trailer as a road train. JC

'One job I remember was to change the clutch on an ERF, so this involved removing the gearbox first of all. The only problem was that we didn't have any lifting equipment with us to remove the gearbox from the chassis to get at the clutch. It was lucky my mate, Johnny Davies, who we called "Doctor Truck", came along with me. He was someone who always knew what he was doing. Johnny grabbed hold of two round steel poles we happened to have with us at the time, which he placed so the poles were positioned sideways across the length of the truck's chassis rails and above the gearbox. We secured the gearbox to one of the steel poles using a length of steel chain to take the weight of the gearbox. A large set of nuts and bolts were then inserted through the links of the steel chain, and by ratcheting up the nuts and bolts using a wrench, the chain was made to take up the weight of the gearbox. This allowed us to disconnect the driveline between the gearbox and the rear axle, and then the gearbox from the engine; so the gearbox could be pushed out of the way of the engine by sliding it backwards on the two poles that had been placed across the chassis members. We were then able to gain access to the clutch housing so we could remove the worn-out clutch from the engine. After fitting the new clutch, the gearbox was put back into position using the same process as before, but in reverse order, applying Johnny's clever pole and chain method.'

on tow, so now I would be towing along a double load of two forty-foot trailers. We were permitted to carry as many as four shipping containers at any one time in this way using a dolly to connect two trailers together. This could mean we were carrying as much as twenty-five tonnes gross in each of the container boxes that sat on each trailer, making a gross overall load weight of a hundred tonnes! These road trains were operated all the way across the interior of Saudi Arabia, running from coast to coast between the Red Sea and the Persian Gulf, and crossing hundreds of miles on a regular route from the port of Jeddah on the west coast to Dammam on the east coast.'

Immense distances were routinely covered to arrive at the scene of many breakdowns, such as the entire 800-mile distance along the Trans-Arabian Pipeline from Thraif to Dammam. After enduring such a long, exhausting drive, carrying out any repair that may have been simple enough in normal circumstances often turned out to be far more difficult than Jerry and the other mechanics could possibly have ever anticipated or even imagined!

Trans Arabia workshops, Jeddah 1982. Last ERF having an engine rebuild as the sump has been taken off. JC

Makeshift repair facilities out in the desert using shipping containers. Note use of canvas and tilting cab to draw the sheet taut overhead! FT

Jerry would take on routine driving whenever Trans Arabia needed an extra driver for a delivery and when he was off-duty from work as a mechanic.

Underlining that old saying about taking coals to Newcastle, Jerry was once asked to carry a load of a special type of engine oil contained in drums, which had been refined in another country and then imported into Saudi Arabia. The job sounded relatively simple, although this went dramatically wrong for Jerry when his 6x4 ERF B-Series suffered two simultaneous burst tyres on the driven wheels. The effects of this were very scary indeed from Jerry's point of view, as both the tractor unit and the trailer were forcibly tipped over on one side, sending the entire load of heavy oil drums tumbling off in all directions, before the trailer landed back on its wheels:

'After seeing to the punctured tyres by fitting a spare set of wheels I had brought with me, I consulted our gaffer who came up with the idea we should reload the oil barrels back on the trailer using the old beer barrel method. To achieve this, we found a couple of planks of wood that were suitable to be used as ramps, and then we handballed each of those heavy barrels which were filled with oil back onto the trailer; this was quite some task considering it all took place in the searing heat of the day!'

Desert driving always required drivers to keep in mind the many perils of travelling in such a harsh environment, with dehydration being an obvious threat to life and limb; there was the need to avoid taking the wrong route and getting lost, and any accidents could be much more serious, indeed life-threatening, when far beyond access to any medical assistance within a reasonable timescale.

There were also the usual hazards to watch out for when travelling through any populated towns and villages on these internal routes, so drivers had to keep their wits about them to avoid any accidents which involved other traffic or pedestrians, as they would soon find themselves spending some time in jail if they didn't take note – even if a traffic offence was of a fairly minor nature.

Jerry recalled a brush with the law that occurred when he was driving through the streets of Dammam and he purposely ignored a ban on taking a truck into the city at certain times of day:

'This policeman stopped me and started talking to me in English, so I decided the best approach would be to pretend I was German by using only a few words of English to suggest my knowledge of the language was limited. So he accepted this and told me that he would come back with another

policeman who did speak German. So this had me really worried. As soon as that policeman was safely out of sight, I saw my chance and made off as fast as I could before he returned with the German speaker. This would have been very awkward for me, as I didn't know any German at all!'

Dave Anslow described an incident when he was locked up in the local jail after falling foul of the Saudi police:

'I went too quickly through a village one day when I was towing a pair of trailers. There were lots of flattened drink tins lying about all over the street. As I was going along so fast, the slipstream from my truck and the two trailers sent all these tin cans flying about in the air. As they had sharp edges where they had been flattened, this created quite a hazard, with the possibility of hurting anyone who was walking down the village street at the time. Shortly afterwards, I was stopped and arrested by the police for creating such a hazard to any villagers, and they locked me up for a while as my punishment.'

One day when Jerry Cooke was taking a break from driving after parking up near the Kuwaiti border he received the fright of his life, which proved beyond any doubt that the desert was not as devoid of life as he had originally believed:

'There I was in the driver's seat, dozing away with the window left open so I could catch the breeze, when I noticed that the side window curtain was slowly moving about, but not from the wind. I then noticed a rustling noise as the curtain began waving more strongly, as if someone was standing there directly outside my cab window. So I struck out with my fist at the middle of the curtain, giving this blow full force in the hope of scaring off any intruder. This was followed by a heart-rending roar just as I swung the cab curtain aside, which exposed a full-grown camel that was looking in through the window at me, just a few inches away from my face! I felt rather guilty for punching the camel, as it was only natural for the animal to be inquisitive. It then moved away, and as if to let its feelings known, it then let out a second bellowing cry. I didn't feel quite as sympathetic with the camel after I came to notice there were some sticky clots of blood and snot that the beast had left all over the window curtain!'

Returning to Mike Dunstan's story that described how he first arrived in Saudi Arabia, together with John 'Percy' Harris, on their very first run working for the Dutch Butrako firm; they found to their surprise that it was now assumed they would continue working for the firm in Saudi even though this had never been mentioned to them before they had set off from Holland. They would be doing internal runs over an indeterminate period of time rather than returning home. However, there was a delay in setting up the internal work, which left Mike and Percy hanging about with nothing much to do, as no work was forthcoming from Butrako. But they managed to turn this situation to their personal financial advantage by doing some work on the side for another haulage firm. Mike described how an offer of some work came their way after they began chatting to a Canadian who was looking for some drivers to do internal deliveries:

'We were in the Medina Hotel in Jeddah, and this bloke called Mike Scully, who worked for a firm called Atco, told us he needed some drivers to take loads of prefabricated building sections from Jeddah to the city of Medina. However, as this was an important religious centre, we weren't allowed to drive into the city as we were not Muslims and this is a holy city. So we were told that we would need to drop our loads just outside town, and these would then be picked up by some Turkish drivers, who were all Muslims, so they would be allowed to complete our deliveries for us. We were asked if we wanted to use the Pegasos as owned by Butrako for this job, or alternatively, we could use some trucks which Mike would supply to us for the job. As we were doing a "foreigner" job that we were going to be paid for, the choice we had to make was obvious – we didn't use the trucks that we'd brought all the way from Holland. The trucks Mike gave us to drive were double-drive White Autocars, each of which was towing a road train consisting of a pair of trailers connected one to the other by a dolly. Percy and I did a couple of trips from Jeddah to Medina and we covered 500 km each way. I enjoyed driving across the desert. It was always scorching hot throughout the day, but the climate meant it could also be very cold at night. Even so, there were many occasions when it was warm enough at night to sleep underneath a trailer. Sleeping outside under the stars was something that I always liked to do until one day when someone told us about those scary-looking camel spiders that were to be found creeping about in the dark! One day when I was brewing up in the desert while waiting for my mates to catch up with me, it felt as if something was crawling about in my underpants. So I immediately dropped my trousers, which happened to be just when all my mates arrived in their own trucks. They were probably wondering what I was doing with my pants down round my ankles, but the answer was obvious when they drew nearer; I hadn't been attacked by a camel spider, but long lines of these huge black ants were crawling their way up both of my legs. One of my

A collection of Butrako Spanish Pegaso trucks and a single normal control Scania Vabis 76. FT

mates was so scared by what he saw that day he refused to get out of his cab.'

Whether this was because of a shared fear of nasty, biting insects or Mike's state of rapid undress is something that's still to be resolved!

Working their own contract didn't last long for Mike and Percy as Butrako sent out Barry Barker as their new boss. Barry then drummed up some internal work for Butrako, starting off with the delivery of prefabricated buildings for the Atco firm, the same task that Mike and Percy had cheekily performed so as to earn a few bob on the side!

Underlining the extreme urgency of unloading ships at the Jeddah docksides, with ships riding at anchor

Street scene in Jeddah with abandoned Volvo F88. FT

On the road to the holy city of Mecca, although only drivers of the Muslim faith were allowed to enter the city. DM

and waiting to unload for months and months because all the quays were choked full of ships, Mike watched as helicopters were brought in by an American firm to pick up pallet loads of cement from a ship, three at a time, slung beneath the helicopters in nets, and deliver them to the firm's compound near Jeddah. The sacks of cement were needed for the completion of a construction project that could not be delayed any longer.

Michael White, who established White Trux based in Kent, operated thirty trucks from a base in Jeddah for about four years, a time when the British seemed to be well favoured by the Saudis, although he was becoming increasingly aware this golden honeymoon period would soon be over:

'The Saudis appreciated what we did, and we had a very good reputation over there, as the local people responded well to our drivers and the quality of all the work they did over there. But things started to change after a while, and a lot of unscrupulous people moved in. The problem was that the Saudis couldn't seem to tell the difference between those who were always so efficient at the job and those who were no good at all, so they started introducing all sorts of laws to control matters. The Saudis were very trustworthy at first, but it was sad that this changed as time went by.'

CHAPTER 12

As Far As You Could Go: Afghanistan and Pakistan

The possibility of going a considerable distance further down the road than the customs warehouse in Tehran airport had always been on the cards. This must have been something that many drivers and hauliers had in mind after taking account of Bob Paul and Michael Woodman's pioneering journey to Kabul, the capital of Afghanistan, in 1964. This trip paved the way for the Asian Transport company, which then became Astran – the most famous British-owned Middle East haulage company!

So following in Bob and Michael's footsteps, some British and other European haulage concerns began pushing further eastwards, which involved travelling beyond Tehran to pass through the holy city of Mashhad, then across the hot and dusty desert plains of Afghanistan towards Herat and on to Kabul. This went well, so the way was opened up to go a lot further. The trucks then passed through the sort of wild mountain scenery and ravines that had inspired Kipling's stirring stories of Britain's distant colonial past and long-lost territories. Onwards through the tribal lands of the Khyber Pass and over the mountains of the Hindu Kush to arrive at the border with Pakistan, which opened the way to the city of Peshawar, a popular destination for unloading. Alternatively, the journey to Pakistan could take a more southerly passage across the arid deserts of Iran before crossing into Pakistan and travelling on towards Karachi, the largest city in Pakistan, where the goods which had travelled so far would be unloaded by a large team of bearded and turbaned labourers.

Mike Dunstan recounted his one and only trip to Pakistan, taken while still working for the Dutch Butrako firm, which turned out to be an unmitigated disaster for all those concerned:

'After my time in Saudi Arabia doing internal runs for Butrako, the firm took on a new job of taking a number of loads to Karachi. But this trip didn't go well, almost resulting in the financial ruin of the company. The trip went so badly because it was the wrong time of year, which meant all sorts of bad weather conditions were encountered along the way. Just about every lorry we took on that trip to Pakistan was wrecked in the process. We all drove Ford Transcontinentals, trucks that usually went well for us but for a few problems with the electrics and the braking systems at times, faults that were compensated for, to my way of thinking, by the excellent Cummins engines and Fuller gearboxes which both performed very well for us.

'I set off some five weeks after the first Butrako trucks had gone, and I was accompanied by Jim Smethurst, who has now passed away. (God bless you, Jim. We did many

The famous Khyber Pass, Afghanistan. GK

Local 'Tonka' Bedford J-Type – Afghanistan. GK

trips together, and you were a very experienced driver.) Jim and I took an unusual route from Iran to Quetta in Pakistan which avoided the more established northern route through Afghanistan. We were carrying some special kind of construction shuttering for a new harbour that was to be built in Karachi.

'One of the problems with the way this job to Pakistan had been organised was the running of seven or eight trucks together at the same time, as this meant that delays would continually arise. There would always be one or another truck holding all the rest back when a driver ran into some sort of trouble or a breakdown. In truth, a couple of the drivers who came on this trip with us were not really up to the job.

'When travelling across Iran we came across a construction company by the name of Marples Ridgway that was building a road out there, and they invited us to stop in their compound for a while, which was handy, as we needed to use their facilities to make welding repairs to our trucks and trailers, and also to renew our stock of diesel fuel. We eventually managed to complete what turned out to be a very difficult trip to Pakistan, although some of the trucks were so badly worn out by then, they were almost completely wrecked and had to be returned home by ship because this was the only option, although my own Transcontinental did manage to complete the return journey. So this was a trip that I wouldn't want ever to have to repeat!

'I finished with Butrako in 1978, and my last trip for this Dutch firm involved taking a load of oil industry equipment for the Ballast Needham company in Kuwait. I travelled with a guy called Alexander Fenwick who could do a good job of playing the blues on his harmonica, which meant we both enjoyed receiving many free drinks along the way.'

Les Rivett was working for Spiers and Hartwell of Evesham when he was invited to take his longest overland journey. This involved a 15,000-mile round trip to Karachi in Pakistan. Les drove a Fiat 619/21 with a trailer on tow carrying an unusual cargo of Old Spice aftershave. This was something that puzzled Les as soon as he arrived in Pakistan, as the blokes he came across sported full beards, so using a splash of aftershave didn't make sense as part of a daily routine! Les described how the journey started off rather badly and then proceeded in the same fashion over the next few weeks:

Scania 110 with refrigerated trailer that could be sent all the way to Karachi! SH

'It was really awful going all the way through Turkey as there had been a terrible earthquake. Not that it affected us directly on the road, but all the damage from this disaster then caused a huge backlog of trucks blocking up the roads. By the time we arrived at the border into Iran, the queue of trucks was so long, it took six days to cover a distance of only eight-tenths of a mile. You could see hundreds of trucks, reaching as far as the eye could see on both sides of the Turkey/Iran border at Gurbulak/Bazargan.'

After successfully arriving in Tehran without any further delays, Les was feeling the need for some help and some tips for how he should continue on with the journey, as he had no foreknowledge of the route which lay ahead other than the bare details that the map he had brought with him could reveal. But none of the drivers that Les chose to question was able to come up with any information that might be of use to him, so it was clear from the beginning that this trip was going to be a step into the great unknown! Les's growing suspicions that this trip was going to be his most difficult of all to date were confirmed beyond doubt when he received some unwelcome news on arriving at the Iran/Afghanistan border:

'I didn't have any papers to enter Afghanistan, so they told me to go back to Mashhad in Iran where I could pick up the paperwork I needed to cross the frontier. So after uncoupling my trailer and leaving this at the border to be collected later on, off I went all the way back to Mashhad. After arriving there and returning with the papers that I needed to get my truck through the border, I was then told that I needed a set of separate papers for my trailer in addition to those I had already collected for the truck, so back I went again to Mashhad for the second time! But at last I was on my way again after collecting the papers I needed for my trailer! I finally managed to make my way across the border, but I was alarmed to come across a sign reading in English, "Beware of Bandits, Do Not Park on the Highway".'

Les encountered a further bureaucratic stumbling block which proved to be a lot easier to resolve when he crossed the next and final border of this trip into Pakistan:

'A customs official had taken all the relevant details on my tractor unit, including the serial number for my truck's engine. He insisted on using a copy of the same form to check the details of my trailer. My problem then was that he wanted me to give him the serial number of the non-existent engine on my trailer, which was nonsense of course! However, as it didn't look as if I could find any way to explain this simple truth to him, it made better sense simply to make up a number. So I read out the engine number of my truck once again, only backwards this time so he wouldn't notice that he'd been tricked! The deception worked a treat, and I was on my way again.'

Les had only gone a few yards when he was greeted by a man who stepped out of an old Studebaker car and approached him to offer his services as an import agent. This was agreed, and the next task was to work out how much cash was needed to pay the import duty on Les's load of aftershave. The payment for the import duty then had to be made by arranging a transfer of funds from a bank in Karachi, which had to be done over the telephone – the only problem being there was no direct line between the border and Karachi, so the call then had to be routed by a long drawn out process that involved a sequence of telephone calls being made over short distances from one hotel business to the next along the way!

After a very long wait, the money finally arrived, so Les paid the import duty and also the helpful agent's fee, and then he was left to his own devices again. The rest of the outward journey went smoothly enough so that Les arrived at his destination in Karachi. The trailer was then unloaded, although all was not well with most of the contents, as Les went on to describe with a touch of irony given the difficulties he had experienced in delivering the load of aftershave over such immense distances and with so many problems along the way:

'The aftershave had become so hot on the journey out towards Pakistan that some of the seals on the containers had broken, causing the lids to come off and allowing some of the aftershave to leak out which then explained why I noticed

Mountain road in Afghanistan. GK

this strong perfume smell most of the time! Some of the aftershave was OK because this was stored in large, forty-five-gallon drums, and the individual bottles were also OK, but imagine travelling all that way with so much of what you had been carrying with you then being totally wasted by the time you got there!'

On the way back, Les met up with a Dutch driver and a Belgian driver, who advised him to take a shortcut by way of the Bolan Pass in western Pakistan, 120 kilometres from the Afghanistan border, which avoided taking a longer route by way of the Khyber Pass. However, this well-meant advice had a serious flaw to it, which made this diversion a lot more difficult for someone towing a box van trailer rather than a continental-style road train as the other two had been driving:

Street scene in Pakistan. GK

'I had to use a road which had a large overhanging rock cliff face above it, which caused a significant problem, as even though I had no problem getting my Fiat truck underneath the cliff to pass on down the road, this did not apply to my box van trailer, as this was too tall to pass underneath the overhanging rock face. So after noticing that the road in front doubled back after crossing a river that I could see across the valley, the answer came to me on what I needed to do. This was to uncouple the Fiat where it was standing in front of the overhanging obstruction. And once the trailer had been removed, I proceeded to drive my truck along a circuitous route that took me on to some place where I could cross the river with my truck. I then drove back along the far side of the river until I arrived at a place where I was facing my trailer, which was on the opposite bank of the river now. My next task was to connect the Fiat to the trailer using a long length of rope that bridged the river, and after taking up all the slack, I proceeded to drag my trailer through the water and across the river bed to the other bank where the truck was!'

This worked well for Les, and after re-coupling the trailer, he was on his way once more. But he began to run out of diesel, something that shouldn't normally have been a problem, except Les's stock of Afghani cash was also running low, with little chance of finding anywhere to exchange his British running money for the local currency, as he was too far out in the sticks.

'I was lucky when I noticed a European truck that was approaching from the opposite direction, so I flashed my headlights on and off to get the other driver to stop his truck. Hopefully, he would have some suggestions on how I could make a deal and swap some of my British cash for local money to buy some diesel fuel. The driver was Belgian, and he came up with the goods, kindly offering to swap the Bulgarian fuel vouchers which I had with me for a pile of Afghani notes. He also helped by telling me about a fuel stop that was only ten kilometres further down the road. After travelling for this distance, an Afghani kid suddenly came out of nowhere, which suggested this was where I now needed to stop and get some fuel for the truck, but I couldn't see where any diesel could be kept out here in the middle of nowhere. The Afghani boy then lifted the lid off a well which I hadn't seen at first and he started filling my fuel tank using some old biscuit tins as buckets. The fuel filler cap on my Fiat was rather small, so there was lots of spillage, but I didn't mind at all as long as I could keep going on my way again!'

When Les returned to the UK from this arduous trip, it didn't take him long to convince his boss at Spiers and Hartwell, Deryck Hartwell, of all the risks he had undergone to reach Karachi and return home. The trip had not been worth the considerable effort that was involved, or for that matter the financial returns that

Gerry Keating, Afghan desert – chai time! 1978. MH

to receive the sort of medical care that's too often taken for granted in this country:

'On reaching Tehran, I headed north over the Elburz Mountains towards the Caspian Sea as an alternative way of going to Afghanistan. The trip over the mountains took twelve hours on the way out, but only three coming back with the truck unloaded. The road was so steep, with no protective Armco barriers along the way, so I didn't like looking down with drops of up to 2000 feet. I could see many wrecks of vehicles that had gone over the edge! Once we had got into Afghanistan, there were no further driving problems at all, even though the roads were as bad as they had been anywhere else. One of the guys that I was running with had forgotten to bring along the inoculation certificates which he needed, so at the border post, he was sent to a hospital to be re-inoculated. The hospital was built of mud, with no glass windows, and when the doctor got out the needle and syringe, he then wiped the needle, indicating that this had already been used many times before! Visiting this hospital convinced me that no-one has any right to complain about the standards of hospital care we receive in this country.'

it made; it was a bad investment of time and money. So ended Les's one and only venture as far away as the Indian subcontinent! He did suggest the only way of setting up and maintaining regular overland truck services to Pakistan would be to send truckloads as far as the Afghanistan/Pakistan border and then arrange onward transport by a local Pakistani haulage concern that would have more experience of the local driving conditions and the customs formalities when entering the country.

Mark Chevalier took a load of coin bullion to Afghanistan, nineteen tons in all, which sounds like a dangerous enterprise in a part of the world infamous for its armed robbers and banditry. But on the bright side, an armed military escort was awaiting Mark's arrival at the border. The soldiers then accompanied the truck and its load of bullion for the remainder of the journey to Herat. Mark had been concerned that a load of newly minted coins may have tempted the officials at the Turkish border to take a look, which did occur, although the load was resealed with care, and the documentation was duly stamped to record this had officially taken place.

Mark described one of the most interesting trips of his Middle East career, which after crossing into Afghanistan, provided an insight into how lucky we are

Tim Smith servicing his Fiat in Pakistan. Did adopting a Yoga-like position help? BC

End of the road for this Birdale truck at Rawalpindi railway station. EW

Warehouse depot in Lahore, Pakistan. Feb 1979. Note local transport. GK

Unloading gang getting busy carting away sacks in Lahore, Pakistan. GK

CHAPTER 13

Venturing Behind the Iron Curtain

Since the fall of the Berlin Wall and the loss of the Soviet Union's control over Eastern European countries during the nineties, it seems strange to consider that travelling in countries such as Hungary, the Czech Republic or Slovakia was a rare, if not at times forbidden, experience for Western visitors. And as for those who lived under the influence of the Soviet regime, they were even more rigorously segregated from the Western world outside, so that if they were caught trying to leave these countries, this was often punishable by death if spotted through the open sights of a border guard's rifle!

From the point of view of anyone wanting to enter an Eastern bloc country, this had a rather spine-tingling touch like becoming part of the plot of a Le Carré spy novel! This impression was further emphasised by the excessive security measures which were in place, with the guard towers mounting searchlights and machine-guns; tall fences topped with barbed wire; and stern gun-parading military personnel always much in evidence.

The irony of all these security measures was that they were mainly directed towards preventing the citizens of all these countries from voting with their feet and leaving rather than keeping out any Westerners and their decadent influences!

There was an obvious disparity in personal wealth that also made Westerners feel uneasy as they travelled through any Eastern bloc countries. By the perceived standards of the local populace, any truck drivers arriving from Western Europe appeared to be fabulously rich, and not surprisingly, this led to the expectations it was only right and proper these affluent travellers should dispense with some of their cash as they passed through a country where everyone seemed dispossessed of life's luxuries or comforts by comparison.

Gavin McArdle showing off an omelette he made from the cab of his Scammell Crusader. KP

Mercedes 1923 driven by Allan Ball just arrived in East Germany. This truck has survived to this day. KP

Owner driver known as 'Budgie' who drove for 'Tanker Bill' beside Johnnie Roberts on the left who drove for Bromilows. Bucharest 1976. KP

So in the old days, making contact with Westerners was something the Soviet-backed governments and law enforcement agencies of the Eastern bloc countries frowned on and actively discouraged so that anyone who was caught getting too friendly with foreigners could be persecuted for the most trivial matters.

Ivor Whittall remembered a night when he managed to get talking to someone in the grounds of a factory in Bulgaria even though this practice was actively discouraged:

'I remember whenever you were in Bulgaria you weren't supposed to talk to the locals under the old Communist regime. I had already been reminded of this one night when we were parked up and the police arrived and said they wanted us to move somewhere else. They explained it was because of the danger from bandits, and they added that they wanted us to move to a camp for TIR drivers that was a few kilometres away. But that wasn't true as the camp was a long way away. The police were only saying this because they didn't want us talking to any locals who might come along. A similar incident occurred one time when I was on my way home and called to collect a return load from a factory in Bulgaria. After trying a number of doors, which showed the workers were all locked up and couldn't get out of the factory, a woman finally came up and spoke in perfect English to say I would be loaded at the factory on the following day. She added I could park my truck in the yard, but I wasn't to talk to anyone who came along. I ignored this advice later on when this lad arrived and told me he was learning English by listening to the BBC's World Service. He started asking me questions, such as how much I earned, and when I told him the amount, he couldn't believe what I'd said, as this seemed so much to him! What was a week's wages to me would have been many months' wages for him. His shoes were so worn the soles were full of holes. I remember thinking, if this is what Communism's all about, you can keep it as far as I am concerned! Bulgarian drivers were earning thirty pounds a month in those days, and it was our belief that when travelling outside any Communist countries, the driver always had to have someone else with him in the cab. And that would be a party member sitting alongside him. His job was to prevent the driver from doing something that they shouldn't have been doing whenever they were in another country; or maybe to stop them running off and then claiming political asylum?'

Graham Cartmail put forward a similar point of view on the poverty and suffering that he observed the locals having to bear as he travelled his way through any Soviet bloc countries, such as Bulgaria:

'They were so poor I would occasionally let them cheat me in any deals they came up with as I felt so sorry for them. It always amazed me in the seventies there were still some people who would say they would be intending to vote

Slavonski Brod, Yugoslavia. Lenny Baylam and Bob Crofton-Sleigh, May 1975. BC

Communist, but they clearly didn't have a clue what they were talking about or they would have known a lot better.'

Graham always found that travelling through countries like Bulgaria was remarkably inexpensive for any Western European truck drivers, which was slightly embarrassing in a way, so to redress the balance, and recognising there was such a strong demand for any Western goods, which had little connection to how much these items had cost, he would obligingly hand over anything that he had brought along with him as an inexpensive act of charity.

Graham commented on the favourable exchange rate that was achieved when swapping Western cash for the local currency whilst transiting through Bulgaria:

'You had to change ten pounds into Bulgarian lev at the border and also collect some tokens that you paid for so that you could buy fuel along the way. When you left the country, any local currency that hadn't been spent would then be converted into Western currency and handed back to you as cash. Sometimes you would get as much as four pounds back after eating and drinking so well all the way through this country, so you had only spent six pounds the whole time you were there on food etc. You could also do well trading any gifts you had brought with you for some cash, the locals were prepared to do all sorts of favours for any Western goods, such as the music cassettes of Tom Jones, the Rolling Stones or the Shadows, as they were not allowed to have any of our kind of music at all!'

The appeal of getting hold of any Western goods was then one in the eye for their authoritarian Communist rulers, and the appeal of such items underlined how poorly their own economic systems performed when it came to delivering luxuries of any kind to such a deprived home market.

Martyn Moulsdale also took a sympathetic approach to anyone who came along asking for small value items such as packets of chewing gum, sweets, crisps; maybe a tin of beans, or even a packet of pork scratchings, that favourite food delicacy of the West Midlands! However, he always kept a close watch on the steel food box that was securely fixed to the chassis frame of his trailer, which was virtually thief-proof after he installed a securing bar over the top that required the correct size of Allen key to gain access.

Many Middle East drivers took the time to pick up a smattering of the German language, as this was well understood in Turkey because so many Turks had worked or were working in Germany at that time. This had a spin-off value when travelling through East Germany, as it was a vast improvement to talk to the police and any other officials in their own language, English not being understood that well at all then.

There were occasions when it paid off not to have a common language, as Ian Taylor recalled when he was stopped one night by a policeman who was standing in the middle of the road and aggressively waving what looked like a large lollipop stick at Ian's truck, which then slowed down and came to a halt:

'When I said I was English this didn't register at all as we had no common language between us, so this then worked in my favour, as he had to let me go! And that was the end of the matter.'

Peter Bamford recalled a similar issue when it came to understanding road directions, or rather, misinterpreting these to his own advantage:

'In Eastern bloc countries you normally weren't allowed to drive straight through the centre of cities; they would want you to use a ring-road that went all over the place. So you would ignore that instruction and then you would go through the centre of town, and if you got away with it, then fair enough.'

Peter commented on a change of route that allowed Yugoslavia to be bypassed when it was no longer possible to obtain insurance for trucks or any loads they were carrying when travelling through this country

Customs house at Vidin, Bulgaria. PB

Crossing the Danube at Russe, Bulgaria – Peter Bamford's Falcongate truck. PB

due to the civil unrest which eventually erupted into open warfare between the various ethnic groups:

'You could bypass Yugoslavia via Romania, but the amount of thieving that you could encounter along the way from locals in Romania was truly horrendous. The only way of keeping out of trouble was to park up at the Romanian border when you were coming in or out of the country, and then set out "early doors" next morning, depending on what time of year it was, so you didn't have to travel in the dark, which was the most dangerous time to be attacked by robbers. If the roads were clear, you would try to cover the whole 600 kilometres nonstop until you were finally out of that country!'

Peter's travels in remote areas of Bulgaria were often, and quite literally, a journey through bandit country, and coming across someone lying on the tarmac could be very dangerous:

'If you saw someone lying in the road, this could mean your truck was about to be ambushed and you were about to be robbed of all the contents in the cab and maybe the load carried on the trailer when you came to a stop to avoid the body lying in the road. I remember little Alfie Jones being attacked in Bulgaria near the city of Plovdiv with lots of stones then thrown at him so his arm was broken. The other problem with people lying down in the road wasn't as serious in one way, but it was in another way. You would come across drunks where they had fallen down in the middle of the road, but couldn't manage to get up again, and if you had hit one, there would have been lots of trouble!'

Offers of sexual services were a much evident feature of life when travelling any routes regularly used by Middle East drivers to cross through Yugoslavia, Bulgaria and Romania. Gordon Summers recalled the occasion when he was propositioned by a woman who had a lot more to offer after he had changed some deutschmarks for some local Romanian lei currency with the woman:

'This was for a fantastic rate of exchange, and afterwards, when we had made the deal, she said to me, "Do you want me as well?" So I replied, "No, you're a bit too old, hen." But back she came just ten minutes later when she turned up with her sixteen-year-old daughter. I made my excuse that the girl would be far too expensive for the likes of me, to which she tried to suggest I had already paid for the girl as part of the money exchange deal. An opportunity which I turned down as you couldn't be too careful!'

TIR-badged trucks were routinely weighed when crossing the borders into Romania and Geoff Morgan remembered a maximum weight of twenty-eight tonnes was imposed at one point in time. So as his truck weighed a good deal more, he always made sure that one set of his truck and trailer's wheels were not on the weighbridge!

David Miller's experience of landing up in court provides a perfect example of the sort of nonsense that could occur if some excuse could be found for parading a foreign driver before a judge for a trumped-up charge in countries such as East Germany, just as if this was a celebrated show trial like those that played out in Moscow during the oppressive Stalinist era!

'This took place when I was working for Grangewood Transport, and we had been delivering part of the European Union beef mountain as part of an eighteen-month contract to deliver supplies of meat to the Eastern bloc countries. But you could see where the meat was really going to end up after you arrived. After unloading my truck at a warehouse that was also an abattoir, the meat I had delivered was reloaded onto Red Army trucks to be taken away to the USSR! Anyway, as I was leaving East Germany, the border guards found this copy of a Dutch newspaper, De Telegaaf, which I had been reading, as I'm half Dutch by right of birth. So I was taken away to face a court hearing where I was accused of importing "the pornography of Western propaganda into the Workers Paradise of the German Democratic Republic". This was a real laugh, as this newspaper was always totally respectable. But the judge insisted it was porn that I had brought with me into what he called the "German Democratic Paradise of East Germany". So I was fined a ridiculously small amount of money, and everyone was very pleased with themselves!'

Despite the differences that existed between East and West, there was little indication of this on a driver-to-driver level, and David had some admiring words to say about the Romanian drivers who were issued with imitation leather trilby hats and drove all the way to Saudi travelling two-up in locally made MAN trucks, sold under the ROMAN name, that didn't have a sleeper cab:

'The really good thing for us at that time was that all the Eastern bloc drivers had to be qualified mechanics before they could manage to get a driving job for themselves, and they were always, in my experience, very willing to help out other drivers with problems. Better still, they carried very comprehensive tool kits with them, and they were always happy to undertake some pretty major stuff right there beside the road. They were excellent lads, with all of them full-on mechanics, who would always stop to give you a hand if this was needed. They would think nothing of repairing a gearbox by the roadside. The Hungarians were also helpful, I remember stopping at the Hungarocamion depot in Budapest because I had a small problem with my Scammell Crusader and they could not have been more helpful. Not only did they fix the problem there and then, but they followed this up by letting a troop of young apprentices loose on the motor who changed the oil, greased it, washed the whole thing down and valeted the cab, all for about thirty German marks!'

Driving through Bulgaria, Paul Rowlands' Volvo at Stara Zagora, Bulgaria, February 1976. PR

Paul Rowlands' Fiat at the National Hotel, Belgrade, May 1975. PR

CHAPTER 14

Tricks of the Trade

Middle East drivers had to live by their wits to ensure any trips were a success so that they paid out enough money to justify all the time and effort that had gone into the enterprise. So self-interest was very important for any operators or owner drivers as they would personally benefit from what was left on the bottom line as profit if a trip had all gone to plan. But what about any employee drivers who received a standard wage packet at the end of each month?

There were opportunities for drivers to increase their basic wage by taking care to cut any costs that were incurred down to the minimum so there was some left in the pot at the end of a trip that they could keep for themselves from the running money they had been given to pay for any expenses at the beginning of a trip. This practice was well accepted in the road haulage industry, and it could be said to work well for both parties by providing an incentive to keep any expenses down to the minimum in order to make some 'profit' for a driver, while benefiting the firm also by ensuring any overspending and requests for extra funding were kept under control.

One practice that was less acceptable to employers involved delivering a return load on the way back while keeping the boss in the dark so that any cash payment went to the driver. This sort of arrangement could also occur when bringing home another driver's damaged or broken-down truck.

There was also the temptation to add a few days to a trip that a driver had made to Saudi so they could tap into the lucrative internal delivery business using their boss's truck and trailer, which he would never find out about as he was sitting in an office over 3000 miles away!

Travelling abroad put drivers under the temptation of exceeding their duty free allowance for fags and booze, and there were many hidey holes on a truck and trailer where some cartons of cigarettes and bottles of spirits could be secreted, for personal consumption, for handing out to relatives and friends, or maybe for earning some extra cash on the side!

So much for the income side of the balance sheet! Now what about the sundry expenses that drivers had to pay out in order to get the job done?

Small gifts placed in the right hands were a good way of smoothing out problems with officials, and in Eastern bloc countries, handing over music cassettes, cigarettes and biros was appreciated by those who could make life very difficult if a donation wasn't promptly forthcoming.

Importing soft porn into these socialist havens of morality was unacceptable of course, and a great deal of effort was exerted by customs officers in rooting out these debauched products of the West. Once any sleazy publications had been unearthed, they would be dutifully snatched away to be confiscated by male customs officials to safeguard and protect the innocence of the proletariat! This then alerted any drivers passing through these frontiers that any soft porn magazines, such as *Playboy* or *Penthouse*, provided a very useful commodity for exchange for any other goods or services!

In order to get over any 'problems' with paperwork at a border crossing, a few deutschmarks discreetly hidden in a batch of documents such as a passport or a carnet could soon iron out any outstanding issues.

Mark Chevalier described an occasion when he came up with a solution just as any chance of making it through a border crossing seemed to be lost for the rest of the day owing to the chief customs officer being in a right old temper as the result of a really bad hangover:

'I was coming back from Basra, and when I arrived at the Iraq/Turkey border, all the drivers I came across were petrified about making an attempt to cross over into Turkey as the chef *in charge of the customs post was so angry because of his hangover that wouldn't go away. The assumption was that any checks carried out on drivers' paperwork were going to be very rigorous because the* chef *was in such a bad temper! So I decided on a good approach to the problem by preparing a glass of Alka Seltzer that I gave him to cure his hangover. This had the desired effect, and he never forgot me from then on, which nicely smoothed my way across this same border post on many occasions.'*

Fred Hodgkins feeding fuel from the trailer belly tank to the main tractor tank. FH

This belly tank lost 1000 gallons of diesel after the two steel securing straps broke in Saudi. Luckily, the fuel bought over there was far less expensive than it would have been over here! GH

In view of the vast distances travelled, and the availability of diesel costing as little as two pence a gallon in countries like Saudi Arabia, most Middle East-bound trucks carried large belly tanks underneath the trailer to take on more cut-price fuel en route, which would then be used to top up the main fuel tanks of the truck, as and when this was required. Low prices and the availability of extra storage capacity added up to some really great savings on fuel compared to the cost of buying diesel at the time in any West European countries. It was also possible to buy and then carry a lot more fuel than was actually needed to complete a trip to the Middle East, so many drivers took the opportunity of entering into the fuel supply business by selling any surplus that they had along the way by making deals with farmers and anyone else who required any cheap diesel fuel.

Peter Bamford narrated his experiences of buying and selling diesel as he passed through Europe in the late 1980s and early 1990s:

'On the way out to the Middle East, we would buy as much fuel as we could carry in Hungary, which came in 2000-litre lots of low-tax, "red" diesel, which was bought very cheaply for only fifty pfennigs a litre. And on the way back, we would do the same by buying as much fuel as we could when travelling through Bulgaria. The going rate for diesel in that country was only about eighteen pence a litre. There was a good profit to be made selling the fuel when travelling through Yugoslavia in either direction, although this was strictly forbidden at the time of the Balkan Wars. British customs officials were appointed to stop and interview drivers along the borders to prevent this practice. But we would say we needed all of the fuel we had with us so that we could complete the journey to wherever we were going, and this was something they couldn't dispute. Later on, when we were further down the road, we would

Glen Harley running fuel from the belly tank to the main fuel tank in Greece. GH

The size of a 500-gallon belly tank is revealed on this Scania 111. MC

The National Hotel was a very popular stopover, so it was often overcrowded! COPYRIGHT UNKNOWN

sell any spare diesel we didn't need for ourselves to a pre-established dealer. I supplied to a bloke who I would meet at the National Hotel in Belgrade. Selling the fuel had always to be an "up front", strictly cash transaction. This worked to our advantage, as dishing out the fuel and collecting money from customers was the responsibility of the dealer rather than mine. The transfer of the fuel was done from the large belly tank underneath my trailer by using a hosepipe and a pump. Everyone was happy, as the sale price was whatever the going rate was at the time, which made a good profit for any of the drivers who brought the fuel into Yugoslavia! However, this happy state of affairs only lasted while the supply of fuel from the belly tank held out, as once it was all gone, the last farmer who had received nothing at all wouldn't be very pleased, as keeping his tractors going with a supply of fuel was a matter of economic survival.'

Peter was once asked to dispense fuel from a lay-by out in the middle of nowhere, although the consequences of running dry didn't bear thinking about as a riot could so easily flare up if any locals missed out when the belly tank had finally emptied!

Chris Stephenson recalled a clandestine meeting out in the Iraqi desert after he had been approached by a Filipino driver who had a very attractive proposal of offering a large supply of cheap diesel in exchange for Western currency:

'It was dark when I arrived at where I was told to go, which was somewhere near Baghdad airport. When I got there, I came across a circle of trucks which were being refuelled from this 30,000-gallon tanker wagon. It turned out that the fuel delivery in the tanker was meant for the Iraqi army base nearby, although after someone had signed to say that the fuel delivery had arrived, the tanker and its load of fuel were whisked away. The diesel was then sold to the truck drivers who'd arrived at the pre-arranged rendezvous out in the middle of nowhere. After I had paid the Filipino for the diesel that topped up my tanks, he asked me if I had any carbon paper, so I gave him some pieces.

National Hotel Belgrade car park. COPYRIGHT UNKNOWN

He explained that by wrapping any money he sent home in carbon paper, the bank notes wouldn't be spotted by the customs officers.'

Finding your way through a major city with few and usually indecipherable road signs in Arabic or Farsi script and Arabic numerals was a particularly refined form of torture, set against a backdrop of local drivers taking scant notice of any instructions or rights of way, which any European drivers may have felt obliged to comply with simply as a matter of course. David Miller described his solution for finding the way through a scene of absolute mayhem and confusion:

'I remember that getting through the city of Baghdad in Iraq was a nightmare. However, I learnt a neat new trick which involved stopping a taxi and asking the driver if he would show me the way to wherever I was going, or the way out of town if that was where I was going, for which he would be paid. This always worked, although you had to remember to give the taxi driver half of the agreed payment before starting out, and you would only pay him the remainder of the agreed money when the job had been done!'

Paying the fee for road tax in Britain didn't seem to be fair at all when a truck was abroad on delivery runs to the Middle East for most of the time. It was only necessary for these trucks to be road taxed when they were making the comparatively short journeys from and to the ports in the UK, so solutions were needed to cut down on what was seen as an unnecessary expense.

Some operators decided to operate their trucks from ports on the far side of the English Channel to avoid paying road tax duty, while defiantly leaving an expired tax disc on display in the windscreen! These British, but now foreign-based, untaxed trucks, would then be coupled to trailers that had arrived by ferryboat from the UK, with the trailers laden with goods bound for the Middle East. The trailers were classed as 'unaccompanied' in that they were loaded on and off the ferries using shipping company tractor tugs.

According to the UK vehicle tax duty laws, it was possible to tax an HGV truck at the same rate as a car at one time, which significantly reduced the amount of duty that had to be paid. This was with the proviso that the truck would not be used for towing a trailer or carrying loads for hire or reward, by which was meant, carrying goods as a commercial enterprise for which payment would be made. So the answer was to send the tractor unit down to the South Coast on its own, with the loaded trailer it was to carry then arriving separately at the same port after being towed by another tractor unit, which was fully taxed as an HGV vehicle. The trailer would then be swapped over to the other truck before this passed through customs control on its way to the Middle East. This process would then be repeated, but in reverse, at the end of a trip.

Les Higgins counted himself lucky after he came across someone who perhaps should have made a fortune as an accountant as he was so good at working out foreign exchange rates to their advantage. This was something Les hadn't anticipated at first owing to the other guy's awkward, geeky appearance:

'I got to know this kid who looked to me rather like a beatnik, but at the same he was wearing the same sort of glasses Eric Morecambe, the comedian on the telly, once wore, which made him look a bit gormless. I met him on the train which carried our trucks across Germany from Cologne towards Munich when we couldn't get permits to drive our trucks on German roads. Despite what he looked like, I learnt to appreciate that this was a really bright lad. I travelled with him a good long way on that trip, and at each of the borders along the way, he would manage to change some money for the both of us at a most favourable rate, as he always knew who to talk to when the time came to change some money, so we were well made up.'

In more remote, wilder parts of Turkey there were occasions when arguments or insults would flare up between drivers and locals for no apparent reason. And when firearms were drawn in a life-threatening manner, it was really time to watch out, as David Miller once experienced, although he was glad the friend he had with him knew how to react in such situations. This was the result of many years acquiring some very advanced military training and battle experience as a member of a famous and select body of fighting men:

'Kenny Searle was the hardest man that I ever met; Kenny had been in the Regiment, the Special Air Services, before he became a Middle East driver, and how this showed on one particular occasion! We'd decided to park up one night in central Turkey, and we were having a beer at a roadside bar when one of the locals suddenly took a dislike to us for an unknown reason, and he pulled out a gun and began waving it at us. So I froze, almost making a nasty mess in my trousers. But Kenny was not someone to be bothered at all by this sort of situation or behaviour. He slowly got up and calmly walked over to the man and took the gun away from him, as gently as you might take a glass from a drunk who was in danger of dropping it on the floor. Kenny

then went outside the bar to where a stream ran underneath the road, where he threw the gun into the water. After he sat down with me at the table again, I remarked on his sang froid in daring to take away the man's gun. He then told me he'd observed that the man who was holding the gun hadn't removed the safety catch. So we weren't in as much danger as I had originally thought. I guess you need a special kind of training to notice an important detail like that.'

Flattery is supposed to get you anywhere, and this well-known saying was one John Buffham remembered to his considerable advantage one day at a border crossing when he noticed the slow, casual way that other drivers' passports were checked over, as this could only result in significant delays before these were processed, stamped and handed back to their owners:

'The customs man was chucking all these passports through a little window so the documents passed from the one room to the next. This didn't look good, so to avoid any delay in processing my own passport, I went through a door into the other room where I got into conversation with the bloke whose job it was to check over the passports. I then dropped this into the conversation: "My word, you speak very good English." He was so flattered, he immediately did what was necessary with my passport and handed it back to me while all the other passports remained piled up high on his desk. So off I went … !'

Had the customs man paid a bit more attention to John's passport, he might have noticed something was seriously amiss with the document that had been given to him to inspect. The reason for this was that John had always been concerned that his passport may have been lost or stolen after he had handed this over and watched it disappear into a back office. What chance was there of obtaining a copy passport from a British Embassy in less than a week or so if you were hundreds of miles away! So in answer to what was becoming a reoccurring fear, John came up with an ingenious solution: he always carried a second passport wherever he went, which had in fact expired, although this was presented time after time at border crossings without the deception being noticed. All the while, John's current passport remained safely tucked away in his coat pocket. And if a customs official had noticed the expiry date had been exceeded, all he had to do was make an apology and hand over the up-to-date passport!

Talking to other drivers was often a good way of getting out of a tight spot. Paul Rowlands once reached the Turkish border at Kapıkule only to be told he couldn't take his truck with its load any farther as he needed to obtain a new carnet before he could proceed and make his delivery in Antalya. The old one was still in credit, although it wouldn't have been by the time he had finished his delivery and returned back to the same border on his way out of the country. As it would have taken ten days to obtain a new carnet from the UK, Paul spent the next few days playing football with the Turkish border guards while he awaited the arrival of the new carnet. However, a White Trux driver then advised Paul he could get his original carnet re-dated and signed for if he visited the offices of the Turkish Automobile and Touring Club in Istanbul. After a 500-mile round taxi trip from the border to Istanbul and back, Paul was on his way again! The lesson to be learned from this situation was that it paid to ask around and establish whether anyone had the know-how to resolve any tricky situations such as this!

Searching out valuable information for both present and future use became second nature to drivers as a way of helping them on their way; this source of information was something that Ian Taylor always tried to latch on to and make good use of after arriving somewhere at the end of a day's run:

'After reaching Turkey, I would head off to the Mocamp in Istanbul, as stopping there was really useful for talking to those drivers who were coming back from any Middle East destinations, as they would tell you what was happening on the route ahead. This worked both ways of course, as you would tell them about all that you'd experienced coming in the other direction from Europe. This sort of chat would concern issues such as any closed borders, or even the state of affairs if a war had been declared, as affected me later on when I made a trip to Iraq. So by stopping to ask some useful questions, I was always well prepared for whatever was going on somewhere ahead of me out there!'

Managing and controlling the expenditure of the running money was as important as the main task of delivering the load safely and keeping the truck on the road, and making sure that enough money was handed out at the beginning of a trip to accomplish all that was required was most important, as Graham Cartmail explained:

'Jenkinson's was a good firm to work for, you always got all the money and any agency cards that were needed to do the job before setting off on your way. From their point of view, this meant there was every chance you would manage

to get yourself and the wagon there and back with it still being in one piece, as well as receiving any payment that was due for completing the delivery. Drivers working for some of the other firms seemed to have nowhere near as much running money as we had to take with us each trip. Some would end up having to pinch things that they could sell, or if necessary, use for themselves, such as fuel or spare parts, so that they could simply get by.'

Carrying a large amount of cash on your person or in the truck's cab could also then be a matter of concern, as Graham went on to explain:

'The locals knew you were carrying a lot of money with you. My wages were about £150 a week at the time, which was a lot of money in those days, but by comparison, I would be carrying up to £2000 in running money along with me. Those guys out there, guarding their sheep and sitting out in the middle of the countryside and carrying a rifle in their hands, they wouldn't get to see that kind of money in ten years or more, if not a whole lifetime in some cases. So it wasn't a good situation. If you broke down, then you wouldn't dare keep all of the money in just one place in case it was stolen. Every transaction for truck repairs, or anything else for that matter, was like bargaining for something that you wanted to buy in an oriental bazaar. This could take ages! You would never let them see how much you were carrying in your wallet, as seeing a couple of thousand pounds would soon increase the price of whatever it was you needed. You would first of all estimate the probable cost, and then, and only then, would you take the required amount with you,

Trucks loaded at Cologne for the trip across Germany to Ludwigsburg. IT

so you would now be in a better bargaining position so you wouldn't end up paying too much.'

The need to carry so much cash was compounded by agency fuel cards only being accepted within Western Europe in those days, and of course ATM cash dispensers had only started to catch on by the late seventies.

Knowing what type of cash resources to take with you was also an important concern for drivers like Graham:

'I would set off with a load of traveller's cheques Jenkinson's had given to me, but these were no use after you had left Germany behind, as everyone wanted sterling, deutschmarks or US dollars – hard currency – not Midland Bank traveller's cheques. So I would change all the traveller's cheques for cash before leaving Germany. Deutschmarks were the best for getting you out of trouble in Bulgaria or Turkey. The simple fact was that I knew the score about money a lot better than they did back at Jenkinson's offices in Salford.'

Middle East drivers had to be good at working out canny solutions to whatever problems or dilemmas fate seemed to throw at them, although there was always the possibility that the solution they came up with wasn't going to work as they had previously hoped. So they would then have to become resourceful once more by coming up with a new solution to resolve any outstanding difficulties, thereby allowing them to be on their way again in the shortest possible time.

Taking a shortcut by using a ferry – Robert-Dods-Brown's Scania 140 in Greece on the way to Kuwait. RDB

Unloading ro-ro ship after travelling from Greece to Syria. MD

Third from the left, Gordon Summers receives instructions from an agent when working for DJ McIntosh of Arbroath. GS

CHAPTER 15

Life on the Road

The life of a Middle East lorry driver involved a lot of time spent cooped up in a cab, and this could be tough on both the nerves and the physical constitution after a while. Consequently, there was a need to look after himself by allowing sufficient time to rest and recover from all those hours behind a steering wheel assumed some degree of importance.

Taking enough leisure time off was essential to a driver's welfare, and in view of the job being such a solitary occupation, the first priority often involved finding someone they could share a conversation with, and preferably in a language that both parties could understand! Those of the same nationality would be preferred, although just about anyone would do after spending enough time in not so splendid isolation in the middle of nowhere!

So drivers would seek out the company of others by the normal means of socialising in wayside bars, cafés and restaurants. Friendships were often forged in minutes out of expediency as a way of compensating for the lack of contact with families and friends they had left many miles away in the UK.

Those of a more individualistic frame of mind often took the opportunity of developing new interests in the history and the culture of the unfamiliar, exotic countries they passed through on the way to their final destinations. Touring the world as seen through a truck's windscreen so to speak; with the opportunity to stop at will and wander around the many historic sites which they came across on the way, such as taking a stroll to see the Crusader castles to be found in Syria for example, or the fabulous Topkapı Palace that overlooks the waters of the Bosphorus in Istanbul.

Reading books, getting a tan or taking a swim in a hotel swimming pool were some of the other ways of recharging the soul's batteries. Each to their own as they say!

Perhaps next on the list of what drivers missed out on were a few home comforts relating to the basic needs of sleeping and eating.

Spending a night dossing down in the cab was accepted by most drivers as something that came with the job, which wasn't too bad providing your truck had a sleeper cab, as trying to snatch a decent kip when stretched across the driver's and passenger's seats was none too comfortable.

No doubt many did have a flutter at casinos, and learnt to regret a night when a good deal of their running money disappeared! DB

Alan Clayton receiving a beard trim and haircut from a mobile barber, money changer and Mr Fixit in Syria. MD

Istanbul skyline at night. The backdrop to one of the most exciting cities in the world. DB

The late sixties saw many design feature improvements introduced in the truck manufacturing industry that were hailed as great advances in driver comfort as well as safety. Volvo and Scania spearheaded this trend, which proved to be a smart move, as these firms scooped up many new truck sales. The sort of cab improvements that particularly appealed to the Middle East hauliers and drivers made life a lot comfier, with bunk beds, and innovations such as air-conditioning, night heaters, a fridge and also a cooker as an alternative to fiddling about with a Calor Gas stove.

Negotiating the narrow streets of Istanbul. UC

It was now possible to have a good night's sleep in the bunk bed of the cab, although a hotel bed and the opportunity to take a shower before having a night out with some mates allowed someone to step away from the job for a while, and as Istanbul represented the halfway mark for both outward-bound or inward-bound journeys, this was a most favoured place to stop over for one or maybe a couple of nights while soaking up the unique atmosphere of this famous city.

On the way into Istanbul, the first overnight stopping place to consider was the Londra Camping establishment, aka the Mocamp, which achieved legendary status in the memory of those who drove the

Nightime view of ferries crossing the Bosphorus. DB

Mike Dunstan's Scania when he was taking the morning off to do some sightseeing at the ancient city of Troy. MD

Ken Ward making his lunch with a cooker inside his locker box. KW

Middle East run. This was where every driver would have stopped at least once to make use of the motel or camping accommodation in an establishment that was pleasantly modern and to European standards for the times. First opened in 1964, the Mocamp had benefited from many improvements by the time its heyday arrived in the mid-1970s when so many TIR trucks passed by its front door travelling east and west, with as many as 200 parked up at any one time.

On arrival, drivers would have to surrender their passports as a form of guarantee they would pay whatever charges fell due before continuing on with their journey. And in the meantime, this was a home from home where they could enjoy sitting round the bar with some newly found mates, drinking a good few pints of the locally brewed Efes lager. Showers and a swimming pool were provided, and after a relaxing day or so, drivers would climb into their cabs feeling pleasantly refreshed for the long drive ahead of them.

The Mocamp had plenty of parking spaces for trucks where servicing and repair was often carried out by the drivers if this was needed. The place always had a multinational flavour, as with four or five drivers sitting round a table, the conversation would drift in and out of the same number of languages, as everyone did the best to make what they had to say understood by the majority of those in attendance!

The driver of this DAF 2800 was most probably taking a kip in the cab after a long day's drive. RW

Ken Shaw and Keith Tabernacle hiding from the sun making breakfast. RR

As an alternative to stopping over at the Mocamp, a night spent at the Harem Hotel on the opposite side of the Bosphorus was also an attractive proposition. This required the will and the nerve to battle on with a truck through Istanbul's fearsome traffic first of all. A field of open combat where ancient trams, battered American taxi cabs, *dolmuş* buses, and horses and overloaded carts jockeyed for position and the right of way, and the devil take the hindmost when it came to making any consideration for pedestrians who were attempting to cross the road!

Everywhere along the kerbsides, porters who were known as *hamals* could be seen carrying impossibly huge loads on their backs like beasts of burden, a reminder to any TIR drivers that some jobs were far worse than the ones they had!

To reach the far shore of the Bosphorus, TIR trucks were driven up the gangplanks of the drive-on/drive-off ferries that took them to the Harem landing on the east shore. This was an opportunity to enjoy the awe-inspiring panorama of the city skyline while enjoying a glass of sugary tea – *çay* – that was served by waiters, and during the 15-minute or so crossing, they could take in the city's architectural splendours while at the same time observing the cavalcade of ships from many ports of origin that plied a sedate course between the open waters of the Mediterranean and the Black Sea.

After arriving on the Asian shore, drivers would park their trucks on the waterfront and then wander over to check in at the Harem Hotel, carrying the *de rigueur* briefcases that were so popular at the time with almost every Middle East driver as somewhere safe to store their passport and all the important documents that were essential to the success of a trip.

Stepping out of the hotel and then meandering down to the waterfront afforded magnificent views towards the Topkapı Palace, which was the seat of a reigning sultan's omnipotent authority for hundreds of years when the Ottoman Empire ruled over vast areas of Asia Minor, Europe and North Africa. Exploring the famous Sultanahmet area where the Blue Mosque and the Byzantine church of Aya Sofia are situated, involved a return ferry ride across the Bosphorus on one of the old-fashioned ferry boats that chugged back and forth from

Two British MAN trucks roll across the seemingly endless steppe lands of Anatolia. RW

Paul Rowlands, belly dancing night at Londra Camping. PR

Paul Rowlands and Micky Prigg wearing leather jerkins and enjoying a few drinks with mates. PR

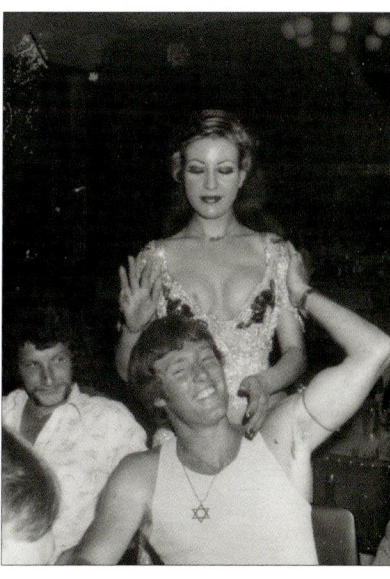

Once again, Paul Rowlands relishing the cultural values of travelling abroad! PR

Paul Rowlands, Micky Prigg and others, also 'One Eye', a popular hostess at the infamous West Berlin Night Club. PR

The en route destination that promised some quality rest and recreation! DB

Paul Rowlands, Londra Camping. PR

Paul Rowlands and Brian Wales, Londra Camping. PR

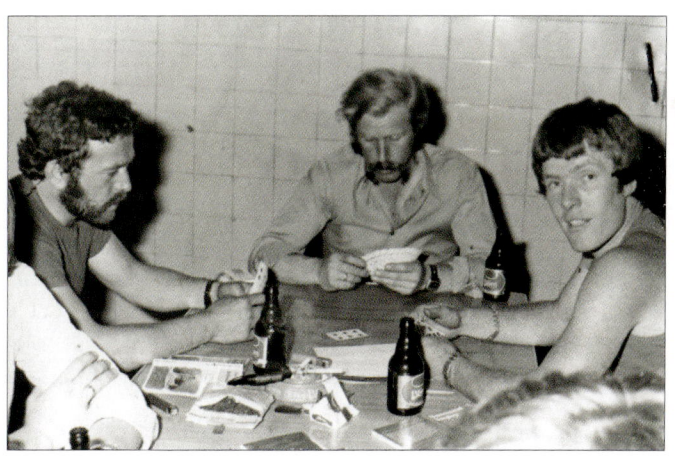

'Sonny', a Frenchman Henk Dutchman, and Paul Rowlands, playing cards, Londra Camping. PR

Ron Slater doing the cooking at the Londra Mocamp. MM

The Pudding Shop, or 'La La' Restaurant, a favourite gathering place for hippies, overlanders and truck drivers. COPYRIGHT UNKNOWN

shore to shore. These small ships provided a reminder of home, as the plaque on each wheelhouse proudly detailed the name of the shipbuilder that built these vessels on the Clyde in Scotland during the 1920s.

After arriving back on the western shore at the Galata Bridge landing, the day was then free to explore the ancient covered Grand Bazaar in the historic Sultanahmet region – a must-see attraction for those who wanted to buy some souvenirs to take home, such as jewellery, pottery, or more ambitiously, oriental carpets and rugs. One story that seems to have been endlessly circulated among Middle East drivers was that antique Colt revolvers dating to the Crimean War could be bought at the Grand Bazaar, although this never appeared to be substantiated by someone actually buying one of these guns to take home with them! Likewise for 'real' gold trinkets, the purchase of which led to an unpleasant surprise as well as a few curses about the integrity of certain bazaar traders when these items were valued by reputable jewellers back in the UK!

Graham Cartmail always took time off to visit the covered bazaar when he stopped over in Istanbul at the Harem Hotel and one of his most pleasurable experiences involved visiting a traditional bath house found in Istanbul and elsewhere in Turkey, known as a *hammam*. Graham always found the process of being scrubbed so clean by a masseuse to be an effective means of getting rid of all the ingrained grime and dust that had accumulated over so many gruelling miles during the intensely hot summer months.

The Pudding Shop café in the Sultanahmet region is still in business today and can be found beside the site of the ancient hippodrome where the Romans held dramatic horse races. This café-cum-restaurant that has always been famous for its confectionary was a popular venue and meeting point for truck drivers although the majority of the customers comprised a multi-national clientele of laid-back, young hippies, who arrived here from all points of the globe. Many of them were on

View of the Bosphorus from the east bank near the Harem Hotel. RW

their way to India in search of what was loosely termed spiritual enlightenment at the feet of a guru, which was something that these youngsters aspired to at the time. There were also the more down-to-earth backpackers, who roamed about the world to satisfy their spirit of adventure, which was something many Middle East drivers could identify with! The more daring of them travelled all the way from Europe to Australia, in one direction or the other! The Pudding Shop was also a meeting point and informal booking office for any travellers who wanted to book tickets for the overland buses, such as the well-known 'Magic Bus' which headed off eastwards to far distant destinations in Iran and further on through Afghanistan, Pakistan and then into India as the final destination for this rickety old bus.

David Miller reported he always made a point of dropping into the Pudding Shop each time he passed by, not least because of the attractive female company to be found here:

'The wonderful Top Deck travel company used elderly double-deck buses with the roofs sawn off to follow the hippie trail all the way to Kathmandu in the Himalayas. The drivers were all "volunteers" from Oz or New Zealand and the buses were only good for about twenty-eight miles an hour. But on the plus side they would always be bringing along some very pretty passengers who were easy to meet and chat with when you visited the Pudding Shop in Istanbul.'

For those hippies and travellers who couldn't afford a bus ticket to follow the well-worn overland trek to India, a notice board was provided on one of the walls at the Pudding Shop where a lift could be requested while sharing running costs, or by prior agreements of a different kind. In the case of some females travelling back to Europe, what was on offer by way of 'personal services' was explicitly detailed without need for further explanation!

Drivers would also meet up with many other travellers along the way out East, this being the era when aged Land Rovers, VW campers and battered Bedford CA vans could be seen struggling eastwards at slow speeds, as many of these vehicles were clearly on the point of mechanical collapse.

Sleeping out on your own at a lonely spot by the roadside could expose drivers to serious danger, as Gerry Holmes underlined with the following graphic account of what could go wrong, an experience that regretfully has been shared by many other drivers over the years:

'I didn't like stopping out on my own in the middle of nowhere and I would always try to pull in for the night whenever I came across a British bloke who had already stopped his truck for the same reason, as this was someone I could then talk to and maybe we could help each other out if anything went wrong later on. One night when I was parked up on my own, I was woken up in the middle of the night as the cab on my truck had started rocking from side to side. I'd left the skylight open to let in some cool air due to all the heat which had built up during the day. And when I looked up at the open skylight, I noticed a rag that smelt strongly of chemicals was being slowly lowered towards my face. I instantly grabbed the rag and caught hold of it. As I already suspected, this had been soaked through with chloroform so that I would have fallen into a much deeper sleep than I was previously experiencing. The objective of the bloke who was on top of my cab was to rob my cab of anything valuable. So I took immediate action by dropping the rag on the floor and starting my truck's motor up so I could drive away from the scene of this attempted robbery as fast I could. This caused the guy on the roof to lose his footing so he would have fallen all the way to the ground as I moved away. For all I know to this day I could have run over him over with my trailer. Not that this would have bothered me, I could not have cared less in view of what he had been up to!'

There was a big surprise in store for Mark Chevalier when he stopped overnight at the Salang Hotel in Herat, Afghanistan. It was still very hot by the time dusk settled over the landscape, but Mark turned down the offer of a hotel room and made his preparations to sleep in the open air on a bed that the staff laid out for him in the hotel garden. It looked as if Mark was about to enjoy a pleasant night's sleep under the firmament of the stars, or at least he would have done had he not woken from his slumbers in terror:

'Out of the dark, the tame pelican which lived all the time in the hotel grounds had come along and grabbed me by the arm. It wasn't so much the bird's grasping beak that I found to be so threatening – that wasn't so bad at all – what was so awful was the terrible smell of the pelican's foul breath!'

Keith Burson grew up as a country boy so he was most perplexed to hear some familiar farmyard sounds when he was stopping in a hotel in one of the world's largest cities.

Breakfast time for Alan Clayton who worked alongside Mike Dunstan with Butrako and Radclive. MD

one problem: he didn't have a clue how to order a fry-up of bacon and eggs because he didn't have a grasp of the local Serbo-Croat language:

'I was accompanied by a bloke called Derek Goddard, and we decided the only way we could get the message across on what we wanted to eat was to make some farmyard noises that should then indicate that we wanted to eat some bacon and eggs. So we started off by grunting like a pig, and then we made some clucking hen noises which finally managed to get the message across on what we wanted for breakfast.'

Paul Rowlands has fond memories of a brand of Turkish beer which was noted for its smooth, thirst-quenching flavour, and also as the perfect complement to kebabs or any other classic eastern meal:

'I always had a good time at the Mocamp when we would drink the local brand of Efes; this was the only worthwhile beer to drink. I was recently surprised many years later to find Efes on sale in UK supermarkets.'

Excessive drinking was something Brian Robertson always tried to avoid as he had noticed drinking too much booze was all too often the cause of mistakes which could make a mess of even the best pre-planned trip:

'I never drank all that much at the Mocamp, but some drivers would be paralytic for the whole time they remained there. I would sit and have a drink, but this was purely as a form of entertainment so I could socialise. Many people lost an awful lot of their driving time through drinking far too much.'

'We used to stop over in Istanbul for the weekend at the Harem Hotel on the waterfront by the Bosphorus. This was a more civilised stay in our opinion than if we had decided to stop overnight at the Londra Mocamp. After we'd booked in, I heard the sound of bleating sheep somewhere close by even though we were in the middle of Istanbul! My mates said I was hearing things when I told them about what I'd heard, but next morning, just as we were leaving the hotel, we all heard the unmistakable sound of sheep bleating away somewhere at the back of the hotel. So we went to take a look and a couple of sheep were tied beside the hotel's kitchen door. These would have been slaughtered for the pot later that day!'

The service area and café on the road between Zagreb and Belgrade which was known as The Trees was one of Keith's favourite eating places since he first pulled over in response to the enticing smell of cooking bacon reaching his appreciative nostrils. There was only

Breaking for lunch while servicing a Chevalier Brothers MAN at a border crossing. MC

Chow down time for Mike Dunstan after parking up his Butrako Transconti. MD

Dave Tickle's well-organised locker box. DT

Les Higgins recalled suffering the side effects of eating something he should have recognised as rather suspect due to the poor conditions where the food was prepared:

'We stopped at a tin shack café in Jordan and I ordered a meal of lamb and rice. First of all, the cook knocked all the flies off a piece of meat that had been left hanging from a hook outside in the open. So I should have known better than to accept any meat that had been covered with lots of flies swarming all over it! But I didn't on this occasion, and as a consequence, I had the runs by the following morning. I reached the point where I needed to take a very urgent toilet break: there was no way I could wait any longer. Even though the floor of an outside squatter toilet was soiled from the toilet hole to the open doorway, there was no alternative, I simply had to go! This involved paddling through a real mess that flooded the floor before I reached the squatter toilet! What made the situation worse when I came out was that someone turned on a hose and sluiced the toilet floor so it was clean again! My running mates were laughing their heads off at me when I came out of the toilet with my shoes in such a state. If only I could have waited for just a bit longer!'

On a further occasion Les and Graham stopped at another café where they sat down to eat without taking in at first that this wasn't such a good idea, as Les went on to explain:

'We had been travelling across open desert when we came upon this place that Graham had told me was just like Charnock Richard services, but it wasn't at all. There was a terrible stench from a dead donkey that was rotting away outside the café. But we went in anyway, where we came across some local Arab gentlemen who were smoking hubble-bubble pipes. This wasn't like any motorway service station I'd ever been to! But Graham had said the cuisine here was excellent, so we sat down to eat. After our meal arrived, we noticed the walls and ceiling were covered by a mass of flies. So Graham asked the chef to turn on the overhead ceiling fans, but as the fan blades started turning, this dislodged

Desert cafe in Iraq. GS

a shower of flies that landed all over our food like lots and lots of little black currants! We hadn't noticed before that all these flies had died long ago!'

Eating at ropey establishments most certainly had its risks for those whose palates and stomachs had yet to be tutored in the exotic ways of the local cuisine. For this reason serving up the homely delights of what was known as 'camion stew' was a popular alternative, particularly with British drivers, for whom cooking was a bit of a mystery until they bit the bullet and bought a can opener at the same time as a cross-section of Heinz's more popular products, with their baked beans often considered to be the favourite addition to drivers' culinary concoctions. The contents of the cans would then be heated up over a small Calor Gas stove, this activity often being of a communal nature as others came along and joined in by donating tins of baked beans, corned beef, spaghetti hoops, or whatever else fell to hand into the pot. The trusty can opener coming out once more to open tins of fruit and rice pudding which were the finale to this delicately prepared, gourmet repast. Other nationalities looked on with ill-concealed horror!

This driver's trying out some exercise on the bumper of his DAF. GB

After everyone had taken care of their stomachs, the evening's entertainment usually followed a well-worn path of recounting old stories about trips that went wrong for whatever reason; competitive bouts of arguing, leg-pulling and joshing; putting the world to rights; or getting genned up on the road conditions further on from drivers who had already passed that way. Games of footie were also very popular, ideally against those of another nationality, adding an international flavour to the proceedings. Playing card games was also a good way of whiling away a few hours, an ideal pastime for drivers when they were holed up in a snowstorm or sitting out the hours waiting to get through a border crossing.

Peter Bamford became aware that quite a few drivers shared his interest in developing their musical skills, so improvised jamming sessions would take place in a roadside bar or around a crackling campfire:

'Quite a lot of us became accomplished musicians, and I started to play a keyboard myself to while away the hours. We would meet up and after preparing and

The driver of a DAF and the driver of the Carmans' Transcontinental share a washing line. COPYRIGHT UNKNOWN

eating plates of camion stew we would start to play our music with whatever instruments we had brought along with us. One of those who took part was so skilled at playing the guitar you could just shut your eyes and think you were listening to Eric Clapton.'

Any possibility of practising and forming a musical ensemble was limited though, as Peter pointed out with the following observation:

'Of those you met along the way, you never got to know their names. Maybe you would travel together for a while so that you became friendly with them, but you might not ever see them again. It was rather like ships that pass by each other in the night.'

Gerry Holmes recalled an evening spent somewhere out on the road when everyone clubbed together to make some improvised entertainment:

'We were all singing that familiar song "Midnight at the Oasis", but with a reworking of the words so they referred to putting your "Scammell" to bed rather than a "camel" – as in the original version. We had joined in to make a communal meal of camion stew which involved everyone coming along and chucking something or other into the pot. After this had been eaten we decided to hold a spiritualist session as someone had brought along an ouija board with them. After asking a lot of silly questions, and a lot of cheating, with the glass pushed in certain directions to spell out the answer which one of us had already decided on, someone came up with a question that was impossible for us ever to predict what the answer should be. We asked the ouija board to tell us the name of the wife of the next British driver who happened to pull over and stop here overnight. The moving glass then spelt out the name "Mary" on the ouija board and after we'd waited for a while, a British driver did pull in where we'd all parked. Much to his surprise, we asked him the name of his wife, to which he replied "Sheila", which was disappointing for all of us of course, as this wasn't the answer we wanted. But after questioning this driver more closely, it turned out that he wasn't actually married to the woman he called Sheila, although he had been married to a women for twenty-five years who had the name Mary! So what a coincidence that was!'

Delays when unloading could be a source of justifiable annoyance, although patience was always a virtue, and rather than getting hot and bothered under the collar, Brian Robertson always tried to make the best of the situation when he was waiting for the last of the customers to sign off any deliveries from a mixed groupage load:

Gordon Pearce sensibly taking some time off to soak up the sunshine! HL

'After arriving at the Abu Ghraib customs facility outside Baghdad, together with some other drivers, we would all go to a nearby lake called Lake Habbaniya taking along ice boxes that contained cold drinks, having a barbecue and reading the books we had brought with us, which we then swapped around after we had read them.'

Christmas was the one special time of year when drivers wanted to make it home so they could join in the festivities with their family and friends, although getting back to the UK in time was not always possible. Graham Cartmail spent two Christmases far from home, and he recalled one occasion when he realised that he didn't have any provisions to make Christmas dinner, or at least he thought so until he suddenly remembered what the load in his refrigerated trailer contained:

'I was stuck on the Jordan/Saudi border with this other driver who worked for Radcliffe Roadways of Nottingham, although I can't remember what his name was. We were carrying loads and loads of different types of frozen food, and after I had watched the customs men removing the seals so they could inspect what I was carrying within my load, they went away again for a while. So before they came back and resealed the refrigerated trailer, I opened up the back doors again and we helped ourselves to some of the boxes of frozen food. Our Christmas lunch that we put together was of good helpings of duck with lots of frozen chips that we fried up; I remember this went down really well!'

Gordon Summers remembered one Christmas Eve when the nearby presence of the Holy Land set him thinking on the meaning of the festive season in a way he had not really considered before this particular occasion:

'I had joined up with a convoy of trucks which was passing through Jordan on Christmas Eve, and we had parked up for the night somewhere outside the capital of Amman. This was at a crossroads where there was a signpost pointing towards Bethlehem in one direction. There was a Jordanian soldier who was travelling along with our convoy, and he came up to me and said, "As you and I are the only Christians out here, do you mind if I share some wine with you so we can celebrate Christmas?" So I then said to him by way of a reply, "Only if you share some of my whisky with me," and I went to bed at least half-cut on that memorable Christmas Eve night.'

Paul Rowlands provided an account of a night which could have turned out rather ugly in view of the sensitivity of some of the locals when he went with a mate to a nightclub in Turkey that had belly-dancers as the star attraction every night:

'After meeting up with this French guy called "Sunny" at Kapıkule on the Turkish border, someone I knew from previous trips, we decided to take a taxi to Edirne to spend time in a nightclub that was in the city centre. After arriving there, we asked the taxi driver if he would come along also before he took us back to the border where our trucks had been parked up for the night. After the belly-dancing act had started, we really got quite into this, so we began stuffing the top of one of the belly-dancing girls' bra with lots of paper money. However, our driver soon noticed this activity of ours wasn't going down at all well with the local men who were also watching the show, so it was time to get going before there was any serious trouble!'

Misunderstandings could occur anywhere when it came to a matter of honour and Les Higgins recalled visiting a village in Czechoslovakia where a wedding party was in progress when he arrived with some someone he had met along the way who went by the nickname 'Black Joe':

'We decided to stop for the night and we met up with this wedding party in what looked to us like a pub. So we had a few drinks and then there was a whip-round for the new bride. We handed over a hundred marks, which would have been a lot of money to them. But things then started turning rather nasty, as the amount of cash we had handed over suggested a transaction of quite a different kind! Luckily, the situation was soon explained and it was resolved, and by the end of the night, everyone was shaking hands with one another!'

Taking someone along with you could be a worthy distraction that alleviated the boredom of spending so much time on your own when travelling solo. But this could backfire quite badly, as Alan Dayson discovered after he agreed to take along a reporter all the way to Saudi so that a report on the trip could be prepared for a local newspaper. After arriving at Riyadh airport to make a delivery, the reporter displayed breathtaking naivety by climbing on top of Alan's truck and taking some photos of any aircraft that could be seen taking off and landing. Alan and the journalist were subsequently arrested and hauled off to jail where they were interrogated and accused of engaging in spying for an unspecified foreign power! After finally convincing their interrogators that all was not as it might seem, they were free, although Alan was left wondering about the consequences had things then gone from bad to much worse!

Keith Burson had the following comment to make on the controversial topic of letting any strangers ride along with him in the cab:

'A couple offered me £1000 to take them from Baghdad to the UK, which was a lot of money in those days, but I refused as I didn't want to find myself in any trouble, as you would never know what they were carrying with them or why they had to get out of the country.'

Camping compound at Saveh Road, Tehran, that was shared with many Aussie backpackers, hippies, etc. FT

Some drivers could be seen driving along and sharing their cab with one or more pretty hippie chicks who had hitched a ride. But Martyn Moulsdale took the view that any backpackers or hippies who may have already travelled through the opium poppy growing regions of Afghanistan may have had a stash of drugs concealed about their person or hidden in their luggage. Or worse still, they may have decided to mask their own involvement in smuggling drugs by hiding these somewhere on the truck, so if found at a border, the driver would be held to blame! Carrying just a small amount of hashish in Turkey during the seventies attracted a three-year sentence if you were caught, and ten years for intent to supply!

Brian Robertson had a more relaxed attitude to taking along a passenger on one occasion when he took pity on a stranded female traveller:

'At that time in the seventies, all the kids were going to India to see the gurus and to "find themselves" and what not, and on one trip I made to Tehran, the embassy sent this girl who was stranded along to the Davies Turner yard as she had run out of money and needed to get home somehow. So I took her along with me all the way back to England, where her dad met her. He was a chief constable or something high up in a police force somewhere, and he was most grateful that I had brought his daughter all that way home.'

Ted Hannant, a professional signwriter as well as a driver, filling in some time with useful work. RR

CHAPTER 16

Camaraderie

As true professionals, truck drivers have always tended to regard themselves as Knights of the Road, represented by helping each other out by the side of the road if there was a breakdown or problem of another kind. So bearing in mind the immense distances to places such as Tehran and Doha, and taking account of the scarcity of recovery and repair facilities when so far away from Western Europe, this unwritten code of honour assumed far more importance for those who travelled any Middle East routes.

Stopping to assist another driver following a breakdown, accident or any other dire emergency could take up quite a lot of valuable time with the upshot that the completion of their trip was delayed. However, this was often viewed as not being an issue worthy of any further consideration. Such thoughts were dismissed by the sobering realisation that anyone could become stranded out in the middle of nowhere with no-one to call on for assistance! So the immediate response was to haul on the brakes and find out how they could assist and resolve the problem! Helping each other out became the unwritten law that should never be broken, and if anyone flew past a broken-down truck, then the driver's conscience would hold him accountable for a long while if he didn't turn his truck round at the first opportunity and retrace his steps so he could assist in any way possible.

Reflecting the multinational aspect of the job in hand, coming forward with a spontaneous offer of help was something which had little to do with clubbing together on the basis of a driver's nationality, or a truck's national registration plates.

The term 'camaraderie' that Middle East drivers all adopted, underlined the will to help each other out with issues such as vehicle repairs and other kinds of emergency, as well as the difficulties in dealing with officialdom. In a more general sense, camaraderie also described 'mucking in' and exhibiting a willingness to help out and share any basic chores, such as cooking meals or helping another driver out with their paperwork if they were in a muddle! It also covered doing one's best to sustain others' morale, whether the situation in question was good, bad or indifferent, with a few jokes and funny stories to lift everyone's spirits!

Getting together with a number of like-minded souls provided much needed relief after spending all those hours driving alone, and in response to this important human requirement, loose social gatherings would form at any stopping places as the day drew to a close. These would be groupings of individuals that may or may not reform further down the road, sometimes retaining a fair number of the original participants at the next stop, or more likely with a few members dropping out, and then some new arrivals joining in for the night's entertainment.

These informal get-togethers allowed for everyone to have a laugh after gathering round a roaring campfire, maybe having a singsong or sharing stories of previous journeys that went well or badly, or telling jokes and tall stories which frequently rebounded on the storyteller! What better way of filling the long waits that occurred at border crossings where a queue of trucks waiting to cross a frontier could stretch back beyond the horizon – delays in these circumstances could take many hours, if not days or a week or so for the situation to be finally resolved and for everyone to get moving again!

Paul Rowlands getting in the mood for some Turkish wrestling with Peter Ransome. BC

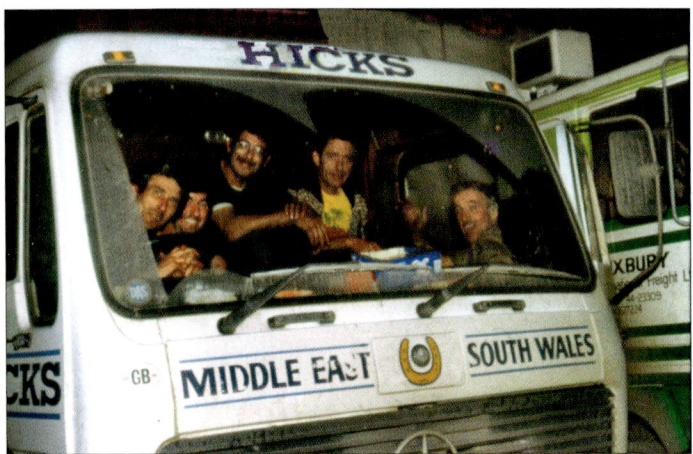

Boardroom conference near Tikrit, Iraq, December 1983. Courtesy of B & T Hicks of South Wales

Talk to any ex-Middle East truck driver and the topic of camaraderie comes up time and time again. This was often quoted as the most important feature of the job by making this way of life more manageable. No doubt there were a few Robinson Crusoe types who took a pride in immersing themselves in the depths of isolation which came with the job. But by all accounts they were in the minority. Gathering together with some mates while sitting on picnic chairs in the shade created by a truck's trailer was just what was needed to heal all the stresses and strains of the day; an opportunity to engage in some light banter while drinking a few beers and watching the sun go down!

Mike Dunstan described the importance of developing a healthy atmosphere of comradeship at all times in the company of others so as to revive any flagging spirits and keep everyone on the up and up:

'Camaraderie between drivers was second to none, and because of this, one of the best aspects of my career was working with all the other guys on the Middle East run. Everyone helped one another, as we were all in the same boat. Time wasn't a factor in those days. If someone needed help, you would be prepared to lose a day or even a week so that you could help them out. It didn't seem to matter how much time was involved providing the problem was sorted. Not like today when drivers are watched every minute of the day by satellites!'

Jeff Kedward commented on the same topic with an overlaying theme that bears comparison with what serving military personnel have to say about the recuperative value of comradeship under any strained or difficult circumstances:

'You became a family as you drove along with those you had started out with or those who you met later on, so that you were all running together. These bonds became tighter over time, even closer than those you had previously experienced when you were back in the UK. Some drivers could not take to the Middle East trucking life at all, and the failure to get along with others was most probably the reason why!'

Brian Robertson remarked on the contrast between spending so long on his own in his cab followed by the relief of finding some like-minded souls who clubbed together and rustled up some good company after they had all parked up at the end of the day, the identity of the participants often coming as a pleasant surprise when they climbed down from their cabs:

'What did I think of the camaraderie out there? Nine times out of ten I would be doing a run on my own, driving

Bob Crofton-Sleigh, centre, with unknown drivers. The broken-down Scania was recovered by Trans UK. BC

Paul Rowlands has drawn the short straw, washing up at the Iran/Turkey border. BC

twenty-four hours during the day and then into the night, travelling almost non-stop when I wanted to, and stopping only when I needed to. By the time I did stop, I would be looking for someone to talk to, and finding someone usually worked out well. What was strange about the situation from then on was that you would get along famously with someone you'd never known before then, and although it was possible that you'd never see that same person until maybe a few months later, it was as if time had stood still as you both got on so well!'

Not that everything always worked out with the sort of easygoing familiarity that Brian expected as his due with so many years of Middle East driving behind him:

'One time when I was in Iraq, no-one would talk to me, and an Astran driver told me why. All the other drivers thought I was a "first tripper", someone who was inexperienced as they were out on their first run, who wanted to tag along with the others so as to draw on their experience. This could be a liability for everyone else if the first tripper didn't know what they were doing. Everyone would get slowed down as they got sucked into sorting out the newcomer's problems. This really amused me because I was absolutely sure that I had done a lot more Middle East driving than any of the others had done so far. They were OK once they realised their mistake, and I was accepted into the group from then on.'

It is true that some drivers were wary of those who could hold them up by being relatively inexperienced. Geoff Morgan recalled a meeting with another driver whom he identified as a source of trouble, although nevertheless, the overriding instinct to help out then exerted its usual strong influence:

'I was in a café after having just crossed over the Czech border when this bloke opened the door and came inside. He then asked who it was that had the British truck standing outside in the parking area. I didn't respond at first, as I suspected trouble. When I came out later, the bloke was sitting in my cab and he then asked why I hadn't said anything when he asked the question in the café. He hadn't eaten all day, so I made him a sandwich from what was available in my trailer box. And as he hadn't any fuel to go on any further, I filled his tank up with diesel. I managed to get him as far as Istanbul, and he sorted himself out from then on.'

Language barriers and any intervening cultural differences could provide convenient excuses for a driver to block out any contact with those of other nationalities, although this could be short-sighted, as demonstrated by Ken Ward, who turned an incidental encounter with a couple of Turkish drivers to his advantage many months after they had parted company:

'My first run out to the Middle East was in a Volvo F88 when I was carrying a refrigerated food delivery for Grand Metropolitan Hotels, as this firm had a contract to supply loads of food to a number of work camps out in Saudi Arabia. I caught the ferry out of Plymouth for Roscoff, a route which had only recently opened. After arriving in France, I met up with two Turkish drivers who were carrying loads of donkey meat. So then I called them over and invited them to share a cup of tea with me. As the evening went on, they kept on

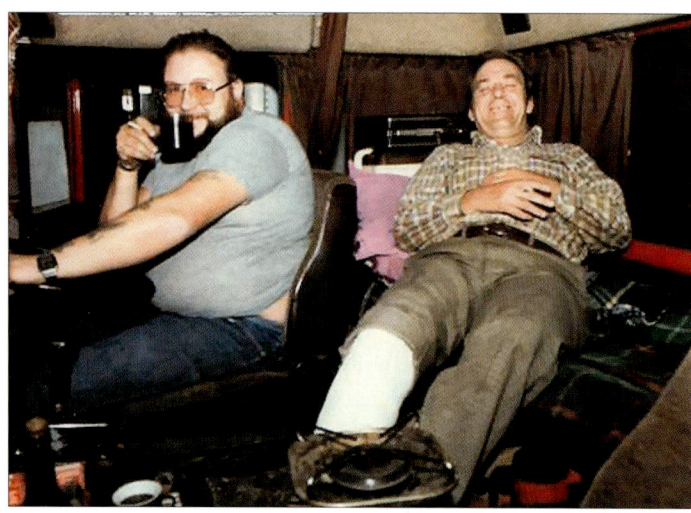

Bob Headley with Alan Canfield who had broken his leg falling down a manhole in Zakho, Iraq. GH

coming back for more tea, so I decided to give them a large packet of my Typhoo tea bags that were still wrapped up in cellophane.'

This simple act of charity was to have a most satisfactory return a few months later when Ken was on another run. He had arrived in Ankara but was unable to travel any further, as he did not have a visa that would have allowed him to transit through Iraq on his way to the Saudi destination.

'I was travelling with a boss who wanted to know more about the business. I tried to convince the Iraqi embassy our load was to be delivered in Iraq rather than to Saudi, which it wasn't of course, but this didn't wash at all, and they wouldn't give me a visa. My request was denied by drawing a red line across the paperwork. By chance, I happened to meet one of the Turkish drivers that I gave the packet of tea to in France. We were at the haulage yard where he worked, and he arranged for my load to be transhipped here to another truck so that it could be delivered to the Saudi destination by a Turkish driver. All was well, but when we were then offered a load to take to Denmark by a Turkish firm, the boss who I was travelling with turned it down, which didn't seem right given the help we'd just received from this firm in getting our load to where it had to be delivered. He had no idea at all when it came down to applying some much needed common sense and diplomacy!'

For someone who was trying to learn about the job, Ken's boss managed to further overstep the mark when he demanded they should now make all possible haste to pick up another load at a distant location that could only be achieved by driving full pelt across Turkey, virtually without stopping at all:

'To cap it all, he expected me to drive overnight all the way from Ankara to the Albanian border in Greece where I was supposed to pick up a load the next morning. He should have known this was virtually impossible given the distance involved. So now in a temper, I drove the whole distance at break-neck speed, with the boss man now finding himself being mercilessly thrown around the cab all the way as he pleaded with me to slow down, which I wouldn't do! What's more, the load wasn't available when we finally arrived, dead on time, at the Greece/Albania border, so we had to hang around for two more days waiting for this to be loaded on my truck. After losing my temper again, he made the right decision and flew home by plane!'

Getting along with someone of another nationality can be easily influenced by prior experience and any presupposed notions, whether these be good or bad, and Ken was surprised when he was so closely cross-examined on his nationality during a meeting with a Turkish transport manager with a view to taking on some new business. The manager went on to hint darkly that maybe Ken was an American who was

Paul Rowlands and Charlie Pennington at Nis in Yugoslavia, July 1975. Dig those bellbottoms! PR

Gordon Summers – left, with some passing-by-night friends he met, but as was the custom, he never got to know their forenames. GS

now posing as a British national for some unspecified reason or other. The general tone of these suspicions demonstrated quite clearly that this wasn't a favourable assessment of Ken's character. After considerably more in-depth questioning, Ken was finally treated in a warmer, friendlier manner, and by way of an apology, the transport manager explained he had fought as a soldier for the Turkish army alongside troops from other United Nation countries during the Korean War in the early 1950s. There had been a situation when the Turkish soldiers were fighting alongside American troops, but to this ex-soldier's everlasting disgust, the Americans had run away in the middle of a difficult battle engagement, which had left his troops in a really bad situation! This, to his mind, showed no appreciation whatsoever of comradeship extending to those of another nationality during a very dangerous fire-fight!

Keeping everyone amused was one of the principal objectives that underlined camaraderie, although taking centre stage to boast about your own achievements wasn't acceptable at all – this was always something to be frowned on and wasn't conducive to being thought well of at all. Fred Hodgkins remembered watching with a smile as a boasting line shooter who had been out to impress received his comeuppance with a dose of humiliation at the hands of someone who was well versed at putting another in their place:

'I witnessed the following situation take place at the National Hotel in Belgrade. I had met up with Alan Kendall of Kendall Trucking who was from Chepstow, together with ten or twelve drivers who were of various nationalities – Dutch, Swedish and Danish. We were all seated at a big table in the centre of the hotel's restaurant at dinner time. While we were noshing away, all the while comparing our experiences and sharing a laugh or two at the same time, our attention was drawn outside to a Ford Transcontinental truck which arrived in the car park. We had no choice but to notice this truck, as the driver was giving it the big-time, making loads of noise by revving up his engine and applying the air brakes when they weren't needed. This was to let us know the "King of the Road" had now arrived in our company! Shortly afterwards, this kid walked in, all dressed in black, wearing a T-shirt with the name "Londra Mocamp" printed on it. I remember he had a set of Turkish puzzle rings on his fingers and he was wearing a pair of clogs to further underline the message: here was a real pro! After standing for a while in the doorway, where he clearly expected to receive a welcoming smile from one and all of us, which was non-existent of course because of the way he had behaved up till then. So our table remained completely silent as we waited to see what this bloke's next move was going to be. He finally sat down with us at our table and immediately tore into an account of the "magic" of everywhere that he had been, how long it had taken to get there, and what he had achieved, etc. This didn't go down too well with all the lads who were just quietly enjoying their meals. We had been talking about all sorts of other things rather than just about trucks and the trips we had made by ourselves. Alan Kendall then stood up and said to this youngster: "Son, I

Ron Slater, Frank Cavangah and Martyn Moulsdale at Gaziantep, Turkey. MM

have a tin of macaroni cheese in my locker that's done more trips than you, so why not be quiet for a while and just look, listen and learn?"'

Mark Chevalier came across an English guy in the middle of a desert whose truck was bogged down to the axles in sand, a situation that was made far worse as the truck had come to a stop in the middle of the no-man's land that lay halfway between the Jordanian and Saudi Arabian border posts, with the accompanying complications of calling for assistance and a recovery truck from either side of the border. All in all, this bloke was in an unenviable plight! Nevertheless, Mark and a few other drivers selflessly spent the next five days working beneath the searing heat of the desert sun to haul the stranded truck onto solid ground using wire hawsers attached to their own trucks.

Sometimes the instinct to help any others out could kick in rather too spontaneously, which was something Jeff Kedward managed to turn to his mischievous advantage. This occurred after Jeff was approached by another driver, who, little realising Jeff was a real professional of the Middle East routes, made an offer to show him the ropes, assuming Jeff was only a first-timer. So Jeff kept quiet about anything that could give the game away, and he played up to the supposition that he was a rookie by hanging on to the other bloke's words of wisdom and advice all the way to the Turkish border. They then came across an agent for the Young Turk concern, who gave the game away by saying: 'Hello Mr Jeff. How are you doing today?' The wicked hoax was now exposed, leaving Jeff grinning like the proverbial Cheshire cat as he faced an unbridled flood of not so nice words from the bloke who had been rather cunningly misled into the role of Jeff's guardian angel!

Making fun of a 'first timer' is a time-honoured tradition in all sorts of industries, and Les Higgins received a few ribbings on his first outing when he was accompanied by Graham Cartmail, who was quick to teach Les a few lessons on not believing everything that he was told. However, Graham didn't have it all his own way and Les Higgins described how he managed to get his own back after he had been told a story that was supposed to scare him rigid:

'We were travelling through Transylvania, and when we stopped our trucks for a while, Graham Cartmail tried to frighten me by telling me a story about Count Dracula and the vampires as supposedly found in this part of the world at one time. These tales did not frighten me at all! But I decided that I still needed to get my own back. I waited until Carty was lying down, now fast asleep on his bunk, and then I thrust a used, but still warm, tea bag at his neck to suggest he was being attacked by Dracula himself! That taught him a lesson! Graham then got his own back on an occasion later on when I was sitting with him and Steve Swaine in one of our trucks. We could hear this really strange noise, which Graham said was the sound of the sirens on a Syrian police car. I realised I'd been fooled when a small donkey came trotting by with a bloke riding on its back, so large his feet were only barely off the ground. The sound I'd heard was the braying of this little donkey rather than any police siren!'

Camaraderie and the willingness to help out others also extended to local drivers. Keith Burson described an incident when he came to the assistance of a Turkish driver who was in deep trouble, which had a spin-off value for all concerned, as if he hadn't acted in this way, the road they were travelling on could have been blocked for hours by an overloaded truck that wasn't going anywhere, and the surfaces of the road becoming as slick and slippery as an ice ring:

'I was coming over the Taurus mountain range when I came across a Thames Trader tanker truck with a six-wheeler conversion as it had an extra axle to carry more weight – which it certainly was doing with a full load of diesel on board. However, as the truck was travelling uphill at a steep angle, gallons of diesel were leaking out of the top of the tank and slopping all over the road surface, making

Tea break with Kermit, Pink Panther and Emu in Saudi, you had to make use of whatever company was available! GHA

it slippery and dangerous. This wasn't a problem for me, as I had managed to get by the tanker, but it was holding everyone else up for a long way down the road, which included my running mates. The Trader driver was assisted by a young boy with a "mobile hand brake": this was a block of wood he was carrying, and his job was to run beside the tanker so that whenever it crawled to a stop he could prevent the truck from running backwards down the hill by placing the block of wood behind a back wheel. Anyway, I noticed the truck had come to a standstill, so I coupled the Trader up to the back of my trailer and I towed him all the way to the top of that mountain until we both reached the top. The old boy driving the Trader was really pleased, he couldn't get over what I'd done for him! This worked out for us also, as my mates were no longer stuck behind the tanker! I was driving an ERF with a 355 engine, a fantastic lorry that had so much pulling power, it was just what was needed to haul along that fully loaded fuel tanker as well as my own load.'

When Keith was on the Bosphorus waterfront the protective instinct to look after others was instantly called into play when he noticed a small shoeshine boy being roughed up by a much older bully:

'I was with Graham Woodward, also Derek Goddard and his wife, when we came across this shoeshine boy on the east bank of the Bosphorus. The lad thought he was speaking to us in English, which he was, but it was just bad language some British lorry drivers had taught him for a laugh! After we had paid him to clean our shoes, he was given a packet of cigarettes so he could sell these on and make some more money. But we saw this bigger kid come along who smacked the shoeshine boy in the mouth and snatched away the packet of fags. So Graham and I stepped in and gave the bully a really good hiding! Later on, we noticed the bully's watch had fallen off during the scuffle, so we kept this for ourselves as rough justice!'

During the time when Graham Cartmail was working for Jenkinson's he noticed that the firm was adopting a 'buddy' recruitment policy to combat the effects of loneliness and isolation by trying to make sure their drivers travelled in twos on a run:

'Jenkinson's would try to send their drivers out in twos so they could help each other out along the way and also for company. You could get very lonely on your own out there. I remember one time when I hadn't managed to talk to another Englishman for a month at a time. If you were left on your own for too long, you would end up talking to yourself after a while, and by the time you finally got home again and went down the pub, you would find you had lost the art of making any conversation! When you first started out on a run you might initially be fussy about who you wanted to talk to. Fellow countrymen were preferred to anyone else, but the further you went, and particularly after leaving Istanbul, you would park up alongside any other drivers you came across. Dutch, German or whatever, it didn't seem to matter providing you understood most of what they had to say. As well as friendship, safety in numbers was also an important factor.'

But travelling with the same person was usually the exception rather than the rule with most firms, as Paul Rowlands further underlined:

'The way the Middle East runs worked meant that although you may have been hired at the same time as someone else, and you may have travelled that first run together, or an occasional trip later on, this didn't mean you would travel with them on a future trip, as they would usually be somewhere down the road from you at any one point in time.'

The old saying, a problem shared is a problem halved, most certainly applied when Martyn Moulsdale ran into difficulties trying to get the engine of his truck started and running for the rest of the day:

'The alternator wasn't working on my truck, so I couldn't charge my batteries and therefore I couldn't restart my engine. Finding a replacement alternator would have been very expensive if not unobtainable. So to get round the problem, a driver I was travelling with offered to share the use of his batteries so that I could get mine started. The idea was to swap the batteries over from one truck to the other one. He would start his truck using his batteries, and then these would be transferred over to my truck, and I could get started as well. My batteries that were low on power were then fitted to his truck so that they could be charged up again on the alternator. As we ran down the road, the sets of batteries would be changed over so the ones which had become discharged were slowly restored to full power. This scheme worked out fine as there didn't need to be much charge in the batteries when you were driving in the daylight. The batteries only lost their charge at a faster rate if the headlights or the windscreen wipers were in use at any time. The trucks in those days had mechanical rather than electrically powered fuel pumps, so running the pump wasn't a problem. I was working for CVH at the time driving an ex-Astran's Scania 111. This driver who helped me out was called Eddie Nixon. We drove all the way from the National Hotel in Belgrade to Istanbul in this way, a distance of *about 500 miles, which is where I arranged for the faulty alternator to be repaired by an auto-electrician.'*

Getting on with drivers who represented other nationalities was often a matter of personal preference. Gerry Holmes recalled that he always seemed to get on very well with Dutch drivers, an opinion that seems to have been shared by other Brits:

'I found the best people to get on with were the Dutch, as they would always do whatever they could to help anyone out. This worked for them as well, such as the time I helped a Dutchman repair the faulty lights on his truck, for example. French drivers seemed to have a tendency to keep to themselves, which was strange, as after all, we are neighbours.'

Ivor Whittall commented along similar lines:

'We got on very well with the Dutch, and they were very pro-English in return. But I noticed many Dutch drivers hated the German drivers. This wasn't long after the war had finished, so after some Dutch drivers had drunk a few beers and there were some Germans about, that's when the trouble started!'

Jeff Kedward summed up the value of camaraderie with the following short observation of how this worked to maximum advantage:

'One of us would go and get the kettle so that we could have a brew and someone else would get out their tools while someone else would be putting on their overalls so that together we could sort out a flat tyre by changing the wheel for the spare one.'

CHAPTER 17

When It All Went Wrong!

There were many considerations to sort out before a truck's wheels were set in motion for a trip out to the Middle East. Making sure the truck and trailer were well prepared was vitally important, so carrying out any service requirements and repairs would usually involve a few days of intense activity in the workshop with the aim of reducing the likelihood of faults or breakdowns occurring along the way. Meanwhile, in the office upstairs, plenty of activity was also taking place to make sure all the paperwork that was needed for the journey had been accurately prepared so it would then withstand the scrutiny of the most pernickety customs official! Then there was the need to gather together all the supplies that had to be taken along; not only spare parts, but food supplies were bought from supermarkets and were stored away in a side locker on the trailer, or less neatly by filling up the spare bunk in the cab so that everything fell out under extreme braking, or as a disorderly pile of canned goods, such as baked beans and Irish stew, and packets of powered potato, deposited in the passenger footwell!

These were all sensible precautions that always had to be taken into account, although however much care was taken in planning a trip, there were always the unanticipated flaws and mistakes which could then lay waste to the most carefully laid out arrangements.

The pressures on a driver could also exert a considerable toll until a load had been safely delivered, as it was within their role to prevent any accidental damage to whatever they were carrying, and it was a real slap in the face to be told they were to blame if there were any problems, particularly if the driver already knew full well that they were not to blame.

Keith Burson was faced with this sort of dilemma when he was in the process of the final delivery of a weighty hammer mill to Baghdad, as this expensive piece of equipment which he had delivered over so many miles was then wrecked by the local crane crew who should have managed the task of gently lifting this off the loadbed of Keith's truck and reuniting it back to terra firma. Keith had to go on the defensive when it became clear an attempt was being made to shift the responsibility for ruining the hammer mill back on to himself even though he had not had anything to do with the unloading procedure and the way the crane had been mishandled:

'The hammer mill was being unloaded from my truck by these Iraqi guys, and they insisted on using only a single chain when a second chain was needed to balance out the load as each item of machinery was lifted off my truck. I tried letting the guys know about this via the interpreter who was with us to assist unloading, but they wouldn't listen to me at all. So the inevitable happened when the hammer mill was lifted off my truck – it broke free of the single chain! After working loose from the chain, the hammer mill, which weighed about five tons, fell down and hit the ground so that each of the support legs were broken. The Iraqis tried insisting this was my fault by claiming the hammer mill had already been damaged before it had arrived. Luckily, I'd taken some photos of the hammer mill when it was still on my truck and later on after it was taken off, so the damage was clearly visible. This meant the Iraqi company couldn't make any claim for compensation against my company or our insurers. Another hammer mill was then ordered as a replacement for the one that was damaged.'

Relatively minor mechanical problems can assume much more serious proportions in the depths of winter when the conditions can compound problems, as Mike Dunstan found out when the batteries on his mate's truck suddenly faded away and then died at a border crossing:

'This trip was to Iran which was for Butrako in 1977, and it turned out to be my very worst ever! Two of us went, my mate Stan Aaron was the other driver, and we took a load of carpets out of Belgium which were to be delivered in Tehran. We were driving Ford Transcontinentals, and we had a lot of trouble with these two lorries both on our way out and on the way back. Stan's first problem occurred when the air compressor that operates the braking system failed to work; so this was fixed in the usual innovative way by some Turkish mechanics; they replaced the compressor piston with one they had taken from an old motorbike engine!

'On the way back, after successfully delivering the two loads of carpets we had brought with us, there was another

problem on Stan's truck concerning the batteries this time. This occurred as we were crossing the frontier from Iran back into Turkey at the Gurbulak/Bazargan border post. We were queuing up to go through the border gate which was about to close for the night, so it was important for us not to get stuck on the wrong side of the border when the barrier went down, as this would delay going any further until the following day. We were right up to the barrier, a pole that was raised to let you through the frontier, and my lorry was sitting right behind Stan's lorry. Because of the poor condition of the batteries, I had previously reminded Stan to make sure that he didn't stall his lorry's engine, as we would have no way of restarting it with so little power available from the batteries to crank the engine over. But of course, that's what he did, without meaning to of course!

'This left us both stranded, and as Stan's truck was blocking the barrier, no-one else was able to get through either! I decided to push Stan's truck over the border using the tow hitch on my front bumper connected to the tow hitch on the back of Stan's trailer. The idea was to drop a towing pin that connected the back of Stan's trailer to the front of my truck, and a couple of Romanians helped out by dropping the securing pin into the towing eye so I could push Stan's truck over the borderline. But as soon as I began letting out the clutch and pushing forward, the pin shot up in the air from the towing eye, and this went straight through the front grille into my radiator, so all the water from my radiator started pouring out onto the ground. This was my own fault as I should have checked the pin was correctly positioned and couldn't shoot out the way it did, which now meant my lorry was also in a bad way.

'Nothing more could be done until the next day, when we swapped over the batteries from my truck to Stan's and we used his truck to tow mine over the border line to where it was parked, awaiting repairs. We then rode in Stan's truck to the town of Doğubeyazıt to see if anyone could fix my damaged radiator. We came across some blokes who were playing cards and they immediately recognised us as a pair of TIR drivers who had lots of deutschmarks to spend on truck repairs which they could carry out for us. Fortunately, it was possible for us to communicate with the Turks using a mixture of their own language and German, and within an hour, the damaged radiator was out and lying on the floor, all thanks to a little grubby kid who expertly worked underneath the truck undoing all the bolts and fittings. The Turkish mechanics then removed the damaged parts of the radiator and spent the next two hours brazing over the exposed ends of the coolant tubes. After filling the radiator with water, they pressure-tested the repair, with washing-up liquid added to the water to see if any bubbles that had been created were escaping, which would then identify any leakage. After the garage owner had satisfied himself there were no longer any leaks in the radiator, some of the water was drained off to enable the radiator to be topped up with anti-freeze, as this took place in the winter months. The temperature in the garage was about –20°C, and we both sat huddled round a roaring

Working for the trailer rental companies, Fred Topham recovered many abandoned trailers. FT

brazier all the while watching them finish the job! The repair to my radiator almost got me all the way home, but it started leaking again when I was nearly there. The leakage was fixed by dropping in a few raw eggs which then sealed any holes. When I got back to Holland, the fitter at Butrako's yard couldn't believe I had managed to get that far with only two-thirds of the radiator core left in place because it had been so badly damaged!'

Ivor Whittall came across a driver whose reserves of endurance had reached rock bottom as he vainly tried to get his truck repaired over a period of weeks when this ordeal should have only taken a few days to resolve:

'I remember rescuing a guy who'd had a terrible experience out there when he was making a run out to Tehran which finally took him a total of three months to complete. I drove past him on the way out and again on a couple more occasions because he still hadn't completed his first trip after his truck had broken down. His troubles began on the way out when someone drove into the front of his Volvo F88 which smashed up his radiator at the Kapıkule border where he'd crossed over into Turkey from Bulgaria. I told him not to try and arrange for a mechanic to repair the radiator as it was too badly damaged, it needed to be replaced with a new one. But he went ahead with ordering the repair anyway, and this involved taking a large lump out of the middle of the radiator core and brazing over the ends of any exposed tubes to prevent any of the water from leaking out. Somehow or other, this makeshift repair allowed the bloke to make it all the way to Tehran so he could make his delivery, and also all the way back to Istanbul. But the radiator failed again, so he was back to the same position he had been in when I had seen him for the first time on his outward journey. I remember he had started to look just like a tramp and he was crying in despair that second time I came across him with his broken truck in Turkey. I felt very sorry for him. The Volvo's engine was also damaged now because of overheating caused by running along with a damaged radiator, so he was actually in a worse position than before. The engine had been taken apart to find out what was wrong, with the pistons and other parts removed, and it was now lying in pieces on the back of the guy's trailer. So I promised to get him home, which involved stripping down the tilt on my empty trailer, and loading his truck on to the back of my trailer. This was after removing all the wheels of his truck to reduce the overall height to get under low bridges, etc. The poor bloke had postponed his up-and-coming marriage on at least two occasions before he finally managed to get himself home at last.'

Ivor also tried to help out when he was running with another truck that was travelling open TIR form with a fire engine on the back, in 1977. This British driver had been stopped by six Turks on the road between Nusaybin and Zakho because a wheel on his brand new MAN truck allegedly threw a stone into the air which had smashed the windscreen of an elderly Oldsmobile sedan that the Turks had been travelling in. The Turks had demanded 700 lira, or about £23 at the current rate of exchange, as compensation for the damage, although the British driver wasn't having any of this and refused to pay up. Recognising no good would come of this uncompromising approach, Ivor tried to intervene and smooth matters by suggesting a lower amount of £18. But no, the truck driver was adamant he wasn't paying, and that was that, he locked himself in his cab as a crowd of locals gathered outside, who were becoming increasingly irate as time went by! Ivor sensibly realised he couldn't do anything more to resolve the situation which was getting more and more heated by the minute, so he set off to leave, although the crowd then wanted to stop him from going. But the Turks from the damaged car said it was OK for him to leave, so off he went, no doubt much relieved to be on his way at last! Ivor later met up with the Brit driver at the border out of Turkey, by which time the smart, new MAN truck was now a very pitiful sight. This was because the driver had continued to refuse to pay for the broken windscreen, and thus all the windows, mirrors and lights on his truck had been put out and smashed by way of revenge. Ivor recalled the driver was very distressed, although he still failed to see the error of his ways, and paying out such a small amount could have saved him so much trouble as well as the difficulties he now faced in getting his damaged truck to its destination and then back home. The explanation he gave for his refusal to pay up was that his boss back home wouldn't have repaid the twenty pounds or so demanded in compensation!

Brian Robertson spoke of the psychological hurdle of starting out on a trip which seemed to weigh more heavily as the miles went by, although as so frequently happens in other realms of life, the passage of time has always been a great healer:

'You would be driving away from your house for a week or maybe two weeks thinking about the fact that you had so far to go before you could turn back. Some days it all went wrong, but you tended to forget the bad times and only remember the good times, such as sitting around with your mates – happy memories!'

George Brooke enjoys a fag while deciding what to do about a leaking oil seal. GB

Mike Dunstan's Volvo F89 'piggy-backed' home by another Radclive's truck after the engine blew up and seized. MD

Further bad news for George Brooke when the windscreen on his DAF was smashed necessitating an improvised, make-shift repair. GB

Queuing to get out of Turkey – a 25-kilometre tailback to the frontier! MM

CHAPTER 18

Crossing Borders

Crossing any frontiers was something that could continually unsettle the most experienced Middle East veteran, and anyone who approached customs formalities with a carefree, come what may sort of attitude, was almost inevitably setting themselves up for a really big fall!

Nothing was ever really set in stone when it came to dealing with customs rules and regulations. Even though the procedures could have been such and such when a driver passed through a border on one occasion, there was always a strong likelihood these had all changed by the time they came the same way on a later occasion. The goalposts had been moved, often to no discernible advantage that anyone could explain or fathom out at all!

If a driver came up against a change in the rules then there was a chance that they could juggle the paperwork around so it was acceptable within the new regulations. But it was more often the case this would involve a new set of paperwork having to be obtained, which often required long journeys to distant embassies and consulates to obtain new visas, etc.

Crossing any border often involved queuing for hours or days at a time due to a build-up of TIR traffic and delays in processing paperwork. A whole day could be spent travelling just a few metres. And then once across the border after completing any lengthy customs procedures, the same lengthy, time-consuming procedures would need to be re-enacted with a new set of officials wearing a different style of uniform to the others, only a short distance away on the other side of the barrier!

The importance of getting any damaged or broken trucks out of Turkey could not be stressed too highly.

One of Grangewood's DAF 2800s leaving the country at Dover. DM

Lenny Baylam on the first trip to the Middle East. BC

David Miller's Altrex Mercedes 1926 at the Jordon/Saudi border. DM

Driving for CVH International, Ron Slater in the Transcontinental and Martyn Moulsdale in the DAF queue up to leave Iraq. MM

The details of the truck were recorded in a driver's passport when they entered the country, and when they came to leave the country, it was expected that they would still be in possession of the vehicle, whether it was damaged, broken down, or still in running order. If they did not have the vehicle with them, it was assumed this had been sold when it was in Turkey, in which case the driver would have to stump up for any import duty that was due! And that sum of money was likely to exceed the amount of cash they happened to be carrying with them at the time!

Chris Stephenson commented on the importance of getting all the paperwork correctly made out and properly stamped:

'It could really cost you if the paperwork wasn't right, particularly when you were transiting through Turkey. And making sure the paperwork was up to date didn't just apply at the borders: you had to stop and have your paperwork stamped at intervals for permission to go any further as you travelled through Turkey. If a document hadn't been stamped somewhere along the way just because this had been overlooked, then you had to go back there and have the documents stamped, perhaps adding many hundreds of miles to your journey as you went back and forward again.'

Chris was employed at Dayson's of Carlisle, so it was Alan Dayson's wife, Ena, who very carefully prepared the detailed paperwork required for any Middle East trip, which included the all-important 20–30 page *carnet de passage* document.

Ivor Whittall further underlined the importance of getting the paperwork correct down to the last detail:

Paul Rowlands in his best truck-driving gear at Kapıkule. BC

'You would hope you did not have a minor error in the paperwork, such

Usual winter mud bath conditions at Kapıkule, Turkey. BC

as the number of your passport not being entered correctly on a document, when you were travelling through Turkey. If this had been noticed by an official as you were leaving the country, then it wasn't something which could be simply corrected on the spot by making any necessary changes to the document. The border people would send you all the way back to the other end of the country if they decided this was necessary, which could involve driving for a distance of more than a thousand miles in each direction.'

Getting the numbers correct on any cargo manifest was of vital importance. Keith Burson was accompanying the late Peter Harborn on a journey across Turkey when a customs inspection revealed Peter's paperwork detailed ten electric motors although eleven motors had been found when the case was opened for examination. It always helped to know someone who knew what they were doing when trying to sort out any problem such as this, because even though the mistake may have seemed insignificant at first, it could soon take on a more critical perspective, as Keith described:

'They tried to do Peter for smuggling some goods into Turkey, so we asked a representative of the Young Turk import agency if he could sort things out for us. He did a

Ian Tyler hanging out the washing at Al Turaif in Saudi near the Jordanian border. ITY

John Buffham's Volvo queueing at the Turkey/Iraq border. JB

Queuing to enter Iran from Gurbulak, 1975. BC

great job and got the problem resolved for us so we could continue with our journey.'

So having the right contacts was often the key to resolving tricky situations, although concealing a few deutschmarks in a passport or other documents could also be most effective!

At a time when many unfamiliar items of equipment and commodities were being imported into Middle Eastern countries for the first time this often lead to confusion in identifying what some of these items were actually to be used for, so drivers would get involved in discussions over the nature of the items with customs officials, which could become very complex to resolve. The scope for confusion when a customs official asked for any such explanation could seem to be never-ending, as Gordon Summers found out when he tried to explain the purpose of a piece of equipment he was carrying on his trailer. He knew this was a most important item of equipment used by the local oil well industry, although from what the customs officer had understood from the paperwork, this should have been adorned with sets of fairy lights and glittering tinsel and decorations, as it was described on the manifest as a 'Christmas tree', when it clearly wasn't at all within the scope of any normal description! He explained:

'I was crossing the Jordan/Saudi border when a customs official spotted the entry for a "Christmas tree" on the manifest. This name was also used in the oil industry for a large steel valve assembly that is used on oil rigs to open and close the valves that control the flow of oil. But because it was described as a tree, they thought that it should have been made of wood, so they wouldn't believe my explanation! In the end, I managed to persuade them after making contact with the client, who thankfully backed up my story. They were probably a bit suspicious of the word "Christmas" in view of any possible connection with Christianity with Saudi Arabia being a Muslim country.'

Trucks on the downward slope at Bazargan. The Iranian flag flies outside the chai house. BC

If the description or categorisation of what was being carried was in any way ambiguous then this could result in a long wait at border crossing posts, as Brian Robertson experienced to his intense displeasure on one notable occasion:

'I was at Gurbulak on the way into Iran, when it was noticed the paperwork for my load described the contents as some kind of "machinery". It was in fact a load of special fire bricks and some kind of cement that were to be used for building a brick furnace. Someone had put "machinery" on the carnet, and the customs blokes were trying to do me over for attempting to smuggle these bricks and the cement into their country, as they clearly didn't match the description of "machinery". I sat there at the Iranian border for nine days before this issue was finally resolved.'

John Buffham remembers a driver having a problem getting through customs procedures as the officials had noticed an entry for 240 'V's on the manifest when he was carrying a load of electric motors. John finally managed to convince the customs man that the 'V's were a reference to the voltage which was used to work these electric motors.

With the relative proximity of the opium-growing crops of Afghanistan, great care had to be taken not to take any narcotics across borders, a precaution which was underlined for David Miller on a trip to Afghanistan:

'I remember this customs officer asking to see the seal on my trailer, and as we walked along, he took hold of my hand, which wasn't an unusual thing to do out there. And after taking a firm grip of my hand, he then said to me, "Have you got any drugs, Mister?" I was later told this was a clever way of getting someone to reveal whether they were shipping heroin out of the country. Any increase in their pulse rate would have instantly revealed whether they had something to be very worried about!'

*Bazargan. On the right, trucks are entering Turkey from Iran.
On the left, trucks are entering Iran from Turkey. BC*

David was working for Eileen Ellingham Middle East when the firm was approached by the *Sunday Mirror* as they wanted to send a reporter out eastwards in a truck. This was a task with which David was quite willing to comply, although he wouldn't have let this bloke within a hundred yards of his truck if he'd known a despicable act of journalistic treachery was to take place a short while later on. Everything seemed well enough on the

Entering Iran at Bazargan. BC

Fred Hodgkins approaches the border at Bazargan with the snow-capped summit of Mount Ararat visible in the distance. FH

journey down to Istanbul, although the journalist then lost interest in travelling with David after they arrived at the Londra Camping establishment. This dedicated newshound then decided to take up residence in the bar, so David continued on with his journey travelling solo. The full implications of what the journalist then did to blacken David's reputation became abundantly clear after arriving back at a Channel port some five weeks later, where he faced stiff interrogation by suspicious British customs officials who'd been alerted to the possibility that a hoard of drugs was carried somewhere on this truck:

'I received a most warm, but clearly false welcome from some customs officials who advised me of my new-found celebrity status by showing me a newspaper with my picture prominently displayed. This journalist had said in his newspaper that I was a drugs smuggler who had brought loads of the opium drugs into this country. So the customs people decided to rip my truck apart, and they even removed all the tyres from the wheels, but they found nothing of course. Nonetheless they continued to give me the full treatment each time I returned back to the UK for my next few trips. I eventually found out where this reporter went drinking from someone I knew who was in the "print"; so I went round to a bar frequented by journalists in London and I floored him, there and then. This made me feel a lot better, although I don't know whether he ever recognised who I actually was! Drugs were not my style at all. You would often be asked if you would carry various parcels from one country to another, but you always had to refuse.'

Breaking the rules on currency exchange could have dire consequences, and there was a thorough tightening-up of regulations at Iranian border posts after the Shah of Iran was deposed to make way for Ayatollah Khomeini. Geoff Morgan was almost caught red-handed after he got involved in a black market money changing deal with one of the locals to obtain a supply of Iranian rials at a most favourable rate of exchange:

'After crossing over Tahir in February, six of us decided to do an illegal black market deal to obtain some Iranian rials, even through the currency restrictions at Iranian borders were a lot stricter than they had ever been before as regards any black market deals. We were caught with the Iranian money we had changed with a dealer as we went through customs. First of all, we tried to say we had exchanged the money in England at an Iranian bank, but this didn't work: there were no Iranian banks in our own country at the time, and to make matters worse, we didn't have any bank receipts to back up our story. So they made us wait for two days while an interpreter arrived to carry out more questioning. In the meantime, I removed a rubber grommet on the cow catcher bar that was on the back of my trailer so that I could hide away the rest of my contraband rials that hadn't been declared when we had been caught and questioned.

Abandoned at a border post, this MAN truck stands next to two ex-hippy vans, a Bedford 15cwt and a Ford Transit. FT

A Merc 309 on a z-plate, a few Tonkas and an abandoned ERF at Bazargan. BC

But I did keep back about twenty pounds in Iranian rials so that I could declare this much smaller amount later on, which was immediately confiscated. So I managed to keep hold of the larger amount that had been safely hidden away in my trailer's rear bumper bar! We were taken to a bank afterwards where we were ordered to exchange our Western money for however many rials we needed. This was at the official exchange rate which the Iranian government had decided on, so the rate of exchange for Western currency was very unfavourable, giving us far less than we'd got on the black market. We were instructed to keep hold of the bank receipts so we could prove where we had got our Iranian money from, if we were challenged again! After we unloaded in Tehran, our passports were stamped "FORBIDDEN" so that we couldn't use these to re-enter Iran on another trip, although the solution to this was quite simple – we obtained new passports after we had got home. At one time, I had seven UK passports which were all in use at the same time.'

Some border crossings required a dip test of the fuel tank to assess how much fuel duty should then be paid, so Geoff always tried to seek out an uneven area of ground so the truck could be parked in such a way that any diesel in the tank would be at its lowest height immediately beneath the open filler cap where the dip test was about to be made.

The most bizarre customs regulation Geoff ever endured was when his entry into Albania was refused on the grounds that he happened to be wearing a beard. As the possession of a beard was forbidden in that country under the instructions of its autocratic ruler, Enver Hoxha, it looked as if Geoff wasn't going to get any further than the barrier across the border line! After hanging around for a long while with a load of Land Rover spare parts still on his trailer, it was finally agreed by the border guards that Geoff could proceed on his way through the country, but only with the proviso that he had to take an armed guard along with him in the truck!

Every border post along the way to the Middle East became an elephant's graveyard of abandoned old cars and not so old trucks which had been barred from entering or leaving a particular country for one reason or another. Gerry Holmes always recognised a sand-coated truck lying out in the desert between two frontiers as he passed by on several occasions when he drove for the firm of H.J. Atlas International:

'We abandoned one of our trucks on the Syria/Jordan border; I remember the registration, it was JAR51N. This truck was a red Ford Transcontinental with a 350 Cummins engine which our local Ford dealer had persuaded our boss, Hussein, to take out for a trial run to the Middle East. But it had broken down, so it became stuck fast in the middle of the area of no-man's land that existed between the two border posts, where no-one could get at it to carry out any repairs, and there it stood out in the desert for a couple of years until it was finally recovered.'

Gordon Summers decided to be his own customs official when he noticed a customs stamp hadn't been issued on his carnet:

'I was bringing a backload out of Greece one time when I noticed one of the entries hadn't been stamped on my documents, so I used a ten drachmae coin to authenticate the document, whereupon a customs man granted permission to let me through.'

Ivor Whittall also used a coin in the same way, but on this occasion he needed to fool a Turkish medical official that his medical records were valid and up to date:

'There was a time when you would be asked to show an up-to-date medical record when you crossed a Turkish border. You were interviewed by someone in a white coat who was no more of a doctor than I am. If your medical record wasn't stamped as being up to date, there was a "problem". So I re-dated my form in biro, and used an ink stamp pad I had found and an old six-penny piece I had in my pocket to leave an official-looking image of the Queen's head on the form I had been given to fill in. No-one noticed the other entries were for a named local medical centre based in the UK! The "doctor" then said "very good". Ridiculously, this medical check took place when you were actually leaving rather than arriving in Turkey. So why were they bothered at all about our health when we were making our way out of the country? This was yet another money-raising scam!'

Trucks queuing up as far as the horizon, a common enough occurence at border crossings. MC

Saudi Arabia was undoubtedly the country with the strictest rules about what could and could not be taken into the country, with alcohol most definitely being *haram* – the Arabic word for forbidden by Islamic law! So it was the usual practice for everything to be taken off a truck for a thorough search of the contents to be carried out. Ken Ward recalled one occasion when the letter of the law was applied in utterly pointless circumstances:

'It was the normal practice that everything had to come off the truck, and I remember seeing lengths of open-ended pipes for a pipeline being lifted off a truck even through you could see right through each of the pipes from one end to the other to confirm there was nothing hidden inside. This practice also extended to the ruinous example of unloading any frozen goods for examination, such as ice cream for example, in temperatures as high as 130°.'

When Mark Chevalier was crossing from Jordan into Saudi a customs man found a bottle of Sarson's vinegar in his truck and mistakenly believed this was some form of alcohol; so the vinegar than had to be poured into the desert sand, in spite of Mark's protestations this was unnecessary!

Treating customs and immigration officials with the utmost courtesy and respect was most important when passing through frontiers, wherever you were, although this basic rule was something a Cockney lad still had to learn to his cost, as making a rather feeble joke about who won the Second World War backfired with a vengeance. Keith Burson recalled watching on with satisfaction as this chap got what he so thoroughly deserved:

'I was crossing the West Germany border when this Cockney boy was giving the customs man all the verbal about how we had won the war. This was a really stupid thing to do of course. Anyway, we all got our papers back but for this Cockney lad, who then started complaining about the delay this was causing him. He eventually did get his papers back, but only after a long delay and the customs man then saying to this lad, "Now tell me who won the war!" I thought this was a really classic way of how to get things wrong.'

In line with their reputation for Teutonic efficiency, German border and customs officials were not to be messed with, a topic which Mike Dunstan went on to describe:

'You had to be very careful how you dealt with German and also Austrian officials. You couldn't really pull the wool over their eyes, and it was pointless trying, which meant all of your paperwork had to be just right.'

Crossing any borders into Eastern bloc countries was something not to be taken at all lightly, as David Miller commented, concerning Bulgaria, perhaps the least-favoured Communist bloc country when it came to customs matters according to some Middle East drivers:

'Bulgaria was a full-on Communist country with all that entails – long and involved border procedures, heavy police presence, almost no other traffic passing through, and no welcome at all. It was always better to leave this country than to enter it.'

Gerry Holmes managed to get his own back when a Hungarian border guard became a little too insistent about getting something he was not entitled to:

'He started off saying, "You have sexy magazine, cigarettes or whisky?" to which I answered "No" each time. But then he replied, "Problem," which then indicated a scam was in progress. So I had with me an old James Last cassette tape that provided a way for me to get round this "Problem". I already knew the cassette wouldn't work properly, as the tape had folded over so the music was played backwards and sounded horrible. But handing the cassette over to the man meant I could continue with my journey. I would have loved to have seen his face when he tried playing that cassette tape! It served him right.'

Brian Robertson frequently managed to ease his way across borders with the offer of a few well-chosen freebies:

'When I was going into Iraq, I used to take some Littlewoods catalogues to give to the customs men as presents, as they seemed to appreciate them. I also remember a chief customs officer whom I got to know at the Turkey/Iraq border. I used to take a supply of Ralgex cream that I gave to him for his mum who suffered from arthritis. I would arrive and hand over my papers to him personally, and he would then send a boy out to clear my paperwork while we sat together all the while drinking tea and chatting away.'

Brian was an exponent of the most beguiling form of flattery when it came to buttering up any customs officials and then getting his own way:

'At Fallujah, the customs post outside Baghdad in Iraq, you had to leave your briefcase in a line outside a caravan; this meant you could avoid the heat during the long delay to clear customs, with the positioning of the briefcases then

Customs car park, out in the desert some miles from Baghdad. RDB

detailing your particular order in the queue. On one occasion when I was running with another driver, I said, "Watch this," and I started shouting out, "It's so great to be back in Baghdad" as we arrived at the doorway to the customs office. We were invited to come in, and jumped ahead of a queue of eighty or so other drivers!'

In addition to all the bureaucratic restrictions, unforeseen circumstances could also be the source of long delays, and as John Buffham explained, situations couldn't get much more out of the ordinary than the following occasion after a customs man had died:

'There was a delay one day at a customs post on the Turkey/Syria border. This was because one of the customs men had been killed in a road crash earlier on, at 8 o'clock that morning. Following the normal procedure in hot countries, he was buried shortly afterwards. The problem was that the customs man was buried in his uniform with the customs stamps in his pockets. So there was a terrible build-up of trucks waiting to cross the border before a replacement set of stamps were sent all the way down from Ankara!'

Chris Stephenson recalled that crossing the border from Syria into Jordan was no joke with everybody trying to jump the queue:

'All the drivers would line up their trucks in a series of concrete channels, and with the engines revving up, everyone would try to creep forward just a few inches at a time to be first to reach the place where the number of lanes had started to reduce as you approached the border. The secret was to get the bumper of your truck just a short distance in front of any trucks that were on either side of you so they couldn't force their way past you!'

Ian Tyler at Al-Mudawara, the Jordanian border crossing when coming from Iraq. ITY

CHAPTER 19

Guardians of Law and Order

Travelling through Eastern Europe and the Middle East could often result in drivers being hauled over for road traffic offences, whether real or quite blatantly fabricated! On the one hand, it could be said there were many occasions when European lorry drivers deliberately flouted any road traffic regulations, although the imposition of a fine for speeding or for some other rule of the road was just as likely to have been imposed as a money-making scam, with the cash received from a driver going straight into a policeman's pocket rather than the money then being handed in at a police station.

Fining the drivers of TIR trucks for speeding and other offences must have been the opportunity of a lifetime for many policemen, something that could have had a lot to do with Eastern European and Turkish policemen receiving a pittance as salary, as well as this sort of corruption being so commonplace and deeply ingrained in these countries at the time.

The perception that many drivers came to after having had to fork out cash on trumped-up charges was that this was a form of low-key highway robbery, a nuisance that had to be put up with as a necessity to getting the job done! At first they may have baulked at the suggestion they had done anything wrong by digging their heels in and refusing to pay. But things tended to go from bad to worse very quickly if this course of action was taken!

When stopped by police there was one word that Middle East drivers could anticipate hearing after they had lowered their cab window. This was 'problem', a word that was expressed with a smile from ear to ear, or maybe a macho, deadpan expression suggesting a more threatening approach was soon to follow! This dreaded word was always expressed in perfect English through so much repeated use! This generally signified it was time for a driver to hand over a few deutschmarks, or maybe a couple of packets of cigarettes, as the means to cancelling out an imaginary transgression concerning the rules of the road. This form of payment by cash or 'gifts' was often regarded by drivers as a form of transit tax that lasted for a number of kilometres until the next uniformed official stepped into the road in expectation of a bounty that would lighten up his day!

Of course, there were a few Middle East drivers who took the view that driving through any foreign lands granted them an unchallengeable right to play fast and loose with any road safety laws and regulations. And this sort of behaviour could be said to have been encouraged by the fact that paying out *baksheesh* gave them licence to flaunt all the rules! Or at least it did until everything went wrong, resulting in a bad accident and death or injury to the local population, which then left them banged up in jail for a long while with plenty of time to study the error of their ways!

David Miller recounted an incident when he took the view that the policeman who hauled him over to the side of the road was merely doing his best to supplement a very poor living wage:

'I was going over Bolu when I was pulled over by a Turkish policeman in a Ford Fairlane police car of early sixties design, which had most probably been given to the Turkish police by the Americans. These patrol cars always

The police or security guards were often present at truck stop locations. COPYRIGHT UNKNOWN

Lorry park security guards kept theft to a minimum – sometimes armed with a revolver. RW

looked ridiculous as they were fitted with such skinny tyres, but with a great big flashing light on the roof that was out of proportion with the rest of the car! Anyway, the policeman gets out of the patrol car carrying a double-barrelled shotgun, and after he had inserted two cartridges in the barrels, he propped himself up against my open side window. So I'm now looking down what looks like a great big pair of railway tunnels! After saying good morning, the policeman starts telling me about what it's like being so poor, and how his children are also poor, and his village is so poor as well. So I offer to help him out, and after giving him the equivalent of a fiver in German marks, he insists on taking me to his village, which was at the bottom of a hill, where he bought me a coffee in a café. I really did make that man's day in return for what was to me, a very small amount of money!'

Traffic policemen would often pick a favourite place of concealment where they could hide, and they would then emerge as a truck came into sight, all the while anticipating picking up a nice little earner. Peter Bamford recalled one such encounter when he finally spotted a lone police officer standing next to a patrol car:

'After crossing the Greece/Turkey border near Ipsala, on the way to Istanbul, there are miles and miles of straight road, and the police would sit on top of a hill overlooking this stretch of road. Along you would come, with nothing on the road in front of you but an old trundling car going along at about three miles an hour, so not seeing any reason not to do so, you would overtake the car. But on one such occasion, a policeman then pulled me over. He would then say: "Problem, mister, no overtaking," before he went on to explain there was a "No Overtaking" sign back down the road. He then demanded some money off me to pay a fine for the alleged offence. But I wasn't having any of this so I dug in my heels saying "No". So he took me down the road in his police car, and after stopping so we could get out, he lifted a "No Overtaking" sign from the bottom of a deep ditch where it had been completely hidden until now! Game set and match – he had won! So I handed over a couple of bob and a pack of Marlboros! You had to be a diplomat, a politician and your own barrister so that you knew how to weigh up any situations such as this one. There was also something else that you needed to remember: if anything ever went wrong, then it was always your fault – if you had not been there in the first place, it couldn't have happened!'

Graham Cartmail was offered a similar deal after he was pulled over for a non-existent speeding offence in Turkey on one of many such occasions:

'There were times when you hadn't even got into top gear before you were stopped by the police; when it was impossible for you to have been speeding, as you hadn't had enough time to build up sufficient speed to exceed a speed limit. The police would ask for your passport, and they would expect you to pay to buy it back from them! I paid up on one occasion, when to my surprise, I was actually given a receipt. The policeman said if any other policeman stopped me for speeding later on that day I should show them the receipt, and I wouldn't be asked to pay them for another speeding fine!'

Not that Graham believed a word of any of this of course!

Pat Seal was travelling with a mate of his, Richard Baxter, through Yugoslavia in the famous blue and white Volvo F88 when a policeman stopped the truck and demanded to see Pat's tachograph recording to confirm that a speeding offence had occurred. Pat's brother, Des, related what happened next:

'Most cunningly, Pat managed to remove a home-made device that was fitted to the tacho which prevented an accurate recording being made of the truck's speed, without the policeman noticing. This device consisted of a piece of cardboard and an elastic band that prevented the tacho from recording any speed above a certain figure. This was something that Pat must have decided was permissible within his present circumstances driving down through Yugoslavia. No doubt disgruntled by the false tacho reading, the policeman then went back to his squad car to consult "the chief" about what to do next. The result of which was that the chief persisted with his demand, insisting that a carton of Marlboro fags should be promptly handed over, a request that Pat eventually agreed to comply with in the spirit of international cordiality. By way of a friendly gesture, the police chief told Pat he could press on at whatever speed he liked all the way towards the Bulgarian border!'

No doubt following this advice would have pleased the next policeman further down the road if Pat had been naive enough to believe a word of this invitation to break the law!

As was the custom throughout the Middle East, road accidents that resulted in death, injury or damage to property, almost invariably resulted in claims by the injured party for compensation, as a form of 'blood money'. This would often lead to a court case that could take many months to resolve, during which time any driver who could be held to be ultimately responsible would have to sit and wait while any legal action was concluded; this could result in them being held in jail for a good long while before the case was heard. The demand for compensation was often conducted with the kind of greed and ferocity that would have made these modern-day no-win, no-fee lawyers look like a bunch of rank amateurs.

Des Seal recalled the day when he decided it was better to make light of the situation after he was taken to task over a trumped-up charge concerning some person being injured that had not been his fault in any way:

'I was in southern Turkey when a Tonka truck pulled up behind me and shunted into the back of my trailer. This resulted in a young lad in the Turkish truck breaking his arm. Over the next two days, there were meetings with the local police and the military, who seemed to have the upper hand over the police. They kept on saying "tercüman, tercüman", which I didn't understand at all at first, although apparently this meant "translator". I had to wait until the local schoolteacher finished work because he was the translator! Meanwhile, the only words I could exchange with the police to respond to their expression "Liverpool Football Club, very good?" was "No, Istanbul very good." In the end, I had to pay up, and that was that.'

Des also remembered the day when he stopped his truck in rural Turkey and he noticed some girls working in fields nearby. After a short while, the girls in the fields began to approach Des's truck, which attracted the attention of a policeman who had arrived, and he began shouting at the girls, who then scattered. But the policeman removed his pistol from its holster and began firing his pistol at the girls. To Des's shock and horror, one of the girls shouted out in pain and sheer panic when a bullet from the policeman's gun hit her in the backside!

'I was absolutely gobsmacked. I was also amazed by the way the police treated their own people later on that day when I came across an incident and saw a taxi driver being violently beaten up by the police for drinking and driving.'

Jeff Kedward recalled receiving the same form of punishment for a minor road offence when he was travelling through Yugoslavia:

'I was roughed up by the police when I was caught speeding somewhere to the north of Belgrade. I took a real beating by this policeman who used a big rubber truncheon to hit me, and I was left with bruises all over me.'

After driving abroad on a trip that took in several countries where just about any kind of motoring offence could be wiped out by handing over an amount of cash or some packets of fags, there could be difficulties in adapting to a different road safety regime on returning to Western Europe. Geoff Morgan described an incident when this was brought home to him, and he had only covered a few miles after setting off from the port of Dover towards his home in Herefordshire:

'I had been travelling through countries where the regulations concerning vehicle safety were a lot laxer than they were in the UK, so it could be difficult relearning what was right and proper according to the road use laws in my own country. I set off from Dover with only two of the three

axles of my trailer actually in use. The third axle wasn't in use because a tyre on one side had been punctured, so I had chained up the axle to lift the wheels on each side off the ground, and I had removed the wheels on both sides of the suspended axle. But I was pulled up by a policeman who told me he was concerned an old lady might catch herself on the exposed wheel studs that were sticking out of the suspended axle on each side of the truck. He asked me if I had any plastic bags to put over the wheel hubs. I said the only bags I had with me contained all of my dirty clothes. So he made me take the dirty clothes that all needed washing out of the plastic bags so I could use these to hide the exposed wheel studs. So what good was this supposed to do to improve road safety?'

Les Rivett's Scania 110 was stopped by the police in Turkey and a policeman examined the truck's tachograph to prove a speeding offence had occurred. Luckily for Les, the policeman failed to notice the tacho readings were recorded in miles per hour rather than kilometres per hour, so the policeman mistakenly interpreted 60 mph as 60 kph! Les took the view he was about to be let off. But not so! A second policeman returned from the back of the truck and said the same word that Les had already heard a few minutes earlier that day – 'Problem!'

'After walking with him to the back of my trailer, the policeman asked why there was no GB sticker, which was something he intended to fine me for. I could see where a GB sticker had recently gone missing from the back of the trailer, as this was clearly outlined by a clear patch of paintwork surrounded by dust. I now knew the second policeman had removed the GB sticker and was offering to sell a new one back to me. But I wasn't having any of this, so I found another sticker from the supply I collected each time I went through UK customs. So what did the policeman want to do next? He wanted to buy all my spare GB stickers so he could then try and pull the same trick of selling these to any British truck drivers who hadn't got a GB sticker on display!'

It could be argued that such confrontations with the law could make someone very cynical about the occupants of a certain country, although Alan Dayson was happy to recount a story of when his faith in human nature had been restored:

'I was arrested in Bulgaria for passing an army wagon at speed, so I had to go along with the policeman to the nearest town for questioning. I took along my tacho card to disprove what the policeman said about how fast I was going, but even though the policeman's word had been doubted during the court hearing, I still had to pay up for a speeding fine. This was a problem for me, as I didn't have any Bulgarian money. But help was at hand as the translator who had been appointed to look after me at the court hearing offered to give me some money which he borrowed so I could pay the fine. This was even though he knew I couldn't pay him back. But we reached an agreeable settlement: he went on to explain that he wanted me to buy him an English dictionary for his studies when I finally got back home, which I sent on to him by post as soon as I arrived.'

Des Seal recalled taking a route through Greece that promised some time to go sightseeing in Athens and to visit the Acropolis, although things started unravelling when his truck became stuck up a side street because a parked car was blocking his way, and the owner was nowhere to be found! Des was stumped, but a policeman then came along who insisted that Des could get through by driving his truck and tall trailer through a gap at the side of the road. Not that Des was convinced, as this route was immediately below some overhanging balconies of the roadside properties! Despite Des's insistence this wouldn't work, he had to do what the policeman said. So after restarting the truck, he drove forwards, which didn't go well, as even though the overhanging balconies remained in place, a shower of electric light bulbs rained down, noisily bursting after hitting the ground, followed by long lengths of live electrical cable! It was time to hop it before any of the property owners noticed the ensuing racket and emerged to vociferously demand compensation payments. Des put his foot down, leaving the bossy policeman to face the irate householders!

Gerry Holmes recounted two incidents when he was asked to dig deep into his pocket to pay off the police, one of which he stood no chance of winning, although he managed to turn the situation round to his own advantage on the second occasion:

'I was stopped in Belgrade by two militia men, and one of them asked for my passport which he then put in his pocket before demanding 200 dinar to give it back to me. I refused to pay him at first, and I resolved I wouldn't do so, even if this took me all night. But then, I thought "What are you going to do without a passport?" I couldn't complain about this theft to the police, as they were the police, and even if I had managed to talk to any of their superiors, they were probably just as bent as the two militia men standing before me. They had me by the short and curlies, so I had to pay up.

'On another occasion, I was breathalysed at ten in the morning by this Czech policeman who insisted I should blow into the breathalyser even though I don't drink. He insisted the test was positive although he wouldn't show me the results. But I managed to make him back down in the end and he got nothing from me at all. I told him that I would need a receipt if I was to pay him any money, which of course he wasn't prepared to do just in case this got him into trouble. They thought we were a mobile bank that would continually pay out on demand to match their corrupt behaviour.'

Persistence in the face of adversity didn't pay off for John Buffham when he was stopped and told he had been speeding, which was clearly untrue:

'It was quite usual to be stopped two or three times each day, so I refused to pay on one occasion. They then put a gun to my head, but I still wouldn't pay up. So then they took me off to the calaboose at the nearest police station, where I was banged up for the next two days. They wanted to show me who was the boss, and this really did work, as I never tried that same trick again!'

Chris Stephenson came up with the unassailable truth that, try as you might, with reasonableness or outright determination, it was better to give up on an uneven contest you had no chance at all of ever winning:

'On being challenged by the authorities for whatever reason, you should argue and shout out your case as loudly as you can, but you should always give in at the end.'

CHAPTER 20

Con Tricks and Scams

Whatever cash or valuables a driver had brought with him had to be guarded at all times to prevent this disappearing in a brief instant. The disreputable means by which this could be achieved were various. There was straightforward theft by those stealthy creatures of the night who silently padded around lorry parks and broke into a cab to steal any valuables, but without waking up the driver, who was sleeping on a bunk nearby all the while. There were also those who used threats or actually carried out violence to rob a driver of whatever cash or belongings he was carrying with him; then there was the more subtle approach involving a confidence trick or sleight of hand.

A scam Des Seal saw one day at the Harem ferry landing stage in Istanbul impressed him as being very cunning indeed and almost foolproof:

'My mate was approached by some youths who seemed intent on buying his jacket as they proposed a very favourable offer. However, the negotiations that had started off so well suddenly fizzled out, and the youths started to walk away. But then they came rushing back, saying they'd just found this wallet, although of course, it had been cleverly lifted from my mate's jacket when he wasn't watching! This was all done with the intention of being offered a reward for "finding" the wallet! What impressed me was, this was such a sustainable scam, as it could be done repeatedly in the same place, and to all intent and purpose, it didn't look as if any crime had been committed.'

One night when Ian Taylor was driving his Scania 111 after crossing the border from Belgium into Germany he was pulled over by a policeman who then stated his intention to examine the truck's tachograph:

'The policeman noticed the needles on the tacho had been bent, so he fined me for having a "doctored" tacho, and I was sent back down the road to a firm which I later thought was rather too conveniently placed nearby to provide me with a replacement tachograph, at significant expense to myself. When I arrived there, I noticed this firm was doing excellent business with a number of other drivers, so I was left wondering whether or not this was all part of a big scam!'

The need to make sure someone was exactly who they said they were became an unbreakable rule for Ian Taylor after he got his fingers badly burnt when he was working for Simon International. Ian was approaching his destination in Baghdad when he was approached by a plausible looking and sounding individual who presented himself as an employee of the shipping agent which Ian needed to contact to concerning the delivery of his load. The supposed representative of the shipping agent offered to travel with Ian in the cab in order to provide directions to the place where the truck would then be unloaded. So Ian went along with this, and while they travelled across the city, the agent made a point of waving to some of the policemen they passed by who were directing the traffic at road junctions. On arriving at the shipping office, Ian was asked by the 'agent' if he would like to deposit any cash he had with him for safety in the office safe. This seemed like a good idea to Ian, although not for long, as after taking the cash and exiting through a back door of the office, Ian's 'helper' disappeared as if into thin air, never to be seen again!

Rather than writing the experience off as sheer bad luck and a lesson to be learnt for the future, when Ian made his next trip to Baghdad, he visited a police station to see if he could identify the thief from police records. After taking a look through a rogues' gallery of low-life rascals, thieves, con merchants and vagabonds, Ian managed to point out the bloke who had run off with all his money! Feeling elated that at last justice was in his grasp and the police were about to swing into action, Ian was amazed to learn from the policeman who was sitting by his side that this con man had already been dealt with for a far more serious crime. One that was so serious it left him lifelessly dangling on the end of a hangman's rope!

The light-fingered brigade would take every opportunity to sell on what they had managed to steal from a driver by hawking these items to any other drivers they came across. But if there was the slightest hint that what was on offer were stolen goods, these would be refused out of hand, as buying from these guys encouraged yet more crime directed against drivers.

Fred Topham ex-Scotland Yard detective on the trail of lost and stolen trailers. FT

This specially adapted Range Rover was also used by Fred Topham later on as a more durable vehicle for Middle East conditions. FT

A quick turnaround is what a thief requires to convert stolen goods into cash, and Gordon Summers was offered a full set of sidelight and brake lenses that he needed for his truck, which was more than a coincidence, as these parts had been cheekily removed from the back of his truck by the person who attempted to sell them back to him!

Counterfeit goods were frequently offered by those who hung around stopping places, such as the customs truck park outside Tehran airport. Even though the items looked authentic enough, it was important to check very closely whether they were a fake, as for example watches that exhibited a textual spelling mistake, such as the name 'Sieko' as the manufacturer rather than 'Seiko' appearing on the watch face!

Fear of theft was something that could easily get on drivers' nerves, and not surprisingly, it was easy for them to think of themselves as a moving target that was about to receive the wrong sort of attention, throughout the day and also the night. The strength of feeling against wrongdoers is best demonstrated perhaps by the following story which went the rounds, perhaps as an urban legend, as the details did tend to change from one telling to the next, or maybe it was founded in an incident which was perfectly true? This tale involved some European truck drivers who had caught a thief red-handed ransacking a truck cab of anything he could find that was valuable. So by way of punishment they drove a truck's tyres over the thief's hands – rough justice!

Fred Topham's Ford Granada estate put in thousands of miles tracking down lost containers. FT

By 1976 the increase in the numbers of trucks and trailers going missing after being sent out to the Middle East was causing increasing disquiet amongst the owners of haulage companies and the firms that rented out trucks and trailers, with insurance firms also

Roger Williams found some locals living in the back of this trailer owned by Willhire. RW

Trailer being recovered. Note the large rip in the tilt canvas. RW

Willhire were a big player in the trailer rental market for the Middle East. RW

Willhire's Volvo F88 as used to recover lost trailers. RW

suffering from having to pay out for any losses covered by their policies.

To summarise the problem, trucks, trailers and the loads they were carrying were being lost, never to be found; or they were being abandoned somewhere along the many thousands of miles which made up the various Middle East routes.

It was recognised that an increasing number of drivers chose to abandon their lorries en route, and the reasons behind this decision were identified as: breakdowns, owing to the difficulties of arranging repairs so far from home; the exhaustion of available funds to continue the journey any farther; or an incapacity to face up to what was a really tough job which the driver now recognised as something beyond his own capabilities. A further, far less worthy reason, was outright, unmitigated fraud!

One hire company lost 300 trailers, and in the face of the rising insurance costs which the underwriters had to pay out, the Lloyd's insurance company hired an ex-Scotland Yard detective to travel the Middle East routes locating any abandoned trucks, trailers, and in some cases the loads as well, so these could be recovered and brought back to the UK. The said detective, Fred Topham, was described in an edition of the *Arab Times* as a 'one-man Highway Patrol with a 2000-mile beat through some of the world's wildest and most dangerous country.' Driving a Ford Granada estate and later on a blue Range Rover that became familiar to British drivers, Fred was indeed successful in tracking down many abandoned trucks and trailers.

Some trucks and trailers never travelled that far at all before they became a semipermanent fixture in a lay-by or roadside truck stop. It was possible to come across such a truck and trailer just a few miles across the English Channel after the driver had blown all his running money by gambling it away at a casino in Zeebrugge.

Closer to home, a police investigation led to a number of fully laden trailers, which were supposedly on their

Mack F700 setting off with a Willhire trailer. RW

Abandoned Mercedes in a Belgrade storage yard. FT

Many ex-UK trucks such as this Merc took on a new life doing internal work in Saudi Arabia. FT

way to the Middle East, turning up in Northolt, which resulted in criminal prosecutions.

Fred outlined what some of the important factors were in creating this undesirable situation which reflected so badly on the Middle East haulage industry:

'The problem was, every man and his dog saw a pot of gold at the end of the rainbow when it came to getting involved with the Middle East run, so they would set off in all sorts of vehicles which were not at all suitable for the job in many cases. They would therefore break down somewhere and the truck would be abandoned together with its trailer and load. The drivers would get into difficulties because they didn't know what they doing or how to deal with any of the problems they encountered along the way. The drivers were generally salt of the earth people, and I got on well with them. Like most people, they liked to talk a lot, which was very useful for me, as they would tell me everything they knew when I was trying to track down any lost vehicles. I enjoyed the work and also the lifestyle. It was a great adventure for me; I met lots of people and I also learnt such a lot doing this job, it was a great experience.

'So how did I get the trucks and trailers home after they had been found? The same way the drivers had managed to leave the country when these had been abandoned: by rights, they couldn't leave the country as the truck, trailer and cargo were recorded on a carnet de passage, but bribery and corruption meant they had managed to get across any frontiers. I used the same method of bribing customs and border officials, as well as showing them some new paperwork: I had letters of introduction made out in Turkish, Farsi and Arabic, which helped to explain what I was doing to recover vehicles for insurance companies. Getting any recovered trucks and trailers out of Turkey was always a problem, as new paperwork would be needed. I would obtain a new carnet in the UK. Then I would fly out to Tehran, as getting vehicles out of Iran wasn't a problem at all. I would then get the new carnet stamped as if the truck in question had in fact crossed the border from Iran to Turkey. Then after picking up the truck where it had been abandoned in Turkey, it would be driven to the exit point at Kapıkule, and then into Bulgaria, to be finally driven home. If a truck and trailer needed to be recovered from Saudi Arabia, I would arrange for this to be shipped through ports such as Jeddah or Oman back home to the UK.'

Volvo F88 and AEC Mandator dumped at Erzurum TIR park, Central Turkey. FT

Fred had some notable successes recovering loads that had gone missing which went on to be sold to a

Right-hand drive steering column indicates this Mercedes truck started out in the UK, but odds on it won't ever be going back that way! FT

new owner by the insurance company, although on one occasion it looked as if finding a buyer was going to be a non-starter at the time:

'On the Jordan/Saudi border, I came across this truck that had sat there for three months with a full load of cheese in the back. Although the refrigeration unit had stopped working, the cheese didn't smell that bad, surprisingly, and it was arranged for an Arab driver to take the truck to Amman where all the cheese was checked out in a laboratory. It was found to be fine, so it was sent off to a new destination in Africa to be sold.'

Fred recalled a story about a British driver who had an enterprising solution to getting home after his truck broke down in Tehran. He decided to take a chance by stealing a brand-new DAF which the Iranian Government had imported from a lorry park. After swapping the UK number plates over from his own, broken-down truck, he drove the stolen DAF all the way to Dover, although any thoughts of selling this truck on were dashed when he was arrested by the police!

The consequences of having your goods stolen could be that the victim rather than the wrongdoer ended up behind prison bars, as Geoff Morgan found out to his intense sorrow:

'I was robbed just as I was crossing into Yugoslavia from Bulgaria on my way back to the UK. I'd been doing some duty free shopping, and after stopping to have a coffee, I noticed the interior light was on in my truck's cab. So I went to the driver's door and a young lad jumped out of the passenger door and ran away down a dark alley. No way was I going after him down there! He had stolen an onyx chess set that I had just bought, but it was lucky I had taken my passport and my money along for safe keeping. But he also took my briefcase containing all my permits for the rest of the trip, so I now needed to replace all of the stolen documents. My next move was to talk to a policeman while he was taking care of another driver. He had suffered a lot worse than I had: someone had hit him over the head using an axe! I went to an identity parade later on in an attempt to find the thief, but this wasn't any use at all. I was advised to go back to Sofia so that I could get some new travel permits to allow me to get out of Bulgaria and continue on with my journey. But I thought I would have a try at sneaking out of the country at the border. So I joined a queue of drivers who had had all their paperwork checked out in the hope that my papers wouldn't be asked for. However, this didn't work out, I was spotted and arrested, and I spent a week in prison before they let me out! In the cell there was a bucket of fruit you could eat and there was another bucket in the corner to do your business in. And at night, you needed to sleep with one eye still open to see what the others in there were up to!'

Keith Burson suffered a similar fate and the indignity of being locked up after his passport and other papers had been stolen:

'This occurred after I had been robbed in Bulgaria and I was locked up by the police for the next three days as the thieves stole my identification papers. They had cut through the rubber sealing strips in the small side windows of the cab so they could free the little release handle and open the window, to get at the door handle so they could then get into the cab and steal whatever they could find. Eventually an embassy official, Miss Lemon, arrived from Sofia, and she was very efficient at helping me to get out of jail – she did very well. We only had greasy soup and stale bread rolls to eat the whole time I was in jail, and I was very glad to get out of there!'

Smashed-up Volvo F86 found far from home on the back of a rented Willhire trailer. RW

CHAPTER 21

Local Traffic and Road Hazards

The condition of the roads out in the Middle East was often mirrored by the poor state of the locally owned vehicles that ran along these routes. Then there was the added dilemma of general driving standards falling short of what could be expected throughout Western Europe, as during the mid-seventies, the provision of driver training and any awareness of road safety issues were still at an elementary stage in countries such as Turkey, Iran and Syria.

Cars, trucks and buses were fairly modern innovations in these parts of the world. They were a novelty that took some time for drivers to become familiar with, and the dangers occasioned by poor driving and lack of safety awareness seemed to go unnoticed in Middle Eastern societies.

Private car ownership in the Communist bloc countries was still a rarity restricted to those with some political clout, with the rest of the population riding around in battered old Skoda buses and equally antiquated trolley buses and trams.

The consequences of becoming involved in an accident are far more severe in any Middle East country, and any TIR driver who was worth his salt needed to maintain a state of constant awareness throughout the day in order to figure out what might happen next, as the unexpected could and did reoccur with startling frequency. The normal rules of the road that applied when driving anywhere in Western Europe meant nothing at all to the drivers of Tonka trucks or fast-moving kamikaze coaches, so anything could happen with explosive swiftness!

As the miles went by, an uneasy state of mind could build up in any TIR driver who had the sense to use their imagination as to what might happen next. Mental images were conjured up and reinforced through the day by the sight of wrecked, fire-gutted vehicles along the roadside or lying upside down on their roofs in the surrounding fields.

Travelling down through Yugoslavia provided the first intimations that driving along the *autoput,* locally known as the 'Brotherhood and Unity Highway', through this country, on the route connecting Zagreb and Belgrade, could be very dangerous. *Gastarbeiter,* Turkish guest workers who were going home from their jobs in Germany, would drive along this road at full pelt, nose to the taillight of the vehicle in front, with an exhausted driver sitting behind the wheel who was slowly losing the struggle to stay awake.

As if as a point of honour, the worker's intention was often to drive all the way from Germany to Turkey in just one hop, barring any fuel stops. Old Mercedes-Benz and Opal saloons that were already clapped out would have been bought in Germany for the express purpose of making this journey, often carrying three generations of the same family at a time, together with a mountain of luggage that filled up the boot. And maybe some

A typical Turkish village scene with a locally owned Thames Trader in the foreground and a licence-built BMC approaching. RW

199

overspill possessions in the form of a television or a washing machine that had been strapped down onto a roof rack, which further compromised the car's already overstrained, sagging suspension!

It was estimated that one in three of the *Gastarbeiter* cars that started this arduous journey failed to arrive. The damaged or broken-down wrecks were left by the roadside as if to suggest a memorial to all the lives that were so needlessly lost each year!

Ian Taylor recalled travelling on the cobbled roads of Yugoslavia and coming across a car bound for Turkey which had an overloaded roof rack bouncing up and down as it raced over the rough road surface:

'If one of these Gastarbeiter *cars was forced to brake suddenly, it wasn't unusual for the roof rack, together with all the contents, to continue on at a speed of 120 kph by skidding along the road surface! I remember seeing many car wrecks along the roadside all the way through Yugoslavia. At the Bulgarian border there was a large pile of crashed cars which had been assembled at the side of the road as a salutary warning about the dangers of the road to those who passed by that way.'*

After crossing the border into Bulgaria, speed was far less of a problem. The main hazard here occurred when a TIR truck rounded a corner in the road and would then encounter a slow-moving tractor and trailer that was hogging the crown of the road, or a wandering horse and cart that also prompted a swift application of the brakes to avoid a collision! Tractors and horse carts were a form of transport for most of the rural

Cars such as this classic piece of Americana once thronged the streets of Istanbul. DB

population as well as farm workers! The horse-drawn carts carried registration plates which seemed so unnecessary given the chance of an owner not being identifiable within any of the close-knit communities to be found along the way in rural Bulgaria!

On arriving in Turkey and reaching Istanbul, a good number of the *Gastarbeiter* traffic would thankfully disperse from the route taken by the TIR trucks – most of these would then head off in all directions to towns and villages across the length and breadth of Turkey.

Most of the remaining contingent of cars still heading eastwards were known as 'Z-platers' on account of these carrying the German export number plates which started off with this same letter – the drivers then being known by the nickname, 'Zoomers'. These cars were usually driven by Iranians travelling at suicidal speeds, with a few adventurous European drivers joining in as well. The second-hand cars were on their way to be delivered and sold in Iran at a considerable profit – if they ever arrived there of course! Some of the cars made the journey piggy-back style, transported on the back of Mercedes-Benz 309 open trucks that were also making a one-way journey to be sold in Iran.

Once over the border into Turkey, those small, four- or six-wheeler trucks most Middle East drivers dismissively referred to as 'Tonkas' began to make their presence felt as an ever-present safety hazard that always needed to be closely watched out for, both by day and by night.

Second World War GMC 'Jimmy' serving as a wrecker truck. RW

Smashed-up front on a Mack imported from Germany, note 'z-plate' registration. 1975. BC

A sixties-style Mack leads a much older truck of the same Bulldog marque; this make of truck was very popular with Iranian operators. BC

The Tonka truck name was derived from the similarity of these small lorries to the toy trucks manufactured at the time by the Tonka toy company. Tonka trucks carried the name badges of American truck firms Chrysler, De Soto or Fargo, and it also seemed to be the case that British truck manufacturers held part of the Turkish market at one time, with the Austin truck name still in evidence as well as the Ford D-Series and Bedford TK lorries, most of which had been licence built in Turkey.

Usually so heavily overloaded that it looked as if the chassis were about to snap in two, these hard-working Tonka vehicles served industry and agriculture interests alike. How hard they were worked was frequently indicated by the poor state of repair exhibited, with badly worn tyres that were almost devoid of any tread, and the heavy loads these trucks carried severely reduced braking efficiency and could badly affect the steering as well.

Adding to the perils of encountering one of these wrecks during the hours of darkness, Tonka drivers had a deeply engrained habit of turning their headlights off when they noticed another vehicle approaching from the opposite direction, which caused no end of confusion!

Keith Burson recalled an anxious moment when he came across a battery of multicoloured lights that seemed to suggest a mobile Christmas tree was coming

De Soto six-wheeler Tonka truck still in service in 2012. DB

Mike Dunstan's modern Volvo F89, the only modern truck parked up in Amman, Jordan. MD

towards him out of the darkness when he was crossing a remote area somewhere in the Turkish mountains:

'I came across one of these Tonka trucks that had lots of fancy lights strung all over it, but no headlights were showing at all. So I assumed I was looking at the back of the truck because I could not see any headlights, but I'd failed to realise the driver had already turned them off! I was getting ready to overtake this truck on the assumption it was going in the same direction that I was travelling in. But then I realised the truck was actually coming straight towards me, and it was getting very, very close! So I only just managed to avoid a collision by getting out of its way! It was also fairly common to come across these local trucks travelling with no rear lights either!'

Peter Bamford added his recollections of following a few overloaded Tonka trucks that were struggling to get over the heights of the Bolu Pass:

'Nowadays, there's the motorway all the way across Turkey to Ankara which took all the fun out of the job: there was no challenge any more, I'd say, after this work was done. But there certainly was a bit of a challenge driving here in the old days! When you were going up Bolu you would come across these Tonka trucks, all loaded up to the nines. They were so overloaded that wooden blocks had to be stuck under the rear leaf springs to keep the wheels turning freely. Otherwise, the weight of the load that was carried on the back would have caused the rear springs to bend so much, the body of the truck would be forced down to rest on top of the tyres, and the rear wheels couldn't go round any more! Travelling three abreast, the drivers of these Tonka trucks would try to overtake each other when there was barely any difference in the speed they were travelling at – maybe three miles an hour between the fastest and the slowest of the three slowly moving trucks. This made life really frustrating for anyone in a more powerful European truck who wanted to get past them. So when the opportunity came to overtake any Tonka truck whose driver had been deliberately holding me back in this way, I would get my own back shortly afterwards when I had finally passed the slow-moving, obstructive Tonka, by bringing my own truck to a dead stop to block the road ahead, forcing the other truck to come to a stop. This was in the knowledge I would be able to drive away again in my more powerful truck, whereas the Tonka would be so heavily overloaded, he would be stuck, and he would have burnt out his clutch if he'd tried setting off carrying so much weight uphill. So he couldn't go on any further without calling for assistance!'

Heavily loaded Tonka trucks could often be seen climbing really steep slopes by driving from one side

Ian Tyler was bemused when some local drivers on the way to Damascus didn't know which side of the road to use. ITY

of the road to the other in order to slightly reduce the angle of approach. But this made getting round these vehicles even more difficult to achieve!

David Miller commented:

'Those Tonka truck drivers had a gruesome reputation for driving badly and a terrible propensity for causing accidents, you had to be really awake all the time when you saw one approaching, either when it was in front of you, or when one was coming up from behind.'

The poor quality and simplicity of tyre repairs was something Chris Stephenson always found amazing, as was the faith the drivers had that all would be well:

'Syrian Tonka lorry drivers would mend their cross-ply tyres with patches that were held in place by coach bolts which had been fitted on the inside of the tyre.'

However, Tonka drivers received a measured degree of approval from Mike Dunstan for the way they managed to handle their broken-down trucks and so keep them going, although his respect and patience soon wore thin when confronted by their pushy antics at border crossings:

'Tonka drivers, I got on well with them on the whole, but not at any border crossings where they were a different animal. They did all sorts of crazy things to be first in the system to get across the border and on to the other side, not least pushing into traffic queues.'

The degree of overloading that a Tonka driver would apply to his truck was brought home to Chris Stephenson when he came across a Steyr four-wheeler flatbed truck that was struggling along when carrying a large load of cement sacks. As Chris drove by at a slow speed, he totted up the number of sacks he could see on the loadbed, and according to his rule of thumb calculations, this amounted to a colossal weight of approximately eighty tons!

A well as providing his thoughts on Tonka drivers, Gerry Homes remarked along the lines that the blame for poor driving could rest on a few British drivers as well:

'Tonka truck drivers, they were quite good drivers but they had a tendency to become overconfident thinking Allah was going to protect them from anything that might have gone wrong. They would always try to keep coming through in the middle of the road if you didn't stop them by fronting them when it was impossible for them to get through anyway. They would then have to reverse to a passing place to allow you to come through.

'But there were a few of the English guys who were just as bad. Some of them were real nutters, or "Cab Happy Cowboys" as I chose to call them at the time. Many small

Improvised repair to get a few hundred extra 'k's out of a locally operated truck! DM

Whether frowned on or applauded, Tonka drivers knew how to brave flooded rivers. GP

Turkish coach drivers were immediately identifiable by their once smart, but now tatty and badly worn uniforms and the battered, peaked caps which they wore that looked as if the suits and headwear had been modelled on the uniforms of airline pilots of the forties era. It was easy to assume that these coach drivers had a death wish as they sped along in their Mercedes D302 coaches with the accelerator pedal pressed flat to the floor! Such were the distances involved on any Turkish or Iranian coach routes, two drivers were usually carried; the second driver would rest up by sleeping on a panel behind the coach's rear seat, and when the time came for a changeover of drivers, they would swap roles so that the second driver would take over from the first one who needed to be relieved, but without taking the precaution of

firms thought they'd have a go at doing the Middle East run without really knowing anything at all about what they had actually taken on. Their attitude was, "We are English, so everyone else is inferior to us, and that means everyone must get out of our way."'

The term kamikaze suggests those fanatical Japanese pilots of the Second World War who deliberately gave up their lives to make desperate suicide attacks on Allied warships. So in view of the poor standard of driving exhibited by Turkish coach drivers, a 'kamikaze' then became the slang word for a Turkish coach that ran between towns and cities to a punishing service schedule to accommodate interconnecting services. The drivers would willingly risk the lives of all those on board as well as anyone travelling in any other vehicles that stood in the way of keeping to time with their schedule!

It was said that the sight of a coach's headlights meant that the driver was about to come through, come what may, so it was very important to move over. Conversely, as coach drivers normally wouldn't slow down or stop for anything that was not really serious; if a coach's brake lights could be seen somewhere in front, this warned of a major problem or accident up ahead!

Ian Tyler trails behind some Tonka trucks on the road between Edirne and Istanbul. ITY

bringing the coach to a halt or even pausing for a while to slow down!

As if grimly intent on proving their reputation for dangerous driving, these coach drivers would cut up any traffic that incautiously got in their way. This all too often caused accidents resulting in multiple casualties and many deaths. On more than one occasion one of these coaches veered across the road in an attempt to overtake slower moving traffic only to plough, full force, into the front of a TIR truck coming from the other direction, causing the death of all the passengers on board as well as the equally innocent lorry driver.

A backpacker travelling on a Turkish coach watched in amazement as the coach he was travelling on was overtaken by a second coach. Rather than using the other side of the road, which was blocked by a third coach that was also attempting to overtake the first coach, the second coach ran off the road, and raced across a stretch of empty wasteland. Unbeknown to the driver of the second coach, a petrol station was fast approaching further ahead, but instead of abandoning the manoeuvre, the fearless coach driver kept his foot to the floor, so his coach then shot between two lines of petrol pumps, where fortunately, no-one was refilling their car with petrol at the time! The coach then exited

Turkish Otosan Ford Tonka truck that's only recently come out of service! DB

Terry Tott as a 'karayollari' road worker. On approaching some road works he had to drive off road as the tar was too soft for a heavy truck and its load. TT

Crashes involving high speed 'kamikaze' coaches often resulted in many casualties. BR

the forecourt before claiming its rightful place ahead of the other two coaches!

One joke that was passed around concerned a priest and a kamikaze coach driver who arrived at the Pearly Gates at the same time and were asked why they thought they should be allowed into Heaven. The priest said he should be allowed admittance as 200 parishioners prayed at his church every Sunday. But the coach driver upstaged the priest saying that 200 passengers prayed in his coach every day.

The need for these coach drivers to keep to their allotted schedule was paramount, with any form of aggressive behaviour justifying the means of achieving this objective, as Alan Dayson explained with the following tale:

'Local bus drivers ruled the road and they behaved as if nothing could ever go wrong. If a coach was coming towards or going past you in order to overtake, it would just keep on coming, whatever was in its way, the driver of these buses would never, ever give in. I held up a bus one day when it was trying to get by me, which it eventually did, and as this bus went on by, I watched the bus boy open up the rear door so he could throw an empty glass bottle at my windscreen!'

Graham Cartmail recalled a similar incident when he was lucky to be driving a right-hand drive rather than a left-hand drive truck in view of what was to happen next:

'If you held up any coach drivers who wanted to overtake you, they would often throw a stone at you as they went on by. This wasn't too bad if you were driving a right-hand drive truck as the stone would be aimed at the nearer, passenger side of the cab. I took this sort of thing in my stride, and I did my best never to get upset as we were earning a lot more money than those Turkish coach drivers ever could.'

Mike Dunstan underlined the need to maintain constant vigilance and keep a sharp look out through your truck's rear mirrors:

'Overland coaches had a right of way legally over any other traffic. You could hear these Merc coaches coming by the sound of the air valves blowing off excess pressure. They would poke the nose of their coach out, and when you saw this in your mirrors, then you knew they were going to try and come round you, while taking no notice at all of anyone who was coming the other way. I've seen them get it wrong so many times, with many passengers lying dead in the wreck of a badly smashed-up coach. Travelling in Turkish overland coaches was a very dangerous thing to do! The drivers had to train in minibuses until they'd earned the status to drive coaches, and then they were as well respected as airline pilots. They always had to keep to their very tight schedules which explained why they went so fast all the time. If any new passengers were standing beside the road waiting for a coach to come by and stop, the coach would only stop still for a few seconds, during which time the passenger door would fly open and the bus boy would forcibly push any new passengers into the coach. If they weren't fast enough at getting on board, they would be left where they were by the roadside!'

Karl Nowotarski learnt to rue the day when he boarded one of these coaches and happened to mention he was also a professional driver:

'If you were a driver out in the Middle East, this gave you a high standing with everyone else out there. So all the kamikaze bus drivers believed they always had the right of way. Going round a blind bend and coming across a coach from the other direction, the coach driver would always expect you to be the one that gave way. And if you didn't, it was down to you if there was an accident. I went on a coach to attend a court trial following a road accident that had involved me. I took care to sit well at the back of the coach knowing how these drivers behaved. But after the driver discovered I was a professional truck driver, he invited me to sit at the front so I was next to him. This was a really frightening experience and it was one I could have well done without!'

Such was the deep-seated habit that Middle East car drivers had of sounding their car's horn at every possible opportunity, that on one occasion when David Miller took a taxi in Istanbul, the driver lost the will to go on when his car horn ceased working. The taxi ground to a halt midway across the Galata Bridge in the centre of Istanbul:

'I was going to see my freight agent to get loading instructions in this ancient De Soto taxi dating back to the 1940s, I would say. However, the taxi driver broke the rim of the car horn push which was in the middle of the steering wheel, so the horn wasn't working any more. He wasn't prepared to go any further without a car horn, so he stopped his car and found me another taxi so I could continue on with my journey!'

In Istanbul, old Chevrolet, Plymouth and Dodge taxi cabs, which would have been scrapped years ago anywhere else, still dominated the roads; often well over thirty years old and quite literally falling apart, the steering was often so badly worn, almost a full turn of the wheel was needed before there was any response transmitted to the front axle and the worn set of tyres!

Gerry Holmes may well have guessed why a taxi driver didn't make all that much use of his aged car's brake pedal:

'I was in one taxi, an old Chevy Impala, when I noticed the driver always slapped the car into first gear using the column change shift whenever he needed to slow down or come to a stop. I said, "Why not use your brakes?" to which he replied, "Brakes kaput." He only had the gearstick and the handbrake to slow this heavy old car down!'

David Miller recalled a moment of abject terror in a taxi cab that was out of control:

'Your taxi driver would hurl his vehicle at a gridlocked junction when he had the traffic lights against him, without slowing down at all, and the only thing he would say was the magic word "Inshallah," meaning, "If it is the will of God." Only then was I beginning to understand these people had a totally different mindset to us.'

The cars to be seen around Istanbul and elsewhere in Turkey attracted plenty of interest from Western truck drivers, the styling being recognisable from films that had Humphrey Bogart in the starring role which had been released maybe twenty or thirty years ago! But by contrast, brand-new American cars could be seen everywhere in Saudi Arabia, although the standard of road safety displayed by the owner of a 1973 Cadillac in Saudi was much the same as their Turkish contemporary who drove a thirty-three-year-old model of the same make!

Alan Dayson provided the following comment on the social one-upmanship that a new car could bestow:

'In Saudi you would see all sorts of new American cars which still had the importer's delivery sticker masking the passenger's side of the windscreen so the driver couldn't see out – perhaps a status symbol attesting to this being a new purchase.'

Paul Rowlands reported you had to be even more careful about road safety when driving southwards through Syria towards the Arabian Peninsula:

'I still can't believe the poor standards of driving in the Middle East by local drivers. The worst drivers were to be found in Damascus, Syria, with Tehran running a close second. I recently travelled to Istanbul and found the situation concerning safety had not improved much at all since the old days, and in some ways you could say it's now

'Hi Ho Silver', MAN tipper truck in Dammam, Saudi Arabia. GH

become even worse due to the increase in traffic volume and everyone going faster than they ever used to do.'

Paul drives for the Transam Trucking haulage firm these days which is involved in providing transport for music events. A recent trip he made to Istanbul brought back many memories, and he adopted a suitably cautious driving style all the way there and back!

Ian Taylor found Saudi truck drivers to be in a class of their own when it came to making erratic progress, as they rarely seemed to know where they were going:

'We would dodge around a Mercedes truck, which would have another truck on its back, with a couple of Mercedes cars then sitting on top of the second truck. These lorries would be driven by Saudi drivers who wore loose cotton clothing like nightshirts. They were always asking us for directions on which way to go, which we would answer by pointing them in the direction of Saudi Arabia for guidance. They didn't have any maps with them that would have told them the correct way to go!'

One of David Miller's favourite memories involved some Iranian-owned trucks which travelled in the opposite east to west direction to make deliveries from Iran to a number of European destinations. He remembers seeing many ancient Mack trucks which seemed to have miraculously made it all the way as far as Europe despite their condition and unsuitability:

'I would be driving along a German autobahn and I would come across one of these vintage, bonneted Macks

Trans UK Volvo at the end of a long haul trip. Missing and smashed fog lights suggest a local ban on halogen bulbs. FT

owned by Sham's Express that would come trundling along the autobahn, looking totally alien sitting on enormous, 14.00 × 20, off-road desert tyres, and with an outlandishly dressed (to our eyes) driver sitting up in the cab. They were also occasionally in the customs yard at Dover, which was as far away from their homes as we all were at the other end of our runs to the Middle East. I suppose there were times when we also looked just as strange to the locals as these Iranian guys did to us when they travelled on our European roads.'

If any spotlights had been fitted to foreign trucks entering Saudi Arabia, then this was something the authorities were intensely concerned about, particularly if the bulbs were of the high-powered halogen type. One theory which went the rounds concerned a Saudi prince who had been dazzled by a set of spotlights, which presumably resulted in a road accident or maybe just a near miss! So after arriving with a truck fitted with these lights at the border, if the spotlights or the bulbs were not removed, or the spotlights were not turned round so they were then ineffective, the border guards would simply smash the lights before allowing access to their country.

Gordon Summers offered an alternative explanation which seemed to be a lot more bizarre as it was grounded in someone's zealous religious fervour:

'This fundamentalist came along and objected to my Volvo having a set of four headlights, a pair on each side of my truck. According to what he believed to be true in a religious sense, you were only supposed to have two headlights; not a set of two headlights on both sides of a truck, as I had on the one I was driving. His reasoning was that the Koran says an animal should have two eyes, not four. So to his way of thinking, it was unnatural for a truck to have four headlights. I've never read the Koran, so this was something I couldn't ever comment on! Anyway, he said, "If you don't remove the two extra headlights, I will smash them for you." So I replied, "You put those two headlights out, and I'll put your own lights out as well!" He went ahead and smashed two of my headlights, one on each side, so what did I do next, I let him have it. I then spent the next two days in prison before the police decided it was time to let me go. You really needed the best set of headlights you could have on your truck when travelling out there, as you needed to spot any camels as soon as you could when you were travelling at night, as these animals had a bad habit of wandering out onto any roads as soon as it was dark!'

Ron Slater driving for CVH in a Ford Transcontinental through Turkey. MM

CHAPTER 22

Accidents

When the poor state of the roads, the condition of the vehicles and a lack of awareness of the need to drive safely were put together, this made for a deadly combination that Middle East drivers soon became aware of, and if they had any reservations about taking on this combination of dangers, then the job clearly was not meant for them at all!

Sadly, nothing much has changed in the last forty-odd years, as accident statistics indicate Turkey still has the unenviable reputation of having one of the highest traffic accident rates in the world. A study of road traffic accidents in Turkey that was conducted in 1998 recorded 440,149 road traffic accidents, resulting in 4935 deaths and 114,552 injuries.

According to a recent UNICEF report, the incidence of road accidents in Iran was calculated at twenty times the average of all other countries, with 28,000 people killed in the survey period and 300,000 injured or disabled. Road accidents in Iran are the second highest cause of death.

It would be fair to say that after each and every trip most Middle East drivers would have come home with a memory of one or two near misses that had caused them to stiffen in fright as they drove along, some of these being serious enough to make them consider whether or not they wanted to continue with this way of life! Or more graphically, whether they wanted to stay alive or take the ever-present risk of dying somewhere out on the road!

By the time most drivers had taken the decision to call it quits and give up what was always a dangerous way of making a living they would have most probably witnessed at least one fatality as well as many other incidents that left someone seriously disabled for the rest of their life. This toll of suffering included many European drivers of course, as the degree of

Multiple pile-up involving a truck and two cars, the second car ending up underneath the truck. BC

This Atkinson truck was struck by a car coming the other way and was then rear-ended by a truck operated by the Wakefield Haulage Company. RW

The driver of the Atkinson was thrown through the windscreen and kept on running just in case he was about to be run over! RW

invulnerability that driving a heavy truck provided was often illusory in a really serious impact.

Geoff Morgan recalled an incident when the need to exercise caution at all times was forcibly brought home to him as he returned from a trip to Iraq:

'This driver who was running ahead of me ran straight into the back of a tractor and trailer that had been abandoned at the side the road because one of the tyres had blown out. When I arrived on the scene, I came across this driver's DAF 2800, which was so badly damaged, the side of the cab on his truck was ripped open, and the steering column had been torn out by the force of the crash. I went to see the police later on to see if I could help out in any way, but it turned out the driver had already died on the operating table by then, leaving a wife and three little kiddies.'

As was frequently the case in many Middle Eastern countries, the only indication of a road ahead being blocked by a broken-down vehicle was when a series of small piles of stones, balanced one on top of the other, were left along the roadside to substitute for a warning triangle or road cones. Geoff added:

'You always had to be careful to spot these stones as you drove along. What made the situation more difficult was that there were so many false alarms when you came across a line of these piles of stones that no-one had bothered to clear away after a broken-down or crash-damaged vehicle had already been removed and there was no longer a hazard. So the next time you came across a line of stones …'

David Miller came to his senses with a start when he was abruptly woken in the middle of the night:

'I was going through Yugoslavia, and after stopping for the night somewhere between Zagreb and Belgrade, I settled down in the cab for the night when there was a sudden huge jolt received from the back of my truck, which left me lying down on the floor of the cab. I got out of the truck carrying a torch with me and I found a car rammed solid underneath my trailer which had a dead man sitting inside it. The interior of the car reeked of booze like a brewery, so I guessed this bloke was as pissed as a parrot when he drove off the motorway flat out onto the lay-by where I'd parked

Another picture taken of the crashed Atkinson which was still there months after it had crashed in July 1975, as indicated by the snowfall on the ground. FT

This Bedford TK was wrecked after running down a steep embankment. BR

British-owned MAN truck left the road and turned over all too easily due to the steep embankment. BC

The damage to this truck indicates what happened when, travelling at a rate of knots, it met a fully grown camel in the middle of the road. TT

my truck for the night! The police arrived and arrested me because they thought I could have been responsible for this man's death. So I was up before the judge the following day, with a translator who was there to help out. I was formally accused of causing the bloke's death, to which I replied, this wasn't fair at all as I had been fast asleep at the time. But the translator advised me not to make any comments other than simply to confirm who I was by giving them my name, and then listen to what the judge had to say. His reasoning was that if I'd stayed at home in England, then this accident could not have happened, so therefore I was to blame for the bloke's death. This judgement had me really worried, but to conclude what was a very serious matter, I was fined about fifty German marks, which was worth only about fifteen quid at the time!

'The carnage of accidents was really something, especially on the route that took you between Zagreb and Belgrade. The road ran through many miles of very low-lying country that was subject to mist in the summer months and freezing fog during the winter. For the first few trips to the Middle East there was always a tendency for new drivers to try and cover as much ground as they could possibly manage in the minimum amount of time. But this involved taking unacceptable risks by attempting to overtake any lumbering Yugoslavian vehicles which were in front of them; but only to end up stuck behind whatever they then came across just a short distance further down the road! So the whole dangerous overtaking manoeuvre would have to be repeated. You soon realised it was far better to stay within the speed restrictions imposed by any local traffic, and not break your heart trying to get by! This was the best policy, and although it took some time to appreciate this to be true, it was also the quickest way through in the long run.'

Fate dealt a cruel blow to the passengers of a Turkish bus when it veered across the road, cannoning into the front of one of Dayson's Scanias near the Turkish border at Kapıkule, resulting in ten deaths and many injuries. The Dayson's driver survived, although by now he has passed away long after finishing his Middle

Astran truck come to grief on the way between Istanbul and Ankara. BR

Double trouble: transporting a broken-down truck ended with a more serious problem. COPYRIGHT UNKNOWN

East career. This person went by the memorable name of Errol Flynn, although any connection with the swashbuckling film star of the same name was purely coincidental. The Errol forename was adopted from his place of birth, Errol in Scotland, and to prove he wasn't joking whenever he needed to confirm his name, Errol carried his passport with him at all times!

Alan Dayson described what happened after Errol's Scania 110 was struck by a long-distance coach travelling at speed so that both vehicles were reduced to twisted wreckage and quite a number of the coach's passengers were killed:

'Normally, you could expect a lot of trouble in circumstances such as this, but what made the situation so different on this occasion was that as Errol's truck had been so badly damaged in the collision, the Turks couldn't believe how he'd managed to survive such a terrible impact. They wanted to touch him, in the belief he was special in some way. Through their religious beliefs, they thought Allah had taken pity on him and had saved his life. Perhaps more to the point, Errol's truck had left-hand drive steering, and most of the damage was to the other side of his truck. If he had been driving a right-hand drive truck to British spec, he would most certainly have died in the crash as well. The locals tried showering Errol with gifts in view of what they saw as a miracle, and the police released him without charge some time later. Whenever Errol went back to Turkey he was often recognised by some of the locals who already knew about the accident; not for his unusual name, but for his miraculous escape. There was hardly anything left of the Scania's cab after it had been recovered and we'd brought it back to Cumbria. It looked just like a pile of scrap metal. But this badly damaged truck made its way back onto the road after a new cab was installed by our fitter, Dave Potter, who was a real marvel at this type of work. I've never seen a Scania as badly mangled as that one was!'

Ken Ward mentioned the day when he met up with a driver who was working for PIE International Carriers, and they got chatting. This man's task was to recover another PIE truck which had been damaged in an accident which killed the British driver, a fate the

The driver of this F88 salvages a few personal possessions. GP

Licence-built BMC Boxer-type Tonka truck that has shed its load after the driver lost control. BR

recovery driver was about to share after he travelled further down the road on what was to be his last trip:

'The first accident had occurred when the driver pulled out to overtake someone else, but another truck was coming the other way, so this resulted in a head-on collision between the two trucks, and the driver was immediately killed. The second fatality occurred when the bloke I had been talking to about the first accident was taking the accident-damaged truck back home through Italy on the back of his PIE truck. This driver stopped and got out of the cab to repair a broken taillight on his trailer, but another truck then ran into the back of the trailer, killing the recovery driver outright.'

Dave Jamieson recalled an incident that could have turned out a lot worse due to the improvised method the driver had adopted to heat up the cab of his broken-down truck:

'Robert Hamilton, who has since passed away, suffered a breakdown with his truck, which was being towed along by another driver called Tommy Greave, with a straight bar connecting the two trucks together. They were passing through a series of narrow tunnels when one of the SOMAT trucks operated by the Bulgarian state transport company came down the tunnel in the opposite direction. As the two trucks went through a curved section of the tunnel, the front edge of the Bulgarian's trailer collided with the side of Robert's trailer, causing Robert's truck to move sideways. It then hit a high kerb running all the way along the wall of the tunnel, and the impact against the kerb damaged the cab and shattered the windscreen, leaving Robert to make his quick escape by jumping through the space where the windscreen once was! What made Robert even more anxious to get out of the cab was that a lighted gas cooker which had been in use to belt out some heat into the cab to keep him nice and warm, had overturned, setting fire to the cab!'

Prompt action smothered the flames, and Robert eventually made it home without any burn marks or further incidents.

Dave also vividly remembered witnessing an accident when a British truck became a runaway as it descended a steep slope travelling westwards from Ankara on the notoriously dangerous Bolu Pass:

'I came across two brand-new Volvo F89s all painted up in black and gold like the John Player Special Formula One racing team's colours in those days. These identical trucks were travelling one behind the other, with both trucks loaded up with twenty tons of welding rods. The driver of the second truck suddenly realised the air pressure which operated the brakes on his truck was well down; so this meant he couldn't stop, to all intents and purposes! He decided the only chance he had of slowing down would be to touch the back of his mate's trailer to take advantage of the other truck's brake system. But before he could catch up with his mate, a kamikaze coach driver nipped into the space between the two Volvos. The driver of the Volvo with the faulty brakes then decided the only way he could save himself was to bail out of the cab before it was going any faster and left the road, plunging into a deep gorge. So he set the steering wheel in a certain direction that would allow the truck to crash harmlessly into the gorge, before leaping out of the cab. But the truck managed to straighten itself out after it ran down the road for a short while, so it avoided plunging down into the gorge, as the driver had planned. It managed to stay

MAN Tonka truck run off the road in Turkey with a collapsed front wheel. BR

This robbed-out Fiat 619 was photographed by Fred Topham as part of his insurance investigations. FT

upright on all its wheels, and then headed off down a side road with no-one at the wheel, where it safely came to a halt. Ironically, the driver was less fortunate as he spent some time in hospital recovering from the injuries which occurred after he'd jumped out of the cab. Later on, the driver of the second Volvo suffered the same problem with the loss of air pressure that also caused the brakes on his truck to fail, but without an accident occurring. The fault on both trucks was traced to a mistake in the way the air lines and valves had been set up for the trailers. Volvo investigated the problem and they recognised and accepted the fault was theirs, so they paid out compensation to the owner of the two trucks for any damage or expenses that were involved.'

Gerry Holmes recalled a similar incident that was caused by a Turkish taxi driver cutting in front of a truck so as to avoid a collision with oncoming traffic:

'I was in Istanbul when I heard about an English guy who had been in an accident near the town of Edirne in western Turkey. A Turkish taxi driver had sneaked in front of his truck after overtaking it. This was done to avoid the taxi hitting some traffic coming the other way towards the taxi. The rear bumper of the taxi caught the front bumper of the English truck, causing the taxi to swing sideways so it was T-boned by the front of the truck. The collision killed a female passenger who was sitting on the taxi's rear seat, and although the English driver wasn't to blame for what happened in any way, he was taken off to jail, as was the usual practice in Turkey, until everything to do with this accident had been sorted out. I volunteered to go and recover his Scania 110, which hadn't suffered all that much damage in the accident at all, so I climbed in, and I drove it to Istanbul, as it was important to prevent it being stripped down by the roadside for any parts, which was what often happened if a truck was abandoned. Later on, I went to see the driver in jail, and it was heartbreaking to see this strong, hairy truck driver sitting there crying his eyes out! He said to me, "Put my children out of their home and put my wife out on the game, but just get me out of here." The experience of being in a Turkish prison had reduced him to a quivering wreck in no time at all. I had to ask myself very seriously, "Why are we doing this job?" '

Gerry Holmes remembered a similar incident when an oncoming coach caused his blood to freeze and he

The end of the road for this Scania 110. RW

Wrecked trucks by the wayside, a common sight throughout Yugoslavia and Turkey. RW

Ford Transcontinental awaiting recovery after a fatal accident in Iran. MC

Chevalier Brothers trailer recovered after the same fatal accident involving the Ford Transcontinental. FT

was lucky to avoid a nasty accident and the inevitable blame for what could have happened afterwards:

'I was carrying a container, which was well freighted, as it was loaded with heavy crockery, so it wouldn't have been easy to stop this truck if there was an emergency. I was running alongside an owner driver called Tyrone Jarvis, who later on became the transport boss for my firm, H.J. Atlas of Avonmouth. I decided to overtake Tyrone, and after managing to get alongside his truck after he had slowed down by missing a gear change, I suddenly saw there was a coach coming towards me from the opposite direction at speed, which it shouldn't have been doing at all, as the section of road we were travelling on was signposted as one-way only! I had to put my truck in the ditch to get out of that coach's way, but the coach driver also ran into the same problem and he drove into the ditch on the opposite side of the road, as he couldn't stop to avoid my truck. So he slid into the ditch a short way ahead of where my truck had come to a halt. All sorts of shouts and screams were coming from the coach as the passengers tried to get out of the wreck. Fortunately, no-one had been hurt, and we managed to get everyone out of the coach, but only by ripping away the roof skylights. The coach driver tried to blame me for what had happened, but as I successfully pointed out to the police that had arrived, the road we were both on was only one-way, therefore the accident couldn't be my fault. This explanation was accepted by the police, who then let me off. A Dutchman and a Bulgarian came along and they used their trucks to pull me out by employing reverse gear, as this was the lowest gear. Luckily, there was no damage to my truck or its load.'

Mike Dunstan remembered an incident when he lost the full load off the back of his truck, but then managed to recover all of this, although finding his briefcase containing his passport and all the other papers assumed much more importance:

'When I was still working for the Dutch firm Butrako, we were running towards the Syrian border in three identical Fiats, which were all travelling open TIR style, as they were loaded with bridge sections to be used for building a flyover at Riyadh airport in Saudi. We stopped at a bus terminal so we could take some time to eat a meal and we all had a haircut before setting off again, but I was delayed and I couldn't keep up with the other drivers because the level of traffic passing through the town had suddenly built up. Further on down the road, after leaving a town called Aksaray behind, my truck was involved in an accident on a section of road which was being resurfaced. The procedure adopted in Turkey was to put some tarmac down when it was hot, but the chippings wouldn't be added until later on. This meant the road surface was of wet, slippery, hot tar, and as I drove along, a tractor towing a trailer carrying cotton workers across a field then climbed a bank on to the road. The tractor driver hadn't noticed my truck was fast approaching in his direction: he had been distracted by a Volkswagen kombi ambulance that was coming down the road in the opposite direction, with its horns blaring and

Mike Dunstan's Fiat after he ran out of road avoiding a tractor and trailer carrying many farm workers. MD

lights flashing. To avoid hitting the tractor and trailer, which had all those people on board, I steered the truck as hard as I could, making it slide on the slippery road surface. But then my truck and trailer leaned over just that bit too far, and they tipped over on their sides and landed in a field. The heavy bridge sections I was carrying had breached their securing chains when the trailer had landed in the field. The force of the impact had damaged my truck, as the cab was all twisted out of shape, and the windscreen had shattered into pieces. I had been left lying in a heap at the bottom of the cab, and I remember seeing people looking in at me through the broken windscreen.

Crescent-Sealand rig hit by a local Tonka truck in Saudi. GH

'After managing to get back on my feet, two blokes held the door open so I could get out. I realised I'd left my briefcase inside the cab, so back I went: they could take anything else from my cab, but they weren't having my important briefcase and paperwork to get in and out of the country! My two mates I was running with arrived after a Turkish driver had stopped them to tip them off about my accident, so they had turned round and come back to help me out. We managed to get the truck and trailer back onto all its wheels later on so it was going again, and the bridge sections I had been carrying were reloaded – they were undamaged – so these were finally delivered intact when I arrived in Saudi Arabia.'

Nevertheless, a few repairs were needed to the truck, although Mike was most fortunate in engaging the services of a garage owner who adopted a novel approach to finding a vital missing part:

'Repairing the damage to my Fiat caused by the accident involved fixing the fuel lines that were leaking, and reattaching the fuel tank as the securing straps had broken. There was also a more serious problem as an essential metal casting on the gearbox had gone missing; without this you could not change gear at all. So the garage owner went out to the scene of the accident, and by using a magnet suspended on the end of a piece of string, he found the missing casting, which he welded back into position to get the gearbox working once again. The handle securing the fifth wheel had also come off, so the mechanic welded it back into position; the only problem then being, we couldn't detach the trailer after we had arrived in Saudi, as it had been welded on solid! In the end we had to cut off the fifth wheel release handle using an oxyacetylene torch so we could detach the trailer for unloading!'

Given that it was usually the foreigner who was automatically held to be at fault for any accidents or collisions that had occurred, irrespective of whether they were actually to blame, this provided a strong incentive to cut and run after an accident had taken place. The aim was then to cover as many kilometres as possible from the scene of an accident so as to reach sanctuary beyond the next border crossing where the driver would be safe from police prosecution, as they would be beyond recall in another country.

John Buffham recognised this as the only way to avoid unfairly taking the blame, moments after he came across two Tonka trucks travelling side by side as they sped onwards towards his truck: it was clear something was now about to go horribly wrong!

Jim Stevens hit the back of a broken-down Syrian truck at night, sustaining serious leg injuries, so he was flown back to the UK. MD

'I had an accident in 1982, and this was when I broke the golden rule of never driving at night if you were travelling anywhere through Turkey. This was because I wanted to get home as quickly as I could, and after rounding a blind bend with a steep drop on my side of the road, I came across these two Turkish trucks running side by side from the opposite direction, both of which were carrying their loads of sheep. One of these trucks had started overtaking the other one, and the only way I could see to avoid a collision was to brake as hard as I could and hope for the best that the two local trucks would manage to stop in time before they had crashed into the front of my truck, or that they would manage to swing out of my way, but then they would have run over the sheer drop that was on my side of the road. The overtaking truck collided with the other one, turning it over and scattering the load of live sheep it was carrying in all directions. This same truck then kept on coming straight towards me, while it was still travelling at speed. It hit my cab mirror first of all, then the side of my tilt, causing the speeding truck to turn onto its side. I remembered another golden rule that night, and that was to keep on going as fast as I could to put as much distance as possible between me and the scene of this accident so as to avoid being caught up with any police involvement followed by a lengthy court case, which could very well have led to a claim for damages, etc.*

An English driver from behind me who had seen what had happened eventually caught up with me after I had covered a safe distance of a couple of hundred miles down the road. He told me I had done the right thing by running away, as no doubt I would have been the one who was held to be at fault for the accident and any loss due to the sheep being thrown out all over the place when that wagon overturned!'

Perhaps recognising that his luck so far was about to run out after this dangerous incident, John decided to call it a day, and he ended what was a most exciting period of his life, driving trucks out on the Middle Eat run between 1977 and 1982, which he had thoroughly enjoyed.

Karl Nowotarski wasn't as lucky when he was hit by a car that came from the other direction, as he then had to wait for weeks before a court hearing allowed him to continue his journey homewards:

'There were three Tonka trucks going in the same direction ahead of me when I suddenly noticed they had all left the road. Their drivers had chosen to hit the dirt to avoid something that was coming towards them which I couldn't see at all. They were all left-hand drive trucks, so they could see the road ahead a lot better than I could when sitting over on the right-hand side of the road in my right-hand drive truck. An approaching car came along the road and struck the front of my truck causing a fair amount of damage. This accident resulted in a court case that then took two and a half months to sort out. I was stopping at the Ankara Telex

Mike Dunstan's Volvo was sold to Swindon International and its driver had an accident when he hit a stationary vehicle on the autobahn. MD

Motel at the time, and my agent kept on saying my case would be settled soon, but it wasn't at all. The delay started to play on my mind, so that it really got to me in the end. I was told my case was due to be heard, but then I was told it had been adjourned. I really lost it on one occasion after travelling 200 miles to the courthouse only to be told my case had been postponed. There I was, losing it by swearing my head off, while not realising the judge who was in charge of my case spoke perfect English! To his credit, the judge went back into the courtroom and my case was then dealt with. What was so annoying was that the car driver had already received a payout from my company for the damage caused to his car some weeks earlier.

'I managed to jump start my damaged truck with help from a local who came along on his tractor, although the engine wasn't running properly: air was being sucked in through the fuel filter, which seemed to be a common problem on DAF 2800s; but some Dutch drivers pointed me in the right direction by fitting a pipe which solved the problem as this bypassed the fuel filter.'

Keith Burson's trip started to go wrong big time when he was travelling back through Yugoslavia and a Swiss-registered F88 lorry and drag came by at speed, the driver of which then lost control while overtaking a parked lorry. This caused the Swiss driver to cross violently into Keith's path so that his tilt trailer was damaged by the impact. The Swiss truck then collided with another British truck driven by Kenny Summerill, causing a much more serious impact, as Kenny's engine and gearbox were pushed back a full eighteen inches:

'Kenny was lucky to get out of that truck alive. The fact that he was sitting in a right-hand drive rather than a left-hand drive truck became a lifesaver! I had to prevent Kenny from giving the Swiss driver a knuckle sandwich. When the Yugoslavian police arrived, they wanted to use a Caterpillar D8 so they could clear the road and get the traffic moving again by bulldozing both of the damaged vehicles off the road, but I wasn't having any of that! We managed to recover Kenny's damaged truck on a Read's transport lorry, which coincidentally was going in the same direction that we wanted to go, all the way to Gloucestershire. In the meantime, I managed to arrange for Kenny's trailer to be repaired. He had been running empty, so I prepared to take his trailer back home on the back of my own trailer. However, the approach of all the Christmas festivities prompted us all into leaving the trucks behind and taking a flight home. After we had arrived back in the UK, Richard Read arrived at the airport in his Rolls-Royce Shadow to take us home. He offered to let me drive his Rolls, which I did, carefully sticking to 70 mph, although Richard then insisted we needed to get home today rather than arriving tomorrow at that sort of speed, so I put my foot down, and we arrived home, on time, and in real style!'

Keith had not let his wife know anything about the accident, but she had heard all about this quite by chance. However, she was unable to establish whether he had been badly hurt from what information was available, so he was in for a really good telling off when he arrived home!

The implications of an accident for the firm in question could be very serious, as Mark Chevalier of Chevalier Brothers learnt to his cost after the irresponsible, show-off antics of one of their drivers resulted in the death of eight passengers when his truck ran smack into a taxi head on:

'This terrible accident happened when one of our drivers was out on his first trip, and he was seemingly out to impress everyone he came across, as he was overtaking as many vehicles as he could possibly manage at the time, which resulted in him hitting the taxi and killing all those people!

'Getting our driver out of Iran was to cost me a fortune. I had to sell my house, and in 1974, the cost of the solicitor's fees reached £23,000. I went out to Iran to see the British Consulate and make any necessary arrangements. My advice to drivers from then on was to make sure they remembered always to slow down when they were going through any villages.'

Brian Robertson commented on the almost inevitability of becoming involved in a road accident, although he was very lucky, as this sort of incident never happened to him:

'By the law of averages, you could normally expect to have an accident every two years or so. Avoiding accidents wasn't down to good driving in my case, this was just good luck. It was rather like going on the fairground dodgems. We were just young kids at the time, so we had no fear whatsoever. The lorries we drove were just something we pointed in the right direction and off we went, without a single care in the world.'

Reports of gory accidents were commonplace; Ivor Whittall reported one incident which played on his mind:

'I saw lots of accidents, people who were dead being left in their cars for hours. I remember seeing a kid getting run

over in Ankara. They just chucked a blanket over the body and left him lying in the road.'

Mark Chevalier had a similar macabre experience:

'There was this dead Turkish guy I could see who was still sitting in his truck, which was outside an army barracks on the way to Istanbul. I was later told that the accident which killed him had happened three days previously.'

Ian Taylor recalled one driver being jailed for six months after a blind man had been killed when he stepped out of a taxi and walked straight in front of this driver's truck.

Attacks against drivers following an accident were fairly predictable occurrences, and Les Higgins was left counting his lucky stars after he was involved in an accident when a Ford Transit minibus ran straight into the front of his truck near the town of Erzincan in Eastern Turkey. The occupants of the *dolmuş* minibus all piled out, spitting and chucking stones at Les's truck before they managed to haul him out of the cab, although the arrival of the police calmed down what was fast becoming a very ugly confrontation.

Martyn Moulsdale had a bad experience in Iraq when someone walked out in the pitch dark in front of his truck so they were immediately killed by the impact:

'I spent the next six months in Iraq, first of all in Abu Ghraib prison that was used by the military in the Second Gulf War. I was in a large cell which was forty-foot square, but with many other prisoners in there, so it was very cramped. If you had no bedding, then you had to sleep just on the surface of the tiled floor. The toilet was a three inch hole in the floor. You had to have food brought in, and if you had no money, then you would have starved. So it was just as well I had some money so I could pay someone to bring in food. I finally went to court, and it was one of the greatest days of my life when I was finally released.'

Ron Slater described the consequences of an accident when he was working for Davies Turner on exhibition work:

'I was driving a Magirus Deutz when an old Thames Trader that had been built into a fire engine ploughed into the side of my truck after the driver lost control when he ran through a large pool of standing water outside Edirne in western Turkey. Even though my truck was badly damaged, I continued on, and I managed to travel all the way to Tehran with one side of my cab all stoved in. After arriving there, I carried out any running repairs that were needed at the Davies Turner yard. Luckily, my Magirus Deutz was a left-hand drive model, but if it had been a right-hand drive truck, the steering column would have been wrecked in the accident, so this would have been the end of my journey.'

Ron also had an accident on another occasion when the Iranian driver of a Fiat Mirafiori attempted to pass by his truck in a tunnel and then came unstuck when he rolled his car over; it was so badly damaged that the car had to be written off. Ron was arrested, and even though his company, Harrison's, had already paid the owner for the loss of his car despite Ron not being to blame for the accident, it was a long while before he was free to return home, as a court case still needed to be heard even though the other party had been fully reimbursed!

Reflecting a rare occasion when it wasn't a European driver who had a bad day after they had been summoned to court following an accident, Gordon Summers had this tale to tell that redressed the balance in the Turkish legal system's favour:

'I was near the town of Sivas in Turkey when a kamikaze coach overtook me at the same time as a Mercedes car was coming towards the both of us from the opposite direction. The coach driver managed to get by me and then cut in front of me, although he caught my truck's front bumper, which was ripped away from the front of the cab. On the opposite side of the road, the driver of the Mercedes had been forced off the road in order to avoid colliding with the coach, and as a result, the car was flipped over on to its roof. We were all arrested, which included all of the passengers who were on the bus for a while until they had managed to sort out who was who! As the accident was obviously not my fault, I was kept under open arrest rather than in jail waiting for a court case to be heard, so I spent my time walking around Sivas, but they took the precaution of keeping hold of my truck and also my passport until the day when the court trial was due to take place, which would finally decide who was to be held to blame for the collision. The case was scheduled to take place a couple of days later, although this was delayed because the circuit judge could not attend after suffering from a dislocated shoulder. When the judge did arrive, it turned out that he had been the driver of the Mercedes car which the coach driver had forced off the road. So the judge threw the book at the coach driver, and I was awarded about three to four hundred pounds as my journey had been held up over a number of days, and also to pay for the damage to my truck's bumper.'

CHAPTER 23

Family Matters

Life on the road and travelling so far from home may have been the adventure of a lifetime for many, as this provided the opportunity of travelling to many foreign lands. Most of the drivers in those days were still in their early to mid-twenties, so they were footloose and ready for some adventure, and not generally of an age when any thoughts of settling down with a wife and family were all that important to them.

Some of the drivers would have had girlfriends or fiancées of course who may have taken a dim view of their prospective life partner disappearing over the horizon for many weeks at a time, although if this was interpreted as an unacceptable state of affairs, the issue could be easily resolved at the wish of either or both parties with a make or break decision on whether to stick together, or alternatively, to finally acknowledge that the time had arrived to call it quits and say goodbye!

For those who were already married, and often encumbered with children to bring up, having a partner who was absent for countless weeks of the year could throw up many matrimonial and family problems. As can be imagined, the high incidence of divorce between drivers and their partners became a well-recognised aspect of the job. Who could blame any wife for deciding that they'd had enough when their partners were only at home for a few precious days before they headed off once more into the wild blue yonder! And no doubt they wondered what it was about the job that their husbands enjoyed so much when it involved so many dangers and often miserable privations!

Many marriages did go on the rocks, and a breaking point was often reached following the issue of an ultimatum along the lines of, 'either it's the job or me.' So quite a few husbands chose to continue a free-wheeling life on the road, but that's only one half of the story, as many marriages did survive the long periods of isolation that both husbands and their wives or partners had to endure.

Maintaining any form of communication was difficult in the days before mobile phones were available and even the alternative of making a call by using a landline became almost impossible after leaving Western Europe behind.

So letters or postcards would be sent home even though these could take days if not weeks to arrive! Karl Nowotarski recalled the growing sense of isolation and home-sickness that could plague him for weeks at a time until a trip was finally completed:

'Communications were very poor in those days; you had to wait six or eight hours just to make a phone call. You would feel so insulated and cut off from the rest of the world, you didn't even know what was going on around you as you travelled along. My wife would write to me and I would arrange to pick up her letters when I got to places where this was possible, such as places where I would stay in Istanbul. This was the only real sort of contact you could have with your partner back then.'

Ian Tyler (front) and a bloke known as 'Taffy' who quite rightly abandoned his truck after his employer failed to pay the bloke's wife back in the UK. ITY

Gerry Holmes would make every attempt to cut off any thoughts of home as soon as he departed, as to do otherwise was to invite depressive, melancholy thoughts that made it even more difficult to do the job that he had set out to complete:

'Once you hit that ribbon of black road you would be gone for a long while, and this was a lot to ask of any wife who had to wait on her own for all that time until you came back. All you would be thinking about during the trip was how well the job was going and the trip itself. If you had begun thinking about what was going on at home all the time, then you would not have been able to concentrate on doing the job properly.'

Brian Robertson reported:

'I was married all the way through my Middle East years, and even though I received a few ultimatums along the lines of "It's either that truck or me," I kept on putting off the decision on whether to quit, as it was always really good money.'

Ivor Whittall took a similar viewpoint as truck driving in the UK was not well paid compared to what was on offer driving to any far-flung Middle East destinations:

'I was married, but we wanted the extra money to buy our own house and to bring up our three children, so the money was why I did it. Drivers in the UK were on about £60–£70 a week at the time, and here was the opportunity to earn £800–£900 on a trip taking as little as three weeks to do. So you were making up to £300 a week; an amount which was far more in real terms than what it is by today's standards!'

So the pay was good, but it was important that a wife had easy access to her husband's pay packet throughout the time he was away from home, and a transport firm that kept the wives of their drivers happy by regularly handing over some of the wages was vitally important, a point that Geoff Morgan commented on:

'One of the good things about working for Hicks, the firm I worked for, was that the wives always got their money every Thursday while we were away.'

Mike Dunstan was one of those who saw the work as his last chance to have a great adventure with the further advantage of receiving a handsome amount of pay while enjoying the experience of a lifetime:

'I was married, and although my wife was a bit horrified when I first raised the issue, she then thought it would be a good idea to get this sort of urge for adventure out of my system. We had two small children at the time, and everything worked out well in the end, as we are still together today.'

Ian Taylor counted himself as being most fortunate by still being with the same woman he married before he took to such a long-distance travelling life, although he knew many drivers who were presented with a stark ultimatum of either giving up the job or agreeing to a divorce, with the latter option chosen in many cases.

Rather like those wounded souls who chose to join the Foreign Legion as the perfect antidote to a romantic disappointment, Graham Cartmail buried his feelings of remorse when the relationship with his wife finally broke down for good, by taking to the road, as the perfect way of learning how to forget:

'I enjoyed the life on the Middle East run, as I was leaving a broken marriage behind me, so this was a release from the distress. I stayed out there as long as I could until 1979, which is when I met up with a new partner that I'm still with today. Many drivers only did the one trip and some didn't even complete their first one because of the loneliness of being away from wives and girlfriends. They just couldn't wait to get home and they couldn't learn to live for the moment! Jenkinson's, the firm I worked for, seemed to have developed a policy of seeking out single men and those who came from broken marriages, such as myself. I remember being asked about this sort of thing when I was interviewed, so they knew exactly what they were looking for, someone without dependents. Going out to the Middle East was a good thing for me as it opened my eyes and gave me such a good insight into so many aspects of life, as well as allowing me to become good judge of character on the basis of meeting so many different people. After I met my new partner, I made the decision to give up the Middle East, preferring much shorter runs to Italy so that I got home each week.'

One answer to keeping a relationship together or providing a partner with an insight into the life of a Middle East driver was to take them along on a trip. Des Seal took his girlfriend Chris, who later became his wife. However, taking Chris along had an unforeseen drawback on one occasion:

'On a trip to Iran, we wandered into a less westernised part of Tehran, and we suddenly had to beat a hasty retreat in the face of a shower of stones which had erupted all round us because Chris was not dressed in the Muslim fashion.'

Terry Tott and his wife and children after he returned home following a bombing raid in Iraq. TT

Chris was highly amused when an Iranian border guard made it known that he had taken a fancy to Des, and suggested they should go off to the toilets for a romantic interlude, an invitation Des emphatically declined! On the next occasion when Des arrived at the Iranian border, he concealed a large rock in his briefcase as a means of fending off any such amorous attention!

At another border crossing from Bulgaria to Turkey, Chris became the star attraction with many onlookers after Des asked her to move their truck along a short distance to close the gap with the next in the line of a queue of trucks advancing towards the border. In those days a woman driving a truck was something to cause amazement, and after Des had resumed his usual place in the driver's seat, he stalled the engine, much to the added amusement of all the onlookers, occasioning many comments on his manhood, as from their limited perspective, Chris had made a much better job of driving Des's truck than he had!

Frank White recalled taking his wife along to give her an understanding of life out on the road travelling through Europe and the Middle East:

'Looking back on those times from today, the Middle East was something which I did in the past as this was a great way of making a living. I had three young kids aged two, four and five at the time. On my first trip, my wife, Anna, went as well. My mother-in-law convinced her it would be the trip of a lifetime, a chance event that was unlikely to reoccur. What an eye-opener it was for her as she had never been anywhere abroad. She wasn't bothered at all about anything that happened to us along the way. To make life easier for her, every third night we would stop in a hotel so that she could get cleaned up, etc.'

Karl Nowotarski wasn't keen on the idea of taking a wife or girlfriend along, as this could soon stir up lots of trouble with the locals as far as he was concerned:

'Taking your partner was a bit dangerous because of the sort of attention this attracted from the locals. I remember one bloke took his attractive wife along with him, and this caused lots of aggravation. Just looking after yourself was bad enough without having to take care of what could only be an extra liability.'

Terry Tott also took his wife, Carol, on three trips out to the Middle East, and although there was a problem with getting a visa when they arrived at the Ramtha border crossing into Saudi Arabia, a trip to Amman sorted that out, but there were still reservations about letting any foreign women into the country. Eventually though they made it, which is when they ran into the sort of trouble that seemed ridiculous at first, but which then took on a more serious edge:

Terry Tott's wife, Carol, in the truck they used as a getaway vehicle from her amorous admirer! TT

'This local in a six-door, stretched Pontiac came to talk to us and he began making an offer that we thought was a joke at first. He said he wanted to buy my wife, Carol, and he eventually made an offer of £60,000, which of course I refused! He wouldn't give up, and in the end we drove away in our truck to get away from him, but he came after us in his fancy car. He tried to overtake us later on by driving onto the desert along our nearside over the next 40 miles. But then his car crashed into a huge hole, so it was badly squashed, rather like a broken concertina. We decided the best thing to do in these circumstances was just to keep on going until we reached the border that allowed us to escape!'

Terry's commitment to the job finally reached breaking point when he was unloading his truck near Baghdad during the Iran–Iraq War. The Iranian air force paid a visit in a couple of Phantom jets that released some bombs which fell a little too close for comfort. This was his very last Middle East run!

The role of a father could be affected if they failed to maintain contact with their children for weeks at a time, which was something that bothered Martyn Moulsdale until he finally gave up on the Middle East and took on local UK work:

'My younger son never really knew he had a dad until I stopped doing the Middle East run when he was fifteen years old. I did make the best of my time with the kids when I was at home, but all too often you were only at home for a couple of days before you would be off again on the next new trip. Today, I resent looking back at any family photos, as I appreciate I didn't see all that much of my kids when they were growing up. I don't know where all that time went.'

Ron Slater expressed similar qualms about the relative advantages and disadvantages of this way of life:

'Although travelling out to the Middle East was an adventure and you would experience things that you'd never have a chance of coming across otherwise, I never saw all my kids growing up, as I was always chasing the good money to be made out there!'

It was hardly surprising that wives, girlfriends and family members who were left behind felt resentful, as suggested by the story of one aggrieved wife who decided to take action on learning her husband was due to depart on a Middle East run in a few days' time – she took command of the situation by burning his passport so he was no longer able to go!

CHAPTER 24

Changing Political Situations

There were many times when the political issues of a particular country could have a bearing on the success or failure of a trip. On many occasions, whatever was happening may well have passed over the heads of any drivers who were transiting through a country or travelling through the country that was their final destination. In these circumstances, the correct response was to press on with the job and then go for a quick turnaround, as getting the job done was their one and only priority, so what business were the politics of a foreign country to anyone who was merely passing through?

As long as they didn't happen to come across a barrier across the road, or a closed frontier post; or the crackling sound of Kalashnikovs greeting a new dawn in a country's future prospects; or some low-flying supersonic jets flashing by and letting loose their lethal cargo of cannon and rockets, everything was still hunky-dory as far as most drivers were concerned!

The Middle East has been the bitter focus of much political and social unrest through the last century, a situation and a disaster that still now seems likely to continue into the foreseeable future.

Oddly enough, the long drawn out problems of Israel versus its neighbouring Arab countries and the Israel/Palestine conflict did not have all that much direct significance to any drivers who were heading off towards the wealthy countries of Saudi Arabia and the Gulf States, or Iraq for that matter, which is something that also applied to the countries through which they transited: Syria, Jordan and Lebanon.

The only precaution any drivers really needed to take notice of was to ensure their passports did not have any Israeli visa of entry or exit stamps marked on the pages, as they would have been refused entry and turned back at the frontiers of any Arab countries, and also Iran for that matter.

Thus any thought of transiting through Israel was a definite no-no, and the borders into this country remained firmly closed as far as any Middle East-bound drivers were concerned!

Some drivers were bothered by the prospect they may have been accused of being Jewish and all that entails as regards then being persecuted. This resulted in Derek Edwards Stephens of Aldershot taking an extra precaution of asking his parish priest to write a letter stating he was of the Church of England faith and had never been a member of Jewish society.

The countries that took a stand against Israel also barred any Israeli products being imported. This was indicated by the wording on an invoice for a consignment of frozen food sent by the food firm, Cobellon Limited of Kintbury, near Newbury, to the Tehran Intercontinental Hotel in October 1977. The paperwork contained the following to confirm the foodstuffs were not of Israeli manufacture:

'We hereby certify that the goods enumerated in this invoice are not of Israeli origin, nor do they contain any Israeli materials and are not being exported from Israel.'

Europeans needed to remember that they should always maintain a degree of discretion in what they said about Israel. If they were to exclaim anything that could even be remotely interpreted as something that provided moral support to the Israeli cause, then they were asking for lots of trouble. Any figures of authority, such as customs and immigration officials or the police, would then really lay it on thick by making trouble at border crossings or road inspections posts with their rules and regulations in addition to being generally obstructive!

Wearing a Star of David wasn't such a good idea according to Paul Rowlands on one trip that he made to Iran, as he was roundly berated by a woman in the street, although not for any alleged support for Israel, it was just that the woman concerned thought Paul was being disrespectful; she approached this situation from the unexpected angle, as she was of Jewish parentage herself!

The Iranian Revolution in 1979 resulted in the overthrow of the Shah of Iran, Mohammad Reza Shah Pahlavi, and his ruling government, and the imposition of a religious theocracy led by the ayatollahs who maintained a tight control of the country. So ended Iran's long, friendly pro-Western stance, and the turbulent years that followed did much to upset the applecart for any future prospects of importing the same scale or amount of goods from Europe as had previously occurred.

Iran's letters of credit were withdrawn, so any trade with Europe came to an abrupt stop. Trade was curtailed so swiftly, any trucks that were already on their way to Iran were ordered to return with their loads still intact.

This political and social upheaval put some Middle East operators out of business, and those that remained voted with their feet and established new routes and contacts for some of the other Middle East countries, the emphasis then changing to Saudi Arabia and the tiny Gulf States dotted along the coastline of the Arabian Peninsula.

Any drivers who had already crossed into Iran just before the Shah was thrown out of the country then found themselves in a most precarious position: the Iranian borders remained firmly closed in the interim so as to allow the ayatollahs' rule to become firmly established.

Gerry Holmes remembered the dilemma that faced some of the other drivers working for H.J. Atlas who became trapped for a while at the Bazargan crossing before they could exit Iran into Turkey:

'A few of our lads were caught out by the Iranian Revolution, and even though they did manage to get out of the country after a while, their trucks had to stay where they were until the dust had settled down and we could go back to collect them at the border. We managed to keep the business going by taking on some other routes to different countries. Although our firm did go back to making deliveries to Iran eventually, there was nowhere near the same amount of business to be had from then on.'

The impact of the Iranian Revolution on Frank White's business was dramatic even though his firm, Frank White Haulage, had only two trucks on the road at the time. As well as Frank and one of his drivers being trapped for weeks at a time, this almost wrecked his business financially, and even after the situation out in Iran had finally settled down, he was not keen about returning in spite of having done so well previously:

'When the Ayatollah Khomeini came to power, suddenly you'd find everyone wasn't as friendly as they had been before. It was as if they wanted to string up everyone who came from anywhere else. The situation reminded me of what it was like with Maggie Thatcher and the miners' strike that caused so much unrest in our own country. Even though the drivers who were stranded in Iran still had some of their running money with them, any Western currency soon became useless: the Iranians switched the value of their own currency so as to stabilise their own economy, which meant any Western money was now almost worthless. So when the drivers changed their money at the official rates provided, this didn't turn out to be a very good deal for them at all.'

Later on, when the Iranian economy was in a bad way, any Western currency – pounds, dollars and deutschmarks – could be exchanged for Iranian rials on the black market at twice the official rates, although the penalty for anyone who was caught out making illegal money change transactions could be a long period of jail time!

Frank remained stuck behind the Iranian border for a number of weeks before he could make his way home, so he contacted his wife to advise her of his plight, which then resulted in his local paper, the *Glasgow Herald*, wanting to run his story with the usual sensationalist nonsense! Frank responded by wisely refusing to cooperate unless he was given the absolute right to edit the content and make any changes he considered to be necessary:

'They kept on phoning my wife back in Britain to give them some details,' said Frank, *'but I knew they didn't want to write this story truthfully. I was very wary from then on about what they wanted to write about me.'*

Jeff Kedward was given some sound advice by Turkish lorry drivers he befriended when they were stopping over in Tehran at the time when news of the Revolution broke out. Jeff chose not to accept what he had been told at first, although he was heartily glad he did finally bow to their better judgement by following their trucks all the way to the border, which he scraped through just before the barriers came down:

'I was with a family of Turkish lorry drivers in Tehran and we were having a glass of çay *when an announcement came over the radio stating the Shah of Iran had been deposed. I was aiming on just driving as far as Tabriz on the first part of my journey towards home, which was still a fairly long way from the Iran/Turkey border, but thankfully, the Turks managed to persuade me otherwise. They convinced me it was far better to cross the border with Turkey as soon as this was possible due to the political situation which was*

developing so quickly. It was just as well that I did follow their example, as the Iranian border was closed for the next three months! So I managed to get out of the country just in time.

Martyn Moulsdale commented on the disquiet he felt after arriving in Iran some time following the Revolution, when he anticipated maybe the dust had all settled and things should now be getting back to normal:

'A short while after the Shah had been exiled I delivered some water pumps to Iran following the Revolution. You would see 15-year-old kids carrying automatic rifles around, so you had to watch out for them always, and you would have to grin and bear whatever they wanted to say to you. You could be in trouble if you were found to be wearing a pair of shorts or a short-sleeved T-shirt as this didn't fit in at all with their way of thinking.'

David Miller had always enjoyed meeting and talking with Iranians, although after the new regime was established, any such contact was not to his liking at all:

'Iran wasn't as friendly after the Shah who had ruled the country was thrown out. I never felt happy in Tehran after this occurred. I remember Pat Seal telling me that he had been made to stand on a pile of wooden pallets when he was going through customs one day and he was then instructed to say all the while "Shah no good" time after time. They wouldn't have let him unload his truck if he had done otherwise and refused to say what they wanted him to say. There was a sense of menace about the place. Some people had become immensely rich, while others were still desperately poor, yet they tried to live side by side.'

What surprised many drivers, and probably many people in positions of political power or advantage, was that no-one outside the country seemed to have a clue about what was about to unfold, which possibly contributed to the ease with which the ayatollahs were able to take control of the country.

Paul Rowlands was surprised that he had not seen anything to indicate that the Iranian Revolution was about to occur, and those he travelled with at the time seemed to have been just as oblivious. This was not unique in Paul's experience, as the outbreak of the Yugoslav Wars, which resulted in a bloodbath of genocide and sheer terror for the population of this fractured country between 1991 and 1999, was also unpredictable. Paul had travelled through Yugoslavia on many previous occasions without recognising any of the social and religious divisions which eventually tore this country apart, resulting in a number of independent nation states coming into existence, which are still in place today.

Further east, any overland trade with Afghanistan and Pakistan was also halted as a result of the Iranian Revolution early on in 1979, and then more seriously by the Soviet invasion of Afghanistan that occurred a few months later in December 1979.

At the start of the Lebanese Civil War, which lasted from 1975 to 1990, Ken Ward delivered twenty tons of frozen fish fingers to Beirut when he was driving a reefer truck for Grangewood's, and he described the situation that he faced after arriving in the war-torn city at the height of the conflict which existed in 1975:

'Two tanks could be seen blocking my way ahead as I approached Beirut. However this turned out OK, as the army provided a military escort which took care of me so that I made my delivery to the dockland area of the city, where it was unloaded. There was a real mess due to the shelling that had taken place; with all the dockyard cranes having collapsed and fallen into the water.'

Ken made a later trip to Lebanon which proved to be more eventful. This involved trying out a new route over the top of a mountain, which turned out to be the right thing to do, even though this contradicted the official advice he had received from those who should have been in the know! He explained:

Ferry from Volos in Greece to Syria as unable to transit Turkey due to political problems and fuel shortages. MD

'A military coup in Turkey in 1980 saw us bypassing this country by taking the ferry from Volos in Greece to get to Lattakia in Syria first of all. I was enjoying a cup of tea in Syria with another British driver when a friendly Arab approached us. My British colleague rudely told the Arab to shove off, so I angrily told him he could shove off himself: I didn't like his attitude at all. I got chatting to this Arab, who was called Mahmud Kara, and he asked me where I was going, so I told him I was going to Beirut. But he gave me some heartfelt advice, suggesting I should ignore the travel manifest I had been given by officials when I crossed over the border into Lebanon, which would have involved taking the coastal road to Tripoli. This was a bad idea according to Mahmud, as the fighting was very bad along that way. He said I should make for Damascus, which is in Syria, instead, as this was the only way to get to Beirut in one piece. I made it through to Damascus, but I then came to a stop at the desolate Masnaa border crossing between Syria and Lebanon. Fighting had already broken out in the Bekaa Valley beyond, and the authorities wouldn't let me go any further. After waiting at the frontier for a few days, I noticed a Jordanian taxi which was making its way from Lebanon into Syria and back each and every day, so I waved to the driver, and after he came to a stop, I asked him what the condition of the road was going to be like on the other side of the border. He said he could only vouch for the road being viable for him to take his taxi along; but he agreed to have a word with the authorities to see whether they would be prepared to let me go if he was showing me the way by leading my lorry through the village of Aramoun and across the Mount Lebanon mountain range. So I set off following the taxi, and the route involved the negotiation of many difficult hairpin bends, also some challengingly steep ascents as I was towing a spread axle trailer which had a broken balance beam and a ripped tyre that added to my problems.

'As darkness fell, the taxi driver had to go on ahead as he wanted to get home all the way to Jordan before a curfew applied. I made it through, and it was with some emotion that I noticed a lone figure waiting for me as I descended the mountain. It was my friend Mahmud Kara, who had sent me via Damascus to avoid any trouble along the other route that I had been advised to take by the officials at the border. He had come out to this road every day in the hope and belief that I would get through and he would see me again.'

Travelling through Syria became risky at one time because of the political situation concerning Israel, and Alan Dayson recounted a few memories of the difficulties of travelling across miles of rough desert

Queuing for a military convoy at Mardin near the Syrian border. IT

country after a convoy of European and locally owned trucks had been assembled with a military escort owing to the possibility of an attack on Syria by the Israelis:

'We travelled through Syria in convoy with army trucks and jeeps, and I had a soldier with me all the time in the cab. It was important to keep your position in the convoy, but this was tricky to achieve because all the Turkish and Arab trucks couldn't keep up, as they were significantly overloaded, and not all that powerful. They would be trying to go like hell to catch up with the European trucks, which did work on the downhill stretches as they could go a lot faster, but they would have to fall back when they came across any inclines. This resulted in a devil take the hindmost free-for-all!'

Alan added that the need to travel in convoy became very apparent when he passed by a European truck that had been rendered immobile as the belly tank containing the fuel had been shot up and thoroughly perforated by machine-gun fire which provided a firm indication of what could go wrong should he have chosen to drive on his own through Syria in such fraught, dangerous times!

Mark Chevalier had a close brush with fate when he heard loud explosions as he was transiting through Syria in a convoy of trucks, which was followed by another even louder explosion after he arrived in downtown Damascus:

'The artillery shelling from the Israeli armed forces was going right over our heads at one time! In Damascus, we called in at the Jordanian embassy to arrange for some visas. We then decided to go and do some shopping while we waited for the visas, and as we walked along, there was a huge explosion at the National Cash Register firm's offices. Luckily, the blast wave from the explosion rolled down a different street to the one we were on. So we considered ourselves to be lucky, and we went back to our hotel for the rest of the time as this was the sensible thing to do until our visas were ready to be collected!'

Travelling through Jordan was usually a pleasant enough run as the country seemed to be generally free of the sort of trouble and strife to be found in neighbouring countries. But Ken Ward became aware of a more volatile behaviour by the locals when he was transiting the country, and the following incident provided a few anxious moments:

'I came to a halt in a long line of trucks as the way ahead of us was blocked by some feuding Arabs, who were throwing stones at each other. As I didn't want any stones coming my way, I hopped out of my cab while shouting "Inglese" all the time to signify that I was English and therefore had nothing to do with what was going on. They seemed to accept this and allow me to pass, my truck remaining undamaged.'

The invasion of Cyprus by Turkish forces in 1974 resulted in increasing aggression by Turkish army personnel still based at home, with soldiers proudly showing off the enamelled badges that depicted the outline shape of Cyprus, which was now firmly divided with the Turkish Cypriot and the Greek Cypriot populations living in isolation on separate parts of the island. David Miller recalled the state of heightened tension that resulted in some exaggerated demands concerning homeland security, even through the Turkish mainland was many sea miles away from the beleaguered island:

'There was a military road which the Turkish army eventually let us use so we could get to the next border crossing out of their country. But following the Turkish invasion of Cyprus in 1974, the soldiers stationed here still allowed us to use this road, but only if we painted our headlights in blue, to prevent them shining so brightly at night, apparently to prevent us from signalling to their enemies in Cyprus, which was ridiculous as Cyprus was well over a hundred miles away!'

David had a problem with his newly painted headlights on the last leg of his journey home, as he passed through Germany. The paint that the soldiers had used on his headlights could not be removed all that easily, so he decided not to drive at night due to the poor illumination now provided by the obscured headlights; driving his truck in this condition at night would have attracted the wrong sort of attention from the ever-vigilant German police.

The Iran–Iraq War that broke out in 1980 and lasted for 8 years brought more tangible dangers to drivers making any deliveries to Iraq, as the need to dodge artillery shell fire and the low-flying jet fighters that discharged bombs was not in any way out of the ordinary! Jeff Kedward was startled when he was driving southwards towards Basra, and as he drew close to the Iranian border, trails of illuminated tracer fire were observed sailing lazily overhead!

Martyn Moulsdale was reminded of the deadly consequences of warfare when he noticed taxis travelling away from the direction of any war zones, bearing unusual loads carried on the roofs:

'During the Iran–Iraq War, I would often see a taxi driving along with a coffin mounted on top of the roof and an Iraqi flag covering the coffin lid. This seemed a strange way of bringing any dead soldiers home. I saw one coffin fly off the roof of the car it was being carried by so that the coffin disintegrated when it hit the ground, throwing out the body from inside, which ended up uncovered on the road surface until it could be retrieved.'

It doesn't take much for exaggerated stories to circulate when any military conflict happens to be in progress, and John Buffham was left wondering what to do when he was told the Iranians had bombed the border crossing he was approaching, which was between Turkey and Iraq. Some lorries were turning back to avoid any danger. But then the true situation was revealed: a truck had reversed into a pillar supporting the concrete roof canopy of the border post, and the roof had then collapsed, landing on top of a bus parked underneath! There is a saying that truth is the first casualty of war!

In 1980, Ian Taylor had been told by his boss back at home to press on to Baghdad even though the Iran–Iraq War had recently started. The reason Ian was

Do-it-yourself funeral transport. DM

given for pressing on was that the war would be over in no time at all. How often has history demolished such reasoning in the past! This sort of analysis of the situation probably sounded OK from the comfortable, unthreatening position of sitting at an office desk over 2000 miles away from any danger that could have arisen, as it did on this occasion!

On arriving in the Iraqi capital, Ian had plenty of time to chew over his boss's statement after seeking shelter from mortal danger in a deep cellar on a Baghdad high street, as Iranian Air Force Phantom jets screamed low overhead followed by the angry crackle of ack-ack guns as the aircraft ripped through the skies of the war-torn city!

Terry Tott had a similar experience when he was parked up in Baghdad for the trade fair and a series of bombs heard falling from Iranian jet bombers suggested it was time to get moving! So after everyone had abandoned their trailers, all the tractor units scurried back over the Jordanian border, and Terry and his mates didn't return until things had quietened down once more.

Geoff Morgan found sanctuary in a place he thought was safe, although any sudden barrage of artillery fire, or a cascade of bombs, could easily have reduced his hideaway to a pile of dust and rubble, leaving his truck as a shattered, burnt-out wreck:

'I went down to Basra in the south of Iraq during the period when the Iran–Iraq War was at its worst. I remember believing that we would be safe enough if we parked up in a school yard because care would be taken to avoid targeting a school with any bombs or shells, but not so, we soon realised this was only wishful thinking.'

Ron Slater wasn't too impressed when he was asked to paint the headlights on his truck blue as a precaution against drawing enemy fire when he was driving through Iraq.

'I went down to Basra many times during the years when the Iraqis were fighting the Iranians. I remember being in Fallujah when the anti-aircraft guns would be going "bang-bang" in the middle of an air raid. When it was all over, the soldiers who were now going off duty would hop on a bus to go home! They would want you to drive all the way down to Basra in pitch darkness without switching on your headlights all the way. Or alternatively, they would want you to paint your headlights blue, and also to cover your truck in a mixture of sand and water as camouflage just in case of any air raids. But we took no notice of the soldiers and we simply switched on our headlights as soon as we were further on down the road where they couldn't see us any more.'

Gordon Summers was in for a shock when he contemplated how close he had come to being killed when an artillery shell landed and sent a piece of shrapnel scything through the cab of his truck:

'I was making a delivery down to Basra during the Iran–Iraq War when all the drivers were suddenly evacuated to Kuwait because of artillery fire coming over the border from Iran. When we got back to where I'd parked my Scania 111, the truck which was next to mine had been flattened by a shell, and when I looked at the cab of my truck a piece of shrapnel had come through into the cab and this had landed just where my head would have been if I had been sleeping at the time on my bunk bed.'

Gordon witnessed an air raid near Baghdad in 1981 when the Israeli Air Force sent jet bombers to attack a nuclear plant which was being built:

'We were in the customs at Baghdad, and all the European drivers were sitting in deckchairs watching the action as the flashes from anti-aircraft guns lit up the sky.'

The homeland of the Kurdish people is located where the borders of Turkey, Iran and Iraq meet, a mountainous and traditionally lawless domain where the Kurds have struggled for generations to establish their autonomous homeland. During the eighties, the Kurdish separatist movement pursued an aggressive policy of sending out guerrillas to fight the Turkish armed forces, although any drivers who travelled through Eastern Turkey during the seventies were well aware that trouble was brewing and of the need to keep away from any conflict areas. Graham Cartmail commented on his experiences of driving through what was becoming an increasingly dangerous and lawless region:

'The Kurds wanted their own independent state, but they weren't recognised by the Turks, the Iranians or the Iraqis in their claim for a homeland straddling the borders of all three countries. So the Kurds became a law unto themselves. As such, you had to be very careful where you parked your wagon in south-east Turkey, as nothing was safe. They would come along and take your fuel or the tyres off your truck, or anything else they could lay their hands on at the time. Never park on your own was an important rule which we always tried to follow!'

Brian Robertson had cause to fear for his life when he broke the rule of never travelling at night as he drove along a lonely road with no other traffic in sight:

'As soon as it got dark, you were supposed to stop somewhere safe and wait until morning arrived and it was light again before pressing on any further. But away I went, taking no notice of this instruction, and of course what happened? I was held up by some Kurdish bandits! My spotlights picked up something on the road, and as I drew nearer, I could see that a telegraph post had been placed so it was blocking the way ahead. After stopping my truck, I watched as half-a-dozen men approached me from both sides of the road. They were carrying rifles and pistols, and after opening up my cab door, they pulled me out of the cab. I had a rifle poking in my stomach and a pistol was pointed straight at my face, I thought that I'd had it, as a couple of weeks previously, a French driver was killed when his throat was cut somewhere near here. They didn't pay much attention to me as they started cutting up the tilt on my trailer with a knife to get at what was inside, and they went through the cab, stealing my money and my watch. But to my relief, I could see some headlights approaching in the distance, and they all suddenly cleared off. So I went back to the nearest village to report this incident to the military gendarmes. I went back with them to the site of the robbery in two Jeeps, where I picked up some of my gear that had been abandoned. The police arranged for a translator, known as a tercüman, who explained why two statements on the theft now had to be prepared. The first of these stated I had stopped to check my tyres when two guys started cutting the canvas on my trailer, and they had run away as I approached them. I was told that if I agreed to sign this, then I could go on my way now. But it was explained that if I signed the other one, which detailed what had really happened, then I would have to stop in this village until the police managed to catch the thieves, so as they probably already knew by now, there wasn't a chance in hell of me ever signing that second statement! I was then escorted by the police to the Turkey/Iran border at Bazargan. There was a four-day-long queue of trucks sitting on the Turkish side of the border, although the police swept past all of these as they took my truck straight into the customs compound. After the police had explained to the customs men what had happened, the canvas tilt was resealed with wire and sewn up so that it complied with the customs regulations for sealed loads and was allowed to cross the border. As for the thieves, all they managed to take away from the load on the truck were some boxes of cornflakes and also some others containing sanitary towels! I was completely happy with the outcome of this incident, although it started to affect me the next day, and I started getting the shakes about what could have happened. They were so bad, I said to myself I wouldn't be coming back this way again. But after a couple of weeks, off I went again!'

Political problems in Turkey during the eighties forced a reappraisal on whether this route was still viable due to the increasing number of problems faced by drivers when they crossed any borders into this country, as Martyn Moulsdale described:

'Turkey became a no-go route owing to problems with the government, difficulties in getting fuel, and also corruption when it came to crossing any border posts. The route we followed later on involved travelling through the Communist countries of East Germany, Czechoslovakia, Hungary, Romania and Bulgaria; we avoided Turkey altogether by going through Greece and taking a two-day ferry trip across the Med to Syria, then heading onwards to Iraq by road.'

CHAPTER 25

The End of the Road

It was the bringing together of a unique set of circumstances that made the transportation of goods by the truckload over the vast distances from Europe to the Middle East economically and logistically viable. So it followed that the gradual fading away of the factors that had made this high-risk business so achievable and profitable led to its gradual demise by the mid-eighties, although less regular deliveries did in fact continue, particularly during the two Gulf Wars, and occasional deliveries are still made to this day! (Subject of course to conflict in the region closing any borders, as exists at the present time due to the Islamic State crisis in Iraq and Syria.)

To recap, the build-up to the creation of the Middle East trucking boom began to gather pace following the closure of the Suez Canal between 1967 and 1975: this was a response by the Arab nations to Israel's military successes against neighbouring countries and American support of the Israeli cause. Part way through this period when the Canal was closed, in 1973 OPEC, the organisation representing many oil-producing nations, particularly those from the Middle East, introduced a sharp hike in oil prices, resulting in the global panic buying of oil and a resultant oil supply crisis, which OPEC responded to by lowering prices, but not by all that much!

The price of oil rocketing brought about a huge increase in revenue as money poured into the oil-producing countries of the Middle East. This provided a mountain of hard cash to pay for a range of goods and supplies which the respective governments needed for ambitious development programmes designed to modernise the infrastructure and economies of these countries where the owning of livestock, such as camels and goats, had recently been the sole indicator of the wealth of an individual or their family.

Sending urgently needed cargoes by road became the solution to meeting the strong demand for goods and materials in spite of the often astronomical costs that were involved. Transport by air, however, was more expensive and also hardly practical for any heavy or bulky items, such as building materials.

So there was no alternative to sending the heavier goods by road, but by then the citizens of these newly wealthy countries had set their sights on a whole range of previously unattainable consumable goods, which further increased the growing demand for overland truck deliveries.

In time, the situation eased, particularly after the reopening of the Suez Canal to ships, although this in turn resulted in further problems, as the docks around the coast of Saudi Arabia were soon blocked solid with an influx of deliveries. There was a decline in overland deliveries from Europe, although this was compensated for, at least in part, by an upsurge in demand for the services of British and other European haulage firms that took on a new role of making deliveries known as internal runs. Goods arriving into port by ship were unloaded and transported by road along the desert highways and mountain roads to destinations throughout the vast interior of the Arabian Peninsula. This internal transport boom lasted until the early eighties before it levelled out, with drivers from other Third World nations then being far cheaper to employ.

The growth in demand for goods and materials by Saudi Arabia and the Gulf States compensated for the loss of business following the Iranian Revolution in 1979, although there was a further reduction in the amount of business that was available to British and European hauliers when the Eastern European hauliers upped their game sending more and more of their trucks to make deliveries to Middle East destinations. State-run transport operations, such as SOMAT of Bulgaria, or Hungarocamion of Hungary, took a huge volume of work from their Western competitors by benefiting from economies of scale and cheaper running costs that allowed them to undercut any previously established going rates. What's more, overall profitability was not quite as important to the Eastern bloc firms as it was to the smaller, private enterprise firms of Europe: securing hard currency for trading purposes was often the prime motivation. So this was always an unfair contest between East and West that could have only one outcome! It was impossible for Western haulage operators to compete with the sort of rates the East

Brian Robertson's forty-year association with the Davies Turner organisation continues to this day with continental work with his Volvo FH12. BR

Europeans could offer. The difference in operating costs was represented by the sort of pay that a Czech, Hungarian or Bulgarian driver would accept, compared to what any British or other West European driver had to be paid in order to support their expectations and higher standards of living.

Alan Dayson outlined in his own words the reasons for the decline in business:

'By 1986, it had become less profitable to go down to the Gulf States carrying any goods by road. This loss of business meant we started to concentrate on much shorter runs to Turkey and to Greece. But business declined further due to containerisation: this went against road haulage in favour of shifting everything by shipping on sea routes. Another turning point was the success of Willy Betz, a German company that started doing very well by employing Turkish drivers at cheaper rates of pay, which allowed this firm to undercut the going rates for road haulage because they didn't need to pay their drivers as much as the firms employing European drivers.'

Martyn Moulsdale further elaborated on how the undercutting of the going rates badly affected British and other European haulage firms:

'The job went to pot as more foreign trucks became involved; the rates went down and down, and in the later days, driving out to the Middle East was no longer a good way of making a lot of money. The Bulgarian and Romanian firms undercut the going rates to such a degree, any British firms were working for virtually nothing at all. If you had a blowout on a couple of tyres, this could be very serious with money becoming so tight. I was working for CVH towards the end of my time out on the Middle East run, and the boss, Gordon Powell, said to me one day; "I've been given £3800 for this Middle East job, but by the time I will have paid all the expenses as well as your wages, with the cost of the ferry and anything else, there'll be nothing left at all!" We did try to get backloads, but these only paid about £1500. So everything went downhill from then on, and you would only travel as far as Istanbul where your truck would be unloaded so a Turkish driver could take the load the rest of the way. So I decided the time had arrived to switch to doing just European work.'

Mark Chevalier operated ten trucks in partnership with his brother Andy, and they recognised their Middle East business had started to decline due to political issues and unrest in Turkey following the American decision to withhold military aid and supplies from the country. Mark commented that this led to a marked escalation in the problems on arriving at Turkish border crossings. And travelling through Turkey was also becoming more and more difficult because of the increase in demands for bribe payments as backhanders by the corrupt officials who controlled the flow of trucks passing through the country.

Mark and Andy then ran into another problem linked to the strike action taken by Ford employees in the UK: as a result of the strike, spare parts for the firm's Ford Transcontinental trucks were now in short supply, resulting in some of these trucks coming off the road, and no longer earning their keep in the normal way, as they had to be cannibalised for urgently needed spare parts to keep the rest of the fleet going.

David Miller recognised that the end of his long-distance driving career was fast approaching when he was asked by his employer to take on more and more European work of a short-haul nature:

'I started with Grangewood Transport of Greenwich in 1979 driving refrigerated loads to the Middle East, and they always looked after me well. They gave me a brand-new Volvo F12 to drive with a Chereau trailer, which was a fantastic combination! Many drivers wanted to work for this company as they treated their drivers so well, and my job with the firm lasted until 1984. By this time the boom years of the Middle East were finally over, so I went back to life at sea as a sailor again, as I didn't want to do just European truck deliveries. That was that, and I never went back to

Taken through the windscreen near Istanbul on one of his Middle East trips © Robert Hackford

doing any Middle East driving again. The magical years were over for me! By the eighties, the major challenges of the job had all but gone. All that was left were the discomforts and the hazards of doing the job. Looking back, I realise we were all unbelievably privileged to have been part of a small piece of history that will never be repeated again.'

Ken Ward also extolled the virtues of employment by Grangewood's. When this firm ceased business, Ken, like many other Middle East drivers, found himself searching for a new role, and with so much valuable driving and operating experience now behind him, the answer was to buy his own truck. So Ken became an owner driver working for Christian Salvesen in the UK and on the Continent, but sadly, his Middle East days looked as if they were now over.

Ken's last run for Grangewood's should have been his last trip to the Middle East, although many years later, he jumped at the chance to return there for one last time when he was offered the opportunity to drive a Volvo FH with a mobile exhibition trailer on tow for the Swedish Ericsson electronics firm. This took Ken on a memory-provoking tour of the Gulf States, of which he commented, nothing much had changed, after his truck and trailer were becalmed by officialdom on the Saudi/Dubai border for a whole five days of waiting about!

Many drivers referred to 'the good old days' that have now disappeared for all time as far as they are concerned; they note the disparity with today's rather joyless, lonely experience of eating up the miles hour by hour rather than living by your wits, and the loss of comradeship that existed between drivers who took on the challenging Middle East routes. Chris Stephenson summed up his experiences as follows:

'I enjoyed every trip, as they were all different. Today, drivers are all programmed by the company they work for not to think all that much about what they are doing, but just to keep on going. Once you were on your own, you had

Ken Ward made it back to the Arabian Peninsula just a few years ago when he was asked to transport this exhibition trailer for the Ericsson company. KW

to rely not only on what you could manage yourself, but on the full knowledge that all the other drivers would come and help out, whatever their nationality, if you needed them to.'

Gerry Holmes was also grateful for what he still views as the opportunity of a lifetime:

'I would come back home to the UK with a pair of crossed palm leaves decorating the front of my truck. This was a page in the book of life, as you can never buy stuff like that!'

Ian Taylor regretted the loss of a job that had served him well in addition to kindling his interest in the history of the regions he travelled through:

'I drove the Middle East from 1975 until 1986, which is when the Eastern Europeans started to take over the business, so it was no longer profitable. It was the biggest adventure of my life, with the certainty that every trip would always offer something completely different. This sort of life also added to my interest in history; I got to see the Crusader castles in Syria and the ancient site of Babylon in Iraq as I went along through those countries.'

When Frank White was on one of his trips he was surprised and elated to see a lone horseman galloping on his steed alongside his truck as they travelled, side by side, over the dry steppe lands of Eastern Turkey. Seeing a horse and rider in this part of the world could be said to hark back to the time when the traveller Marco Polo passed by on horseback making his way to China.

As a result of the demand for silk by the West, the Silk Road has become a much-travelled route with caravans of horses and camels carrying exotic goods across the two continents of Europe and Asia, and this route became an important intercontinental route which connected the capital cities of Europe with those of India and far distant China.

Just as in the old days when European merchants set out on the Silk Road to conduct trade across the length and breadth of Asia, those truck drivers who headed out this same way also had to put up with extremes of heat and cold through the scorching summer and the

Homeward-bound near Bazargan on the Iran/Turkey border with Mount Ararat in the distance. FH

freezing winter months. Although separated by many centuries, those Middle East truck drivers shared the same physical discomforts and strain of having to spend so much time travelling along poorly maintained roads on a venture that was often just as bold and challenging as it was all those years ago.

Most Middle East drivers will have their own memories of the times when they battled along in trucks against the odds, travelling through all sorts of weather conditions and taking many other difficulties in their stride, and the stories from these pages should now live on as a reminder of what was a unique adventure that stands little chance of ever being repeated in the future!

THE END

The author, Dave Bowers